CATULLUS AND THE POETICS OF ROMAN MANHOOD

This book applies comparative cultural and literary models to a reading of Catullus' poems as social performances of a "poetics of manhood": a competitively, often outrageously, self-allusive bid for recognition and admiration. Earlier readings of Catullus, based on Romantic and Modernist notions of "lyric" poetry, have tended to focus on the relationship with Lesbia and to ignore the majority of the shorter poems, which are instead directed at other men. Professor Wray approaches these poems in the light of new models for understanding male social interaction in the premodern Mediterranean, placing them in their specifically Roman historical context while bringing out their strikingly "postmodern" qualities. The result is a new way of reading the fiercely aggressive and delicately refined agonism performed in Catullus' shorter poems. All Latin and Greek quoted is supplied with an English translation.

DAVID WRAY is Assistant Professor of Classical Languages and Literatures at the University of Chicago. He received his doctorate from Harvard and has previously taught at Georgia State University and Kennesaw State University. He has published articles on Roman and Hellenistic Greek poetry and literary translation and is currently an Associate Editor of the journal *Classical Philology*.

CATULLUS AND THE POETICS OF ROMAN MANHOOD

DAVID WRAY

CAMBRIDGE
UNIVERSITY PRESS

PUBLISHED BY THE PRESS SYNDICATE OF THE UNIVERSITY OF CAMBRIDGE
The Pitt Building, Trumpington Street, Cambridge, United Kingdom

CAMBRIDGE UNIVERSITY PRESS
The Edinburgh Building, Cambridge CB2 2RU, UK
40 West 20th Street, New York NY 10011-4211, USA
10 Stamford Road, Oakleigh, VIC 3166, Australia
Ruiz de Alarcón 13, 28014 Madrid, Spain
Dock House, The Waterfront, Cape Town 8001, South Africa

http://www.cambridge.org

© David Wray 2001

First published 2001

Printed in the United Kingdom at the University Press, Cambridge

Typeset in Baskerville and New Hellenic Greek [A O]

A catalogue record for this book is available from the British Library

Library of Congress Cataloguing in Publication data

Wray, David, 1959–
Catullus and the poetics of Roman manhood / David Wray.
p.   cm.
Includes bibliographical references and index.
ISBN 0 521 66127 7
1. Catullus, Gaius Valerius – Criticism and interpretation. 2. Love poetry, Latin – Male
authors – History and criticism. 3. Epigrams, Latin – Male authors – History and criticism.
4. Masculinity in literature. 5. Rome – In literature. 6. Self in literature.
7. Men in literature. 8. Intertextuality.
I. Title.
PA6276.W73 2001
874′.01 – dc21   2001025549

ISBN 0 521 66127 7 hardback

D · M · S
Louise Scott Wray
1931–1997

Deiner Mutter Seele schwebt voraus.
Deiner Mutter Seele hilft die Nacht umschiffen,
Riff um Riff.

Paul Celan

Contents

Preface

Like Catullus himself, this book about his poems came to maturity in exciting times. A first version of it, well under way when the monographs of Paul Allen Miller and Micaela Janan gave their names to a Catullan year, had only just been submitted as a dissertation when William Fitzgerald's *Provocations* first came into my hands. Since that time, ongoing dialogue with these refined and complex Catullan voices, and with others as well, has brought fuller elaboration and sharper focus to the critical views expressed in these pages. But exciting times never come as an unmingled gift of fortune, and what began as a revision for publication took, in the event, nearly as long as the original writing. The end result is not so much a rewritten book as a new one.

By all accounts, Catullus still commands a wider audience than any other Latin poet. I have written with a varied readership in mind throughout, perhaps especially in the first two chapters on literary and critical constructions and receptions of the Catullan corpus and its author. The second chapter's discussion of Louis Zukofsky and postmodern poetics, while ultimately crucial to the broader arguments of the book, keeps Catullus' own words largely out of the debate for a longer time than some readers may have expected. Patience and indulgence, if tested in Chapter 2, will, I hope, be compensated in Chapter 3, where the contours of a Catullan poetics of manhood are traced through a sustained and nearly exclusive focus on the text of the poems. Chapter 4 brings comparative material drawn from the work of cultural anthropologists to bear on a delineation of what has always seemed to me a defining and irreducible aspect of Catullus' poems: the aggression personated by their speaker. It was Marion Kuntz who, as a dissertation reader, first suggested to me the idea of eventually attempting to situate Catullan invective in a comparative Medi-

terranean context. That advice is among the many debts I owe
her, and the line of inquiry is one I think might fruitfully be taken
much further in a separate study. The fifth and final chapter, on
Archilochean and Callimachean intertextual presences as "code
models" of manhood in Catullus, poses the question of what remains of the "Catullan persona" after the collapse of the critical
and metaphysical certainties that underpinned Modernist "persona criticism," and offers a partial answer to that question in a
postmodern model of Roman manhood, and selfhood, as performance. Translations are my own unless otherwise noted.

I come to the end of this project owing much to many, and
owning no coin of payment other than gratitude. Richard Thomas
(as director), Marion Kuntz and Richard Tarrant read the dissertation and made all manner of unlikely things possible. Others
who have kindly read all or part of various and variant versions,
and who have improved the end result by encouragement, advice,
championing or challenge include, in more or less chronological
order, Gregory Nagy, Ralph Johnson, Robert Kaster, Peter
White, Richard Saller, Shadi Bartsch, Robert von Hallberg,
Niklas Holzberg and Brian Krostenko. I am grateful to the Press's
two anonymous readers for their thorough, insightful and every-
where helpful criticism, to Michael Sharp for unflagging patience
and enthusiasm as editor, and to Muriel Hall for expert, painstaking copy-editing. Many colleagues at the University of Chicago
(alongside those already named), and many of my students as well,
have contributed to this book in subtler but no less real ways. A
book that announces so sparkling a list of friends and benefactors
runs the risk of setting its reader's expectations far too high. Re-
sponsibility for any and all hopes dashed by what follows herein
must of course rest with the author alone.

The cover jacket image, David Fraley's "Golden Boy" – a rivet-
ing performance, and aptly illustrative of this book's concerns by
its Hellenistic allusivity and self-allusivity, by its "palimpsest" technique of competing textures and lines, and by the delicately fierce
wit of its title – is a gift of the artist, graciously confirmed by his
estate after his sudden and untimely death. His words, from our
twenty years of conversation about art and the postmodern, have
superimposed their rhythms, like the Epicurean *clinamena* of his
canvases, across these pages. As for his works, death will not put
a hand on his nightingales.

Alongside the debt recorded in the dedication, I wish also to thank the following people for help and support of every kind: my father Jack Wray, my late grandmother Grace Scott, my Latin teacher Ruth Wells, Earnest and Mariana Atkins, Bruce Mattys, James Powell and Elizabeth Vandiver.

And the most important thing of all: Kristen, you loaned me your copy of Fordyce's Catullus that summer and I never returned it. Good thing you married me. The next book is for you. So is everything else.

CHAPTER I

Catullan criticism and the problem of lyric

All the new thinking is about loss. In this it resembles the old
thinking.

                              Robert Hass, "Meditation at Lagunitas"

"CELEBRATE YOUR CATULLUS"

New thinking from a new book: a fair enough expectation, even
when the new book is a literary study of an ancient poet, and even
when the ancient poet is Catullus. But if "new thinking" is to
mean thinking away the intervening centuries to reveal a timeless
classic preserved under the aspic of eternity, then new thinking
about Catullus is neither possible nor even desirable. The tradition of an ancient text – both the discourse that transmits and
mediates that text (reception) and the discourse that the text itself
mediates (intertext) – is not an obstacle to its proper understanding, something to be set aside, got over. Rather, its ancient and
modern tradition is precisely that thing which renders Catullus'
text comprehensible in the first place. Forgetting reception history,
including scholarly reception (starting with all those emendations
of a garbled text), would be as helpful to a reading of Catullus as
forgetting the Roman alphabet.[1]

Still, there is a sense within Catullan studies that surely we can
do better than the Romanticism of the nineteenth century and the
neo-Romanticism of much of the twentieth.[2] Surely we have done
better already. The work of T. P. Wiseman, combining detailed

---

[1] On reception, see Jauss (1990) and, notably among literary Romanists, Martindale (1993)
1–34; on intertext, Still and Worton (1990) with references there.
[2] The danger of overcompensating for the excesses of Romantic readings, as of any earlier
critical stance, is of course a real one. Wiseman (1985) 116 and Thomas (1988) 54–5 suggest that Catullans may have fallen into it long since. On Romanticism and the critical
valuation of Latin literature, see Habinek (1992) and (1998) 15–33.

historical reconstruction, informed speculation, and an insistence
on reading Catullus' text as a poetry collection rather than the
novelistic journal of a love affair with its entries shuffled, is one
example of how much better we have done.[3] A more recent
example, to cite only one among several, is William Fitzgerald's
Catullan Provocations: the work of a sensitive reader who takes
poetry seriously, even as his Foucauldian *ressentiment* teases and
prods us, with elegant churlishness, towards an escape from over-
sentimentalizing of a poet "we have taken rather too much to our
hearts."[4]

If it seems that at last something close to the palette of its true
colors is being restored to Catullus' poetry, then a question
imposes itself, homerically: How did that image first begin to be
denatured? When did the smoke start to cloud the fresco beyond
recognition? I seem already to have laid the blame implicitly at
the feet of Romanticism, and probably many readers will have
accepted that attribution as just. Was it Ludwig Schwabe who led
us astray, then, Schwabe with his seductive (in its way) amalgam
of empirical historicism, encyclopedic philology, gushing sentiment
and – perhaps most importantly – keen novel writer's instinct,
expressed in elegantly clear Latin prose?[5] If it is true that "the
founding act of modern scholarship on Catullus is [Schwabe's]
identification of the woman behind the name Lesbia," it is also
true that there are modernities and modernities.[6] Schwabe's act,
at the head of a century-long modernity now several decades past,
consisted in mapping Catullus' written Lesbia onto Clodia *Metelli*,
wife of Q. Metellus Celer and the only one of Clodius' three
sisters about whom enough is known to tell a really good story.
Cicero's *Pro Caelio* is a "conspicuous source," and a damning one
for "Lesbia" construed by identification with Cicero's Clodia.[7] His
portrait of a "two-bit Clytemnestra"[8] has provided plentiful grist
for a misogynist mill, one that often mystified the mechanics of its

---

[3] Wiseman, esp. (1969) and (1985).

[4] Fitzgerald (1995) 235.

[5] Schwabe (1862), esp. 53–157, "de amoribus Catulli." Other nineteenth century Catullans
whose voices continued to resonate in the twentieth include Ribbeck (1863) and Westphal
(1867).

[6] Fitzgerald (1995) 21.

[7] On the allure of the "conspicuous source," Wiseman (1985) 1–4.

[8] The nickname *quadrantaria Clytaemnestra*, given by Caelius to Clodia, is preserved by
Quintilian (*Inst.* 8.6.53). On Cicero's smearing of her character through derisive humor in
the *Pro Caelio*, see Austin (1960), Geffcken (1973) and esp. Skinner (1983).

own grinding behind an exalted veneration for the "tenderest of Roman poets."[9] Modernities and modernities: when the "long" modernity, now half a millenium old and counting, welcomed Catullus into its ranks as a printed book, what it took aboard was a text already received, with an author already precooked for readerly consumption, already constructed – even already "romanticized."

The *editio princeps*, dated 1472, came out of the printing house of Wendelin von Speyer at Venice.[10] None of the chapbook intimacy of our slender scholarly Catulluses: this is a large quarto volume containing, along with all of Catullus, the elegies of Propertius and Tibullus and the *Silvae* of Statius. On the verso opposite the first page of the Catullan collection stands this notice:

Valerius Catullus, scriptor lyricus, Veronae nascitur olympiade CLXIII anno ante natum Sallustium Crispum diris Marii Syllaeque temporibus, quo die Plotinus Latinam rhetoricam primus Romae docere coepit. amauit hic puellam primariam Clodiam, quam Lesbiam suo appellat in carmine. lasciuusculus fuit et sua tempestate pares paucos in dicendo frenata oratione, superiorem habuit neminem. in iocis apprime lepidus, in seriis uero grauissimus extitit. erotica scripsit et epithalamium in Manlium. anno uero aetatis suae XXX Romae moritur elatus moerore publico.

Valerius Catullus, lyric writer, born in the 163rd Olympiad the year before the birth of Sallustius Crispus, in the dreadful times of Marius and Sulla, on the day Plotinus [*sic*] first began to teach Latin rhetoric at Rome. He loved Clodia, a girl of high rank, whom he calls Lesbia in his poetry. He was somewhat lascivious, and in his time had few equals, and no superior, in verse expression. He was particularly elegant in jests, but a man of great gravity on serious matters. He wrote erotic pieces, and a marriage-song to Manlius. He died at Rome in the thirtieth year of his age, with public mourning at his funeral.[11]

This publisher's blurb was composed or compiled, we now know, by one Gerolamo Squarzafico, a "modest and ill-paid humanist who worked for Wendelin."[12] The dates of birth and death come from Jerome; the rest may be invention, or extrapolated from the poems, or possibly drawn from an ancient source available to Squarzafico but now lost to us.[13] Of course Squarzafico is follow-

---

[9] Tennyson, "Frater Ave atque Vale."   [10] Gaisser (1993) 25–31.
[11] Text and translation from Wiseman (1985) 207.   [12] Gaisser (1993) 26.
[13] Jerome *Chronica* 150–1H; Wiseman (1985) 270–1.

ing the traditional form used by ancient *grammatici* in composing similar Lives of the Poets: life, works and literary *color*. But even within that convention, the glamor of the Life seems already to have encroached upon the artistry of the Poet. After the (probably fabricated and in any case inaccurate) synchronicities accompanying the nativity comes a sentence with its verb emphatically fronted: that "he loved" (*amauit*), we are to understand, is the central fact of Catullus' existence. And the object of his love is identified first as Clodia – presumably on the authority of Apuleius, *Apol.* 10, though the description *primariam puellam* ("girl of high rank"), not found in Apuleius, sounds genuinely ancient. Only subsequently does Squarzafico give the name "Lesbia" (we are to understand a simple one-to-one correspondence), glossed as the name by which Catullus referred to her *in his poetry*, that last phrase tacked on almost as an afterthought. Eerily modern (or is it eerily Romantic?) of Squarzafico to have writen "Clodia" before "Lesbia." Apuleius, at least, had had the good taste to say it the other way around: "by the same token they should indict Gaius Catullus for using the name 'Lesbia' to stand in for 'Clodia'."[14]

Already present, somehow, in Squarzafico's early modern words is "our Catullus," intact and entire, "biographical fallacy" and all: life privileged over work, and the Lesbia poems (or should we say "Clodia poems"?) over the rest of the collection.[15] This construction of an author named Catullus addressed to the users of a new technology has become familiar to us, through frequent citation, as part of the story we tell about the journey of Catullus (the name of a book and an author) through the centuries into our hands.[16] The story is an odd one, dramatic for all its familiarity: if a single manuscript containing all the poems of our modern editions had not turned up at Verona in the late thirteenth century or the first few years of the fourteenth, Catullus would be for us little more than a name and a series of fragments and testimonia. Textual criticism calls that manuscript V, for *Veronensis*: "Veronese," like Catullus himself, though in fact we have no idea where it had been or where it was actually discovered, or by whom (except in an unsolved riddle). V was copied at least once before it dis-

---

[14] Apuleius *Apologia* 10: *eadem opera accusent C. Catullum quod Lesbiam pro Clodiam nominarit.*
[15] Gaisser (1993) 28.
[16] The entire paragraph is reproduced in Wiseman (1985) 207, Gaisser (1993) 26 and Miller (1994) 52.

appeared again, this time apparently for good. From a copy of V, denoted as A (also now lost), we have one direct descendant (O) and two grandchildren (G and R) by a different parent (called X, also lost).[17]

Catullus the book, then, reached us just before our modernity. Sometime in the first decade of the fourteenth century – possibly in the same year that Dante, recently exiled from Florence, was taking consolation in the hospitality of the Scaligeri at Verona – a contemporary witness of Catullus' return, Benvenuto Campesani, composed a Latin poem to mark the occasion:

> Ad patriam uenio longis a finibus exsul;
>   causa mei reditus compatriota fuit,
> scilicet a calamis tribuit cui Francia nomen
>   quique notat turbae praetereuntis iter.
> quo licet ingenio uestrum celebrate Catullum,
>   cuius sub modio clausa papirus erat.

I who was an exile am come to my country from a faraway land. The cause of my return was a fellow countryman: namely, the one to whom France gave a name from *calami* (reeds) and who marks the path of the passing crowd. With all the wit you may, celebrate your Catullus, whose *papirus* (papyrus/light) had been hidden under a bushel.

This epigram, like many of Catullus' own poems, is inhabited by a series of indeterminacies.[18] First, the middle couplet appears to offer a pair of etymological riddles, presumably on the given and family names of the manuscript's discoverer, whose identity remains undiscovered to date. *Compatriota* (2) would seem to assign him Veronese origin, though in that case *Francia* (3) is a difficulty.[19]

Next there is the Foucauldian question: "Who is speaking?"[20] To answer that the verses are "put into the mouth of Catullus himself" is unobjectionable, but what does "Catullus" mean in that answer?[21] "I who was an exile am come ...": the thing that was missing and now returned is after all the *book of poems* in the reader's hands. At least in its opening words, the epigram harks

---

[17] McKie (1977) 38–95 demonstrated that O and also X, the lost parent of R and G, were copied not directly from V but rather from a lost copy of V, now designated A. See Thomson (1973), (1978) 3–63 and (1997) 22–38.

[18] On Catullan indeterminacy, Selden (1992).

[19] Gaisser (1993) 18 suggests, toward solution of the riddle, a given name of Francesco.

[20] Foucault (1979).

[21] Fordyce (1961) xxvi.

back to a very ancient mode of writing: a first-person inscription by which the inscribed artifact or surface is turned into a "speaking object."[22] Such inscriptions make sense only when attached to the objects they ventriloquize: in this case, a copy of Catullus. Ancient poetry bookrolls often bore similar prefatory inscriptions, some turning the book into a speaking object, others ventriloquized in the voice of the author. An example of the former type, written by the author himself, was attached to Ovid's *Amores* in its second edition: *Qui modo Nasonis fueramus quinque libelli,* | *tres sumus* ("We who had recently been Naso's *five* books are now three"). An example of the second type is the spurious (probably non-Virgilian, that is, but genuinely ancient) opening of the *Aeneid*: *Ille ego qui quondam gracili modulatus auena* | *carmen* ("I am he who once composed a song upon a slender oaten pipe").[23]

The speaker of Benvenuto's epigram sits indeterminately between these two choices; neither choice has its full meaning without the pressure exerted by the other one. Both those choices, of course, are subsumed under the name "Catullus." The corporeal presence of the poet, and the trace of his absence in his *corpus*, are both represented by the signifier of the proper name.[24] English still says "reading Catullus" or "liking Catullus" when it means the *poems*. Latin employed this effaced trope even more readily than our language; the Roman author said, not "my works are read," but "*I* am read." The mistaking of the verses for the poet, for the author, that we generally ascribe to outmoded ("Romantic") forms of literary criticism, and that Catullus' Poem 16 seems to attribute to Furius and Aurelius, is in fact already imbedded in the language used, in both our own tongue and Catullus', to describe the act, desire and enjoyment of reading.

A further locus of indeterminacy in Benvenuto's poem resides at the level of its Catullan intertext. The first verse speaks of absence

---

[22] Burzachechi (1962), also Svenbro (1993) 26–43, a chapter entitled "I Write, Therefore I Efface Myself."

[23] Conte (1986) 84–7 has argued compellingly that Ovid's epigram at the head of the *Amores*, when read together with the opening of the first poem of the collection, makes an allusive gesture both toward the "fake" opening of the *Aeneid* (which Ovid must therefore have known, perhaps as the inscription beneath a portrait lozenge at the head of a deluxe edition) and toward the epic's "real" opening. On the "fake" opening of the *Aeneid* and its (in)authentication, see Austin (1968).

[24] On the (Derridean) "trace" as the textual presence of an absence, Barchiesi (1984), also Riffaterre (1980b).

and of faraway lands: does Benvenuto (Benvenuto's Catullus) have in mind Poem 101 on Catullus' brother's funeral rites, or perhaps a passage or two from Poem 68? The first couplet's joy in homecoming: might this be an echo of Catullus' verses on his own return to Sirmio (Poem 31) or on a friend's homecoming from Spain (Poem 9)? Possibly; but the fact is that there is no verbal affinity close enough to guarantee that Benvenuto had actually read *any* given poem of Catullus (though it is likely on the face of it that he wrote the epigram fresh from a reading of all or part of the collection). Certainly there are no outright Catullan *allusions* here, and it may be that the perceived reminiscences are instances of "readerly" rather than "writerly" intertextuality.[25] The closest and most obvious model for the situation of V's (Catullus') return is the *Odyssey*, unknown to Benvenuto as a text but undoubtedly known to him as a model, just as it was known as a model to his aforementioned contemporary who, without having read Homer, would soon put a series of "Homeric" references into the mouth of Ulysses at *Inferno* 26.90–142.[26]

There is however one unambiguously clear intertextual presence in the epigram, and the reference Benvenuto makes to it is, in the most classical sense of the term, an allusion. Learned and witty, it would be tempting to call it "Callimachean" (since that is what Catullan scholars often say when they mean "learned and witty"), if only it sent the reader's memory to any ancient text other than the one that the tradition of modern classical philology has tended to rope off and quarantine, whether for reasons of Protestant reform, of secularism or, in a word, of modernity. The reference to a gospel parable, coming at the end of the final verse, gives a pointed epigram its point, its pirouette.[27] The presence of the irregular word *papirus*, and even more so the syllepsis upon the word's two meanings – one common ("paper"), the other recondite ("lamp") – performatively mark the poem's author as *doctus*

---

[25] The dichotomy "readerly"/"writerly" invokes the work of Barthes, esp. (1970) and (1973). Both "readerly" and so-called "writerly" intertextuality are of course construed in the only place they can be: at the point of reading, by the reader. The comparable distinction between "explicit" and "implicit" intertextuality, drawn by Jenny (1976), is critiqued by Culler (1981) 100–118. On the heuristic value of reintroducing intersubjectivity into a pure (Kristevan) intertextual model, Hinds (1998) 47–51.

[26] Poem 101 itself makes an intertextual gesture toward the opening of the *Odyssey*, as Conte (1986) 32–9 has shown. See 50–1 below.

[27] Skutsch (1970).

("learned"), *uenustus* ("sophisticated"), and, in short, a worthy reader of Catullus.

The epigram's point is in fact still sharper, and cuts deeper. The "*papirus* under the bushel," once read, retrospectively lights up the entire epigram. Recontextualized by this Christian allusion, the "distant lands" to which the epigram's speaker had been exiled now represent, metaphorically, not merely the centuries during which there was no Catullus (manuscript), but rather the bourne of death, that place "from which," at least in Catullus' poetry, "they say no one returns" (*unde negant redire quemquam*, 3.12). But Catullus *has* returned, to confound his own pagan wisdom. He is with us once more, bidding us celebrate him and call him our own, and his return, in the odd logic of Benvenuto's epigram, has more than a little to do with the communion of saints. If such an interpretation seems a fanciful overreading, it did not seem so to the copyist of G, who in 1375 captioned the epigram: "Verses of Messer Benvenuto Campesani of Vicenza upon the *resurrection* of Catullus, Veronese poet."[28]

Benvenuto's epigram instantiates something that all poetry, all art, ultimately, lays implicit claim to (at least under a certain model of reading): the power to charm away the absence of death, daring us to resist the charm even as it flaunts that charm's failure.[29] What renders Benvenuto's "technology of immortality" foreign to a modern classicist (to this one, at least) is perhaps precisely the fact that it is neither classical nor modern, in any ordinary sense of either term.[30] We are no strangers to poetry's negotiations with death, but in Benvenuto we miss the anxiety, the delirium, the vampirism of a Propertian Baudelaire or a Baudelairean Propertius. For such a poet as those, Benvenuto's wordplay on Catullus' *papirus* might have suggested another play, on Catullus' *corpus*, and the accompanying images of corruption are unsavory ones. But if Benvenuto and his Catullus belong to a different "thought world" from ours, a world also inhabited by Dante and

---

[28] Italics mine. The original caption reads "*Versus domini Beneuenuti de Campexanis de Vicencia de resurrectione Catulli poetae Veronensis*" and appears in G, copied in 1375. Thomson (1978) 195.

[29] Compare the powerful reading of a posthumous stanza by Keats (supposed to have been addressed to Fanny Brawne) by Fitzgerald (1995) 3–4. On Romanticism and the "absent dead," see also Fry (1995) 159–180.

[30] On the immortality conferred by Indo-European traditional poetry, Nagy (1979) 174–210 and (1990) 146–198.

nearing its historical close, there is another sense – and this is the point of reading his poem here – in which Benvenuto's "reception" and "construction" of Catullus, no less than Squarzafico's, is fully familiar to us, and not so very different from the moist and intimate embrace in which Romanticizing novelists and poets, and (to our embarrassment) Romanticizing scholars, have clasped Catullus, that extraordinary case among ancient poets, "one of the special lyric darlings of Europe."[31]

What conclusions can be drawn from this opening look at two cardinal moments in Catullus' reception after antiquity? For one, authors are "always already" constructed. (That much we knew already.) And if that is the case, then perhaps a second conclusion suggests that the essentialist/constructionist binarism is itself a bit facile from the outset; or at least, perhaps we have been too quick to use the terms as if we knew precisely what they meant. (No less a "constructionist" than Judith Butler has recently suggested as much.)[32] A third conclusion takes the form of a question. Should we, then, as Catullan critics, (1) keep our "critical distance" from our author (which sounds proper, moral and grimly pleasureless, even if we believe in that approach's promise to bring us eventually closer to our text rather than take us farther from it), or might we (2) ease up a bit on our modern (and Modernist) earnestness and follow Benvenuto's advice to "celebrate our Catullus"? To explore that question, and the possibility of an answer to it that subsumes both choices, is among the aims of this study. I begin with one of the critical terms of art under which readers have most richly celebrated their Catullus.

SPLENDORS OF THE LYRIC ...

Catullus scriptor lyricus: lyric has long been a Catullan problem, or at least a Catullan issue. Whether it was so for Catullus is another question, and probably unanswerable. He specifically mentions several other kinds of poetry, but never lyric, and no extant source earlier than Jerome refers to Catullus with the epithet *lyricus*.[33] On

[31] Johnson (1982) 108.
[32] Butler, discussing the work of Irigaray in interview with Cheah and Grosz (1998) 19: "[The] utopian dimension actually led me to reconsider what it is that we've all been talking about under the rubric of essentialism when we use that term." See also Butler (1993) 4–12, and de Lauretis (1998) 851–3.
[33] Jerome *Chronica* 150–1H.

a pure historicizing view, ancient lyric was a category of poetry written in the strophic metres once used, or believed to have been used, by archaic Greek poets (who spoke of *melos*, never "lyric") for songs accompanied by the lyre.[34] If we apply this etymological, diachronic and ultimately anachronistic definition of a Hellenistic literary critical term to the Catullan collection, exactly three of the fifty-seven short polymetric poems qualify as lyric: the Sappho translation (Poem 51) and the malediction-valediction addressed to Lesbia in care of Furius and Aurelius (Poem 11), both in sapphics; and the hymn to Diana (Poem 34), in glyconics.[35]

Quite apart from the fact that the critical meaning and value of the term "lyric" is thereby reduced nearly to nil, this identification of genre with metrical form already runs aground even on its own historical terms.[36] Catullus surely knew, for example, Callimachus' fifth hymn *On the Bath of Pallas*, composed in elegiac distichs rather than hexameters, a bold and experimental juxtaposition of *forme* and *fond* in the Hellenistic mode of genre-crossing. More specifically, and closer to the case of Catullus, if "lyric" is to mean "strophic" for Roman poets, then the evidence of Horace is difficult to explain away.[37] The programmatic dedication of the first three books of *Odes* seems to lay explicit claim to lyric status (*lyricis uatibus*, 1.1.35). Even if we do not interpret Horace to mean that *every* poem in his collection is lyric (though I suspect he does mean that), surely it would be perverse to argue that the Leuconoe ode (1.11) is *not* meant to be read as a lyric poem while the Pyrrha ode (1.5) *is*, simply because the former is in the stichic "fifth Asclepiadean" metre and the latter is in the strophic "fourth Asclepiadean." And if lyric could be stichic for Horace, then why not equally so for Catullus, who used the fifth Asclepiadean in an abandoned friend's complaint to Alfenus (Poem 30)? And if one stichic choriambic metre is good for lyric, then why not the hendecasyllabic Phalaecian metre of the sparrows (Poems 2 and 3)

---

[34] See *OCD* s.v. "lyric poetry." On the "absence of ancient lyric theory," see Johnson (1982) 76–95.

[35] Quinn (1972) 31.

[36] If this simplistic view of genre in ancient literature seems now to be more straw than substance, that is so thanks to such work as Cairns (1972) and Conte (1994), esp. 105–128.

[37] Quintilian, interestingly and very clearly, did not classify Catullus among lyric poets (to the consternation of Havelock [1939] 175). At *Inst.* 10.1.96 he names Catullus (along with [Furius] Bibaculus and Horace) among Roman exponents of *iambus*, and in the next sentence pronounces Horace "basically the only [Roman] lyric poet worth reading" (*at lyricorum idem Horatius fere solus legi dignus*).

and kisses (Poems 5 and 7)? The evidence of Martial suggests that those four poems were as central to Catullus' ancient reception as they have been to his modern one, and most readers would probably contend that those poems are "lyric" if there is anything at all of lyric to be found in Catullus.[38]

Another set of critical views has tended, broadly, toward viewing all the polymetric poems – sometimes the epigrams as well, sometimes the whole collection – under the heading of lyric. Taken literally to mean that every poem in the collection is best classified as a lyric poem rather than belonging to some other type – such as *iambus*, which Catullus mentions several times[39] – such a view presents obvious difficulties.[40] But lyric is understood here in a wider sense, implicitly or explicitly, and in any case such an approach has the advantage of offering, in principle, a way to read the poetry collection as a whole work. In practice, however, the attempt to take in the corpus from a single vantage point of "lyric" has had, among other results, a way of throwing the spotlight on a select group of poems to the disadvantage of the rest.

At this end of the critical spectrum, Eric Havelock's enthusiastic formulation, informed by high Romantic critical definitions of the terms "poet," "lyric" and "genius," represents a kind of foundational moment, one that still exercises a certain gravitational pull:[41] "The total of a hundred and nine poems and fragments ... deserves to be regarded as a single body of work displaying certain common characteristics of style and substance, the work in fact of a lyric poet."[42] More than one scholar has made the fair observation that, despite his vast vision of the entire corpus as unified by a single breath of lyric inspiration, Havelock's actual *reading* of Catullus confines itself almost exclusively to the twenty-six "lyrics" he translated.[43] There is no need to rehearse here the limitations

---

[38] Surviving ancient references to Catullus are assembled at Wiseman (1985) 248–50.

[39] The fourth- (or early fifth-) century Roman grammarian Diomedes defines *iambus* as "an abusive poem, usually in ⟨iambic⟩ trimeters." Keil, *Gramm. Lat.* 1.485.11 ff.

[40] Newman (1990) 43–74, on the other hand, stakes his claim for unity on the argument that Catullus is above all an iambic satirist; he consequently reads even the Lesbia poems as partaking of the carnivalesque and grotesque features of the ἰαμβική ἰδέα.

[41] Romantic poetics, we could say, dawns at the late eighteenth-century moment when the poet no longer *has* genius, but rather *is* "a genius": Meltzer (1994) 12. Chateaubriand's notion of "mother geniuses" (*génies mères*) is a central instance of this Romantic conception of literary creation, on which see Bakhtin (1984) 123–4.

[42] Havelock (1939) 75. In the "Alexandrian" longer poems, Havelock finds that Catullus' "writing becomes significant and important only in so far as it is lyrical" (78).

[43] Quinn (1972) 36–7.

of Havelock's important contribution to Catullan studies. Among the valuable and instructive qualities of *The Lyric Genius of Catullus*, certainly, is its sense of "heartfelt, soulswept elevation." The sublime was an aesthetic emotion that high Romantic criticism had been, to put it mildly, less than eager to associate with any poetry of the Latin language.[44]

Havelock's example might have given one to think a Romantic reading of the Catullan sublime to be irreconcilable with powerful and precise critical thinking about the poems and their relation to the lyric genre, had not W. R. Johnson's *The Idea of Lyric* come to prove otherwise. Johnson's conception of the lyric – poetic utterance marked by a heightened rhetorical intensity in the expression of an identity, achieved principally through the dynamic configuration of pronominal forms – is still widely influential in contemporary discussions of the genre both within and without the field of classical literature.[45] His penetrating reading of the lyric Catullus as "a very great neurotic poet, almost in the modern mode" is among the primary reasons why "lyric" has continued to be a central term in Catullan literary studies to date.[46]

An important recent work on the lyric genre characterizes Catullus' poetic production in a way that bears comparison to both Havelock and Johnson. Paul Allen Miller, by a very different route from Havelock's Romanticism (lyric poetry, for Miller, "has little to do with spontaneous outflowings of emotion"), arrives nonetheless at a cohesive and unifying characterization of "the work of Catullus as the first extant example of a true lyric collection."[47] Like Johnson, Miller brings to his Catullan readings a wide literary culture, including an affinity for and deep understanding of Romantic lyric poetry.[48] In Miller's definition, the lyric genre emerges only with the advent of the written poetry collection – a Hellenistic invention, then, though none of its Hellenistic examples survives (not, at least, in the form of single-author collections of short poems).[49] Miller likens the act of reading and rereading the Catullan collection to a "Garden of Forking Paths,"

---

[44] Miles (1974), cited in Johnson (1982) 22.
[45] See, for example, Bahti (1996) 2–7.
[46] Johnson (1982) 122.
[47] Miller (1994) 52.
[48] His work includes, for instance, Bakhtinian criticism on the poetry of Baudelaire: Miller (1993a).
[49] On Hellenistic poetry books, Gutzwiller (1998), also Bing (1988).

after Borges' short story about a mysterious novel in which "whenever a character makes a decision, all possible outcomes are envisaged. The result is a labyrinthine text, which although at first seems to contain no linear plot, in fact possesses a plurality of them."[50]

For Miller, "lyric consciousness" resonates with the temporality of "our own divided psyches."[51] This infinitely complex consciousness emerges in the act of reading, precisely to the extent that the reader becomes engaged in the attempt to construe a *narrative* out of, and in, the poetic collection. Both meaning and "lyric," for Miller, come into being in the Catullan collection through a "will to narrative" that belongs not only to readers but seems to have been "programmed into the text itself."[52] The story told by that narrative, not surprisingly, is the story of Catullus' affair with Lesbia, with the consequence that Miller's actual reading, like that of most Catullan literary critics since Havelock, operates under a principle of selection, or at least of focus. The three pairs of kisses, sparrows and sapphics, and such poems as *Miser Catulle, desinas ineptire* ("Poor Catullus, stop playing the fool," Poem 8), are all central to that narrative; other poems come into focus primarily to the extent that they bathe in Lesbia's light. So, for example, an epigram that otherwise "might appear to be nothing more than a sentimental trifle" gains poignancy not from its own intrinsic merit but from its relation to the rest of the collection, "the dominant theme of which is the poet's love for Lesbia."[53]

Miller has more recently put forward his model of Catullan "lyric consciousness" as a piece of counterevidence for which the narrative spun by Foucault in the third volume of the *History of Sexuality* seems unable to account. Foucault would have it that the Roman imperial period witnessed the invention of a new culture of "care of the self" characterized by an individuality constructed in a way radically different from the culture of "self-mastery" that obtained in Greek society of the fourth century BCE. In its broadest scope, Miller's argument makes the following point: Foucault's synchronic, "archaeological" models posit a given historical era as informed discursively by a single epistemological grid or paradigm (*épistémè*), which "functions as the precondition for the produc-

---

[50] Miller (1994) 75.   [51] Miller (1994) 76.   [52] Miller (1994) 57.
[53] Miller (1994) 56.

tion of all positive knowledge" in that era.[54] Any resistance to an era's dominant *épistémè*, for Foucault, must necessarily be "co-constituted" with the very power by which that *épistémè* is maintained, and therefore not negative, not productive of real historical difference, but rather merely "transgressive."[55] In other words, by making his discursive models – "self-mastery," "care of the self," "sexuality" – into "virtual monoliths"[56] which no subject can negate (let alone escape), Foucault's version of history seems to render impossible precisely those sea changes that would produce the kind of radical grid shift, the kind of quantum leap between reigning orders, that Foucauldian "archaeology" necessarily posits. Miller's more specific point is that between the two synchronic moments defined by Foucault yawns a considerable historical lacuna, and "in that lacuna we find Catullus, whose representation of the subject's self-relation can be accounted for neither by the ethic of self-mastery nor by that of the 'care of the self.' "[57] Remarkably, what makes the literary representation of such a self-relation possible, what enables our reading to call forth into expression that "vertiginous flux of a complex multi-leveled and multi-temporal subjectivity whose relation to itself can never be reduced to the rational normative model implicit in the discourse of Seneca, Pliny and Musonius Rufus," is in Miller's view nothing more or less than the generic form, the generic identity of Catullus' work: "lyric collection."[58]

While Micaela Janan's Lacanian reading of Catullus, and of his (and its, and our) modulations of narrative desire does not explicitly take "lyric" as a term of art, it points toward a "recombinatory reading" of the corpus in a way that has much in common with Miller's approach. Here is a particularly elegant and clear formulation of her position:

[T]he tropological changes rung on our desire as readers are not fundamentally different from those we experience as lovers or as philosophers. We seek meaning – we interpret – in noticing the points of resemblance

[54] Miller (1998) 193; Foucault (1966) 179 (= [1970] 168).
[55] Foucault's (1980) central and most famous example is of course his recharacterization of Freud and the entire "project" of psychoanalysis as operating under a "repressive hypothesis" whose effect is first to invent and subsequently to maintain the modern construction of "sexuality."
[56] Miller (1998) 196.
[57] Miller (1998) 192.
[58] Miller (1998) 192–3.

and difference between different parts of the Catullan corpus. We are
invited to do so, by repetition and difference in subject matter and imagery ..., but as well in meter, vocabulary, and the like. We are simultaneously frustrated, because the Lesbia cycle falls far short of the
totality of a novel, a play, or an epic poem. Resemblance and transformation in key terms assures us that these poems are not simply "an as-
semblage of facts." Yet the gaps in what we are given obscure the
meaning of this particular discourse – rather like a painting or a statue
of which only parts remain.[59]

What makes "narrative desire" desire, as Kermode and Brooks
have taught us, is the "sense of an ending," the enticing promise
of *jouissance* in catching a glimpse of the work (at the end) in its
completed totality, "the totality of a novel, a play or an epic
poem" – but especially of a *novel*, the genre within which Genette,
as well as Kermode and Brooks, elaborated theories of narrative
and reading that have become central to critical thinking about
literature in many genres.[60] We tend to take it for granted now
that one reads an epic, for instance, as if it were a novel, and ac-
cordingly we turn to our great novel readers to learn how to read
epic (with some remarkable results).[61] Once stigmatized as ignoble,
unworthy of serious attention and even morally suspect, the novel
has long since become for most Western readers the zero degree
of genre: the sort of literature you think of when you think of
"literature."[62]

The desire that Catullus' text simultaneously arouses and frus-
trates, in Janan's reading, is a novelistic death drive, focused
nearly exclusively upon the *Liebesroman* – or, in its anagram, the
roman (de) Lesbie.[63] The problem with reading Catullus as if he were
a novel, as Janan well brings out, is that while Catullus himself
gets the *jouissance* of dying young (and leaving, we trust, a beautiful
corpse), he refuses to kill *us* off, as every good novel, and even
every bad one, must. The novelistically desirous reader might, for
instance, latch on to Poems 51 and 11 as the respective beginning
and end of the "affair" (many have done so), and then proceed to

---

[59] Janan (1994) 43.
[60] Central critical texts in this line include Kermode (1966), Booth (1974), Genette (1980), Brooks (1984).
[61] Examples include de Jong (1987) on Homer and Fusillo (1985) on Apollonius.
[62] On "the novel of Catullus," Fitzgerald (1995) 27–9.
[63] It should be pointed out that Janan (1994) 33 defines her study from the outset as focused upon the "Lesbia cycle" rather than the whole corpus.

fill an Aristotelian middle with the other "Lesbia" poems.[64] And yet, assuming that we can reconcile our critical consciences to the notion of shuffling the poems like a Tarot pack to make them tell a story, as in Italo Calvino's *Castle of Crossed Destinies*, even then the text's oscillations and repetitions never allow any given linear sequence to fit the collection seamlessly.[65] Janan's text dramatizes the appetite for narrative cohesion, plenitude and meaning aroused by reading Catullus (by reading him in a certain way, that is), and dramatizes no less the hunger to which that appetite is ultimately left by a book of poems that refuses to be a novel, or even a (lyric) song cycle. There is arguably a sense of the "lyric" implicit in Janan's reading, both in its modulations of the "subject-in-language" (a translation of Lacan's portmanteau word *parlêtre*, but "subject" and "subjectivity" are notions central to recent definitions of lyric),[66] and perhaps even more in her own literary formation as a sensitive critical reader of poetry in the Romantic lyrical tradition: "When the lamp is shattered," a short lyric poem by Shelley, furnishes Janan's book with its title and one of its two epigraphs (a lyric of Coleridge furnishes the other).

The last major literary study of Catullus of the twentieth century, like the first one, has positioned itself under the sign of lyric (once again in a configuration very far from Havelock's notion of "lyric genius"), taking it as a central critical term and featuring it prominently on the cover. "Lyric poetry and the drama of position" subtitles William Fitzgerald's *Catullan Provocations*, a work already praised here for its project of questioning Catullus' seeming diplomatic immunity among critics of ancient poetry, of displacing him from the cushioned armchair that even Paul Veyne was at pains to draw to the table in Catullus' honor.[67] The second reagent in Fitzgerald's critical aqua regia, alongside Foucauldian *ressentiment*, is a distillation prepared from the powerful analytical models elaborated by Paul de Man through readings of Romantic lyric poetry.[68] Applying this heady corrosive, Fitzgerald now inter-

---

[64] On Poem 11 as the end of the "Lesbia cycle" – already so designated by Schwabe (1862) 128 (*quod carminum ad Lesbiae amorem spectantium omnium ultimum a poeta conpositum esse credimus*) – see Fredricksmeyer (1993), also Janan (1994) 66–76. See Miller (1994) 61–77 on Poems 11 and 109 as alternate ends of the "affair."

[65] Calvino (1973).

[66] See, for example, Meschonnic (1996), Jeffreys (1998) xvii–xix.

[67] Fitzgerald (1995) 6–8, 242 n. 15. Veyne (1988a) 34–6 pronounces Catullus' illusion more "classical" than that of the Roman elegists.

[68] de Man (1979).

rogates, and now just as provocatively celebrates, an "ethic of slightness" posited as the generative aesthetic of Catullan lyric. The notion of lyric as a "drama of positionality" gives a foothold for resisting the tendency of many critics to vindicate, through "interpretation," the slightness and even vileness of many of Catullus' poems back into an exalted poetic of depth, seriousness and nobility. Fitzgerald's aim, instead, is to explore "the unconscious of the lyric genre," precisely those things that we as readers, implicitly and all too obviously, license poets to do when we submit ourselves to the silent position of an audience before a lyric speaking subject who never yields the floor.[69]

Whether implicitly or explicitly, then, whether as a given notion or defined with theoretical rigor, the "lyric," as a term and as an idea, was throughout the twentieth century – and even more so at its end than at its beginning – a splendid standard beneath which some of the most important and forward-moving critical thinking about Catullus ranged itself. I hope that my respect and admiration for the critics whose work I have just now reviewed is clear from the pages above; I trust that the extent of my debt to them will be made even clearer at length, even in the following sections in which I set forth my present project of exploring aspects of Catullan poetics in which "lyric" plays no more than a small and decentralized role. If I part company with them, at least for the length of this study, on the question of "lyric," it is certainly not with a view to supplanting the results of their work. If nothing else, I could plead the inevitable perversity that accompanies the sense of belatedness, and a feeling that all the exciting new books on the "lyric" in Catullus have already been written. Less frivolously, I wish to suggest, as others already have both within and without the field of Catullan studies, that certain inevitable associations attached to the term "lyric", associations belonging both to the Romantic tradition and to that version of Modernism that is continuous with rather than disjunctive from Romanticism, still continue to precondition our focus as readers of Catullus.[70] The empiricist, "commonsense" solution to the problem of getting around those preconditions – forgetting modern reception and just reading the poems in their ancient context – tends to produce

---

[69] Fitzgerald (1995) 237.
[70] Batstone's (1993) important essay is more far-reaching in this regard than its own conclusion (framed in terms of Romanticism and "the old New Criticism") explicitly allows.

some perverse results.[71] Perhaps it would be less so if our empirical knowledge were less fragmentary. In any case, it was precisely in an attempt to sweep away the intervening centuries of reception history and get at Catullus "as he really was" that Schwabe produced his Romantic biography of Catullus and spawned an entire tradition for us to regret at our leisure. But perhaps it is possible to get closer to what lies beneath a Romanticized Catullus by moving not farther behind the Romantic but farther past it.

... AND THE LYRIC'S SORROWS

Lyric is more than a Catullan problem, and complaining about its imprecision as a term of art is no new critical occupation. "The very definition of 'lyric,' in the Oxford Dictionary, indicates that the word cannot be satisfactorily defined": so T. S. Eliot, famously, in a 1953 lecture on "The Three Voices of Poetry." The definition he read aloud on that occasion is still of interest:

Lyric: Now the name for short poems, usually divided into stanzas or strophes, and directly expressing the poet's own thoughts and sentiments.

Particularly objectionable to Eliot were the prescription of brevity and the mention of strophic form, a residue from musical performance.[72] What Eliot likes in the definition is the bit about the poet directly expressing his own thoughts and sentiments, but he decides that "meditative verse" is after all a better term than "lyric" for poetry written in the first voice, the voice of the poet "talking to himself, or to no one at all."[73] The term "meditative," however, stands at an even farther remove than "lyric" from the qualities of Catullus' poetry upon which I intend to focus.

If rejecting the (indispensable) term "lyric" has a distinguished modern tradition, the same can be said of the gesture of removing a poet widely considered as lyric (such as Catullus) from the lyric's sphere. To take a single instance: Walter Benjamin, in the face of the vast and rising critical success of Baudelaire's *Les fleurs du mal* during a time when, in Benjamin's judgment, "the conditions for the acceptance of lyric poetry [had] become less favorable,"

---

[71] On "common sense" in literary criticism, Belsey (1980) 1–14.

[72] Strophic form, as suggested earlier, was probably a musical residue for Catullus as well, rather than a synchronic marker of generic identity.

[73] Eliot (1961) 105–6; cited in Quinn (1959) 91–2, also Johnson (1982) 1.

resolved the apparent paradox by pronouncing Baudelaire *not* a lyric poet at all.[74] Benjamin's example is not much more heartening than Eliot's. "Lyric" seems, frankly, an apt enough epithet for Baudelaire. If he is arguably the first "modern" poet of the French language, Baudelaire also inherits the traditions of both French and German Romanticism at their height. *Poète maudit* whose mother shakes her fist at heaven for having engendered such a monster, albatross trapped on a ship and tormented cruelly by sailors, Parisian Andromache wandering amidst the scaffolding of Haussman's construction sites in a city no longer recognizable as home: Baudelaire's self-representation fits very many of the Romantic and modern associations, even the vaguer ones, commonly attached to the term "lyric."[75] More than that, the collection of *Les fleurs du mal* conforms tightly both to W. R. Johnson's conception of lyric by its pronominal dynamics, its rhetorical urgency, and its frequently meditative stance, and also to Paul Allen Miller's definition of lyric as a genre instantiated in a written collection of poems from which there emerges, through the act of reading and rereading in all directions, a multi-layered and multi-faceted consciousness of infinite complexity.[76] Baudelaire's poetry book, I think, fits both the broader and the more rigorously defined notions of the lyric to a significantly greater extent than Catullus', whether by "Catullus' poetry book" we mean a one-volume *libellus* containing the polymetrics alone or the entire corpus as we possess it.

To point out that "lyric" is an apter term for a poet like Baudelaire than for Catullus does not of course amount to saying that the term is useless for Catullan criticism (the work reviewed in the previous section has amply demonstrated the contrary). And it is certainly not to suggest that the kind of emotive self-representation just now described as lyric in Baudelaire is absent from Catullus: for sheer pathos, Catullus as flower at the meadow's edge cut by the passing plow (Poem 11) stands up to, probably even trumps,

---

[74] Benjamin (1974) 607–8, cited in Bahti (1996) 147.

[75] But then, I am writing about Catullus not Baudelaire; it is likely that I would think otherwise if my purpose were to bring Baudelaire's poetry into sharper critical focus. See, for example, de Man's (1984) 239–62 essay on two Baudelaire sonnets in which he argues powerfully that, while "*Obsessions*" is a lyric poem, the more famous "*Correspondances*" is not. See also Jameson's (1985) argument for the presence of a "postmodernism" in Baudelaire.

[76] Johnson (1982) 1–23; Miller (1994) 52–77.

Baudelaire as albatross burned by a cruel sailor's pipe-ashes (and Catullus never consoles himself with the thought that *ses ailes de géant l'empêchent de marcher* ["his giant's wings keep him from walking"]).[77] Nor is it anything close to a move toward deconstructing the term "lyric." It is all a matter of focus, obviously, and what I wish to focus upon are the differences rather than the similarities between, on the one hand, Catullus in the context of his own generic and intertextual traditions and, on the other hand, the traditions of the Romantic and modern poets associated with the term "lyric" in its most unmarked uses.

Its unmarked uses in fact constitute a chief difficulty with the term. "Lyric," when used even slightly imprecisely, comes quickly to mean simply "poem," with the tacit and unquestioned implication that "lyric" is the only kind of poetry, or at least the only real kind, the only kind deserving of the name of poetry and worthy of serious study. Kenneth Quinn, writing in 1971, pointed out that "lyric" for Eric Havelock, writing in 1938, "mean[t], indeed, I think, little more than 'poem,' but 'poem' in the Romantic sense."[78] I doubt if anyone is surprised either by Havelock's usage or by Quinn's characterization of it. But this slippage is by no means limited to Catullan critics, nor to classical scholars, nor even to neo-Romantic high Modernist literary critics. An example: Timothy Bahti, an acute and sensitive critic, neither a Catullan nor a classicist, and writing in 1996, casually makes the following admission near the end of a book on lyric poetry: "My study has not much worried about the distinction between 'lyric' and 'poem.'"[79] Similar instances are not hard to find in other recent critical writing. It is no simple matter, this confusion between the "lyric" and the "poetic," and certainly not something easily dismissed as merely symptomatic of the theoretically retrograde classical philology of a past generation.

On a more public and popular level, current expressions of critical and pedagogical hand-wringing over the widespread decline of interest in poetry tend to slip seamlessly from the "death of the lyric" (a cliché for some time now) into a global demise of

---

[77] Baudelaire, "L'Albatros."
[78] Quinn (1972) 34; Havelock (1939) passim. Though Quinn (1959) 85–100, in an earlier critical sketch that was to have wide and vivifying influence on Catullan studies, had not hesitated to associate Catullus with "the beginnings of modern lyric."
[79] Bahti (1996) 148.

"poetry," the latter usually portrayed as taking place at the hands of the discourses of science and the media.[80] Conversely, and interestingly, the most innovative of our contemporary *poets* have for some time now been experimenting with ways of making new poetry (and making poetry new) precisely by incorporating or "cutting" into their poetic production disparate elements of the prosaic and quotidian discourses of science, of television and computers (among other sources), often juxtaposing these elements with emotively and rhetorically urgent modes of discourse characterizable as lyric. In English, some of the most interesting work along these lines in recent decades has been done by poets described in Britain as "linguistically innovative" and identified in the U.S. with a movement known as "Language poetry."[81]

Precisely this point is made by Marjorie Perloff in a series of studies on poetry in the tradition of Ezra Pound. In an essay entitled "Postmodernism and the impasse of lyric," Perloff examines a number of "high-brow" and "low-brow" variants of that same implicit identification of poetry with the lyric that Quinn criticized in Havelock. Among the "high-brow" versions is Harold Bloom's notion of "internalized quest romance" or "crisis poem" (whose subject must of necessity be the poet's own lyric subjectivity) as the essential form of post-Enlightenment poetry.[82] Another is Mallarmé's "separatist" doctrine of poetry as a language apart, elaborated in *Quant au livre* and elsewhere in Mallarmé's prose and letters as a dichotomy between "The Newspaper" and "The Book." Against the trivial newspaper with "the monotonousness of its eternally unbearable columns," Mallarmé champions the "fragile and inviolable book" whose intimate foldings have an almost religious significance and whose content "is perfect Music, and cannot be anything else" (a lyric collection, in other words).[83]

Chief among Perloff's "low-brow" versions of lyric's hegemony is a poetry collection that constituted a central piece of the furniture of literary competence for English-speaking readers and writers of poetry for well over a century, and still exercises a wide sway, indirectly and intertextually, even over those who do not

---

[80] On Romanticism and the "death of lyric consciousness," Rajan (1985). On lyric's continued postmortem flourishing, see for example Hamburger (1993) 238–44.

[81] On language poetry, Andrews and Bernstein (1984).

[82] Perloff (1985) 172–200. Bloom (1973) and (1977) 1–26; 375–406.

[83] Mallarmé (1982).

know it.[84] *The Golden Treasury of the Best Songs and Lyrics in the English Language* first appeared in 1861, under the editorship of Francis Turner Palgrave, a recent Oxford graduate who later returned to Oxford to occupy a Chair of Poetry. Known as Palgrave's *Golden Treasury* or simply "Palgrave," the anthology has had numerous editions and a few updates, most notably those of C. Day Lewis in 1954 and of John Press in 1964, and has never gone out of print.[85] True to its title, the collection has been treasured by readers and writers of poetry on both sides of the Atlantic; Perloff mentions copies owned, and lovingly annotated, by Thomas Hardy and Wallace Stevens.

In an introduction to the book's first edition, Palgrave effuses: "Poetry gives treasures more golden than gold, leading us in higher and healthier ways than those of the world." The mining of that gold is to be effected by a principle of exclusion stricter than any Roman neoteric version of "Callimachean aesthetics": "Lyrical has been here held essentially to imply that each Poem shall turn on some single thought, feeling, or situation." Narrative, descriptive and didactic poems "unless accompanied by rapidity of movement, brevity, and the colouring of human passion" (qualities that would render them *lyric*) are to be excluded. "What is strictly personal, occasional, and religious" is again dross to be cast out, as is humorous poetry, "except in the very unfrequent instances where a truly poetical tone pervades the whole" (and here, as Perloff notes, the slippage is complete: "truly poetical" has become another way of saying "lyrical"). The residue of those exclusions, Palgrave is confident, will be poetry's very essence: "It is hoped that the contents of this Anthology will ... be found to present a certain 'unity,' 'as episodes,' in the noble language of Shelley, 'to that great Poem which all poets, like the cooperating thoughts of one great mind, have built up since the beginning of the world.'"[86]

To make Palgrave sound ridiculous – an unfair, even a churlish aim, and in any case not much of a challenge at this remove – is not Perloff's point, or mine. It is rather to suggest how pervasive this and related views of poetry continue to be at every level of

---

[84] Newman (1990) 51 has already drawn the connection between Palgrave and discussions of the "lyric" in Catullus.
[85] Palgrave (1861).
[86] Palgrave (1861) a–c, cited in Perloff (1985) 176–7.

contemporary discourse (including the level inhabited by literary studies of Catullus). To several generations of Anglophone readers (budding poets included), "getting to know poetry" meant Palgrave, and therefore poetry meant, in the first instance, *lyric*. But even on the high road of poetic tradition, the dominance of certain Romantic norms for poetry has accompanied us into and through the twentieth century under a number of Modernist guises. Mallarmé's notion of a "Grand Oeuvre" has more in common than not with Shelley's "great Poem," just as Mallarmé's Symbolist aestheticism, from our point of view, now looks more aligned with Romanticism than opposed to it.[87] And, as Perloff points out in another essay, Wallace Stevens' "Supreme Fiction" (from the title of what is perhaps his greatest poem) can be read as another instance of a poetics of Romantic plenitude and cohesion, just as Stevens' version of Modernism is arguably more conterminous with than disjunctive from Romantic visionary humanism.[88] So much is this the case that Harold Bloom was able to assert in the wake of Stevens that "Modernism in literature has not passed; rather it has been exposed as never having been there."[89]

There has been, in other words, a twentieth century whose Modernism, passing from Romantic and Symbolist lyric through Stevens to various contemporary "Modernisms of accommodation," never made the initial break with the Romantic, a twentieth century for which a Romantic poetics in Modernist guise has been as invisible, universal and "natural" as air. In consequence, even at this late date, it is difficult to invoke a term such as "lyric" in any context without (as the spirit says in *Faust*) sucking on the sphere of Romantic paradigms, or of Modernist ones amounting to encrypted versions of the Romantic. This point and the ones deriving from it have, I think, particular importance in the context of Catullan literary studies precisely because of the fact that the major twentieth-century literary criticism on Catullus was produced by classical scholars who, seemingly without exception, were also critically informed, sensitive readers of poetry belonging to Romantic and Modernist traditions (and other traditions as well; Catullus attracts great lovers of poetry). Hence the possibility that a discussion like the present one may provide a means both of

---

[87] Perloff (1985) 177. See also Todorov (1977) on the rise of the Romantic aesthetic.
[88] Stevens, "Notes Toward a Supreme Fiction"; Perloff (1985) 4–6.
[89] Bloom (1975) 28, cited in Perloff (1985) 2.

engaging debate with important Catullan scholarship of recent
and less recent decades and also of focusing attention upon the
tints of the various critical lenses through which Catullus' poetry
has been read – and suggesting ultimately that we try looking at
him through a different shade.

There has of course been another twentieth century alongside
that of the so-called "Stevens tradition," a century whose Modernism spelled rupture rather than continuity with the previous
century's Romanticism. The central poetic production of that
twentieth century, for Perloff and other critics, belongs to Ezra
Pound and the poets of the "Pound tradition." Hugh Kenner's
1971 critical study, by its title, dubbed the modern century's first
half *The Pound Era*.[90] Harold Bloom's *The Poems of our Climate* (1977)
parried with the suggestion that perhaps it was high time to call
the period "the Age of Stevens (or shall we say the Stevens
Era)?"[91] Indeed, the poetic projects of those two Modernist giants
are so radically different, at least in Perloff's view, as to preclude a
meaningful definition of Modernism wide enough to contain them
both. In an essay whose title references that poetic and critical rift
("Pound/Stevens: whose era?"), Perloff contrasts the poetic models attached to these two names.

For Stevens, and for the poets and critics of his tradition, the
poet is above all a *maker of meaning*. The poet gives us "what will
suffice" (Stevens) in a world where established truths have col-
lapsed; he is a kind of "priest of the invisible" (Stevens) whose
"triumphantly desperate humanism" (Bloom), as the only remaining compensation for the traumatic collapse of religious and other
inherited systems of belief and value, "helps us to survive" and
"teaches us how to talk to ourselves" (Bloom). The historical past,
a place from which we try vainly to escape, is both dead and
deadly, full of "rotted names" (Stevens). Poetry is "a part of the
structure of reality," showing us the way to "a life apart from politics" lived in "a kind of radiant and productive atmosphere"
(Stevens). Key terms that regularly appear in Stevensian criticism
include *being, consciousness, self, reality*; literary historical evaluative
terms applied to Stevens' poetry tend to be derived from the
names of Romantic poets: "Keatsian," "Wordsworthian," "Bla-
kean."[92] Behind Stevens' vision of poetry as a kind of aesthetic

⁹⁰ Kenner (1971).   ⁹¹ Bloom (1977) 152.   ⁹² Perloff (1985) 13–23.

religion compensating for the collapse of religious belief and (in Palgrave's words again) "leading us in higher and healthier ways than those of the world" stands of course a long tradition, one that includes Wordsworth and the other great names of high Romantic poetry, later poets like Mallarmé, and such critics as Matthew Arnold and Walter Pater.

Nothing could be further from Pound's definition of poetry. For Pound and his tradition, the poet as "inventor of meaning" is an impossibility. This is so firstly because "the medium of poetry" is not ideas but "WORDS" (as against Stevens, for whom "the thing said must be the poem not the language used in saying it").[93] In consequence, the Poundian poet is above all a crafter of language (Eliot called Pound *il miglior fabbro*) for whom, as for Dr. Johnson, poetry is in the first instance "a species of metrical composition," and whose poetic art at its highest consists in what Pope defined as "true wit": finding words for "what oft was thought but ne'er so well expressed." Secondly, the Poundian poet does not invent meaning because meaning is not made but received; there are no invented meanings. As Kenner put it, in Poundian time "the gods have never left us. Nothing we know the mind to have known has ever left us. Quickened by hints, the mind can know it again, and make it new."[94] No crisis of belief or of meaning inhabits the center of this poetic universe. Poetry, in this vision of it, is neither a language apart nor a world apart from the one in which we live. Instead of Romanticism's, and Stevensian Modernism's, disgust and dyspepsia before the "rotted names" of the historical past, Poundian Modernism evinces a Jeffersonian curiosity for knowledge of every kind from every cultural tradition, a robust appetite for texts to be incorporated – as intertextual presences, as allusions, or as cut-and-paste citations – into a poetry of "encyclopedic collage." Where Stevensian critics apply to their poet such epithets as "Keatsian" and "Wordsworthian," the literary historical terms of Poundian criticism, following the *Cantos*, must range widely over time and space: "Homeric," "Confucian," "Provençal," "Augustan."[95]

Even more telling are the abstractions taken by Pound critics as central terms of art. In place of Stevensian *being, consciousness, self* and *reality*, Poundian criticism tends to privilege such terms as

[93] Stevens (1957) 165; Pound (1934) 34.   [94] Kenner (1971) 554.   [95] Perloff (1985) 13, 22.

precision, particularity, image, structure, and – an approbative critical term of Cicero and Quintilian whose usage one might have thought to have died with Dryden – *invention.* The eighteenth-century references are not coincidental, just as it is no coincidence, in Perloff's view, that some of the most important critical work on Pound has been done by classicists (D. S. Carne-Ross, Guy Davenport, J. P. Sullivan). The late twentieth-century poetry of the Pound tradition, in breaking from neo-Romantic Modernism, can be said to recapitulate a time "before the flood" of Romanticism, and so to point the way to a Postmodernism whose "poetics, it may yet turn out, has more in common with the performative, playful mode of eighteenth-century ironists than with Shelleyan apocalypse. It wants, that is to say, to re-inscribe its initial letter into the story of its arrival – to turn a Poe into a Pope."[96]

We are left with the conclusion that the great question of Modernist poetics, the aesthetic dichotomy at its center, has been whether poetry ought to be Stevensian or Poundian, expressionist or constructionist, "lyric or collage, meditation or encyclopedia, the still moment or jagged fragment."[97] The neatness of Perloff's dichotomy, of course, in some measure blurs the specificity of the two poets occupying that dichotomy's poles. It is perhaps more than a little unfair to Stevens, a poet whose "blessed rage for order" was not exactly equivalent to a blithe indifference in regard to form. But then, that is the way with critically imposed binarisms: they tend toward neatness, simplification, generalization, and even caricature, but they can be good to think with.[98] This one may be good for thinking about Catullus, at least to the extent that it invites us to pose the following question: Between these two twentieth-century paradigms of what poetry is and what the poet does, the Stevensian and the Poundian, the "modern" and "postmodern," "meditative lyric" and "encyclopedic collage," which one sounds closer to Catullus in his current critical reception, closer to "our Catullus"?

---

[96] Perloff (1985) 176.
[97] Perloff (1985) 23.
[98] For a welcome complicating of Perloff's dichotomy, see Campbell (1997). But see Perloff (1999), where the relations between Romanticism, Modernism and Postmodernism are viewed from a broader perspective. And Perloff is by no means the only critic to have pointed to the imbeddedness of specifically modern and Modernist metaphysical certainties in Stevens' poetry: see for example Bruns (1999) 165–79.

MAKE CATULLUS MODERN

I think it safe to say that a fair response to that question would incline toward the first member of each of its pairs, and that twentieth-century Catullan criticism was profoundly influenced by a paradigm of the true poet as chiefly a maker of new meanings in an age of waning belief in a disintegrating system of received values and signs, rather than a wordsmith whose central project is to revivify the expression of received meanings.[99] At the very least, the Romantic and Modernist poets whose names are attached to the former vision of the poet's true work have had paradigmatic value for many Catullans. Add to that the fact that the most influential twentieth-century historical narratives of late republican Rome, Syme's version prominent among them, drew a series of implied and stated parallels between "the modern century" and the generations surrounding Rome's passage from republic to empire.[100] Among the corollaries of this Modernist view of ancient history was an implicit model of historical change as separate from, anterior to, and preconditioning cultural change. That model is now being called into question for the neat distinction and causal relation it posited between the "historical" and the "cultural," a relation that privileged the former, aestheticized the latter, and put their homologues, "politics" and "literature," into the kind of separatist relationship they also occupied, not coincidentally, in the thought of such modern poets as Mallarmé and Stevens.[101] But that calling into question is quite recent, and its work is still continuing; for most of the century, in Roman literary studies as elsewhere, there obtained, widely and implicitly, a vernacularized Modernist model of literary production as something like (1) the aesthetic response of (2) an emotionally intense individual subjectivity to (3) a cultural climate preconditioned by (4) historical (read "political") forces, with those four elements arranged in ascending order of importance and causational power.[102]

---

[99] Put in those terms, Perloff's version of "Poundian" poetics begins to sound close to Mallarmé's "*donner un sens plus pur aux mots de la tribu*" ("to give the tribe's words a purer meaning," from the *Tombeau d'Edgar Poe*), and the neatness of her dichotomy is thus further fretted.

[100] Syme (1939).

[101] Wallace-Hadrill (1997).

[102] For an alternative (Althusserian materialist) twentieth-century version of "literary production," see Macherey (1966).

The tacit assumptions of this critical ideology (it is at least nearly an ideology, as invisible and unnameable as any other) operate in ways considerably subtler than, for example, the Romantic "biographical fallacy" against which Modernist Catullan critics continued to caution themselves and their readers. No one has written seriously about Catullus the Romantic Poet for some time now.[103] But it may be that we are still working to get past Catullus the Modernist Poet, and that it still requires a considerable act of will to reverse, for example, the implicit separation of the literary and the political in Catullus and to entertain the possibility that the poetics of Catullan self-fashioning may be an instance of politics carried on by other means, the possibility of Catullan poetics as what Henri Meschonnic calls a "politics of rhythm."[104]

It is arguable, again, that neo-Romantic Modernist notions of (in Bloom's powerful formulations) "internalized quest romance" as poetry's essential nature and "crisis poetry" as the (lyric) poet's highest and truest work have exercised a degree of paradigmatic allure over Catullan criticism, both at that criticism's most psychologizing and even at its most historicizing, causing it to swerve, to a greater or lesser degree, in the direction of the almost irresistible nobility of Modernist poetics. I am not suggesting for a moment that Catullan studies would be somehow improved by a prescriptive exclusion of such "Stevensian" and psychological terms as *consciousness* or *self*. Nor am I setting out to refute the proposition that Catullus' poetry, by all appearances, bears witness at many levels to cognitive dissonances and anxieties whose sources almost certainly include the facts of his being an Italian of Veronese origin living and writing at Rome (and at Verona, and in eastern Roman provinces) during a time of political, cultural and social upheaval on a massive scale. It may even be true that Catullus' poetry bears witness to an individual crisis of values and

---

[103] The last to do so may have been Blaiklock (1959). A significant date: after Quinn (1959), an avowedly Romantic reading of Catullus stood little chance of being taken seriously enough to be published.

[104] Certainly the last two decades of Catullan scholarship (from, e.g., Skinner [1980] and [1982] to Tatum [1997]) have witnessed a salutary increase in focus on the political in Catullus. I wish to suggest that the personal *is* political in Catullus, and that it is significantly more so (and differently so) than in the Roman poets of the next generation. On "self-fashioning": Greenblatt (1980), esp. 11–73. On "politics of rhythm": Meschonnic (1995) and (1996).

meaning. It may be true to an extent, but to the extent that such a narrative about Catullus is implicitly taken as not merely true but axiomatic, central and complete, it needs questioning.

If Catullus as "crisis poet" has been an unstated modern axiom, at least two modern assumptions have underpinned it, and Christianity, strangely enough, seems bound up with both of them. First is the notion called "Stevensian" by Perloff and often called "Wordsworthian" by other critics (it is in any case a pervasive Romantic and Modernist idea to which many other names could be attached), the notion that poetry, and art in general, serves in its highest and truest form as a kind of aesthetic religion, a compensation for the traumatic collapse of a system of belief and values.[105] Second is, again, the notion that Catullus' time, like ours, was characterized by just such a collapse of belief in the norms of an inherited sign-system, a collapse whose results included a sense of loss and emptiness at the level of individual subjectivity. Both of these assumptions are predicated upon a construction of the term "belief" that appears to be specific to the tradition of Christianity, as Denis Feeney, drawing on recent work in anthropology and religion, has pointed out.[106] For the high Modernist poet and critic, poetry (what it says, far more than how it says it) *matters* in just the way that belief once mattered; by giving us "what will suffice," the poet saves us, narrowly, from a world in which *nothing* matters. I think it would not be an exaggeration to suggest that in consequence, many twentieth-century readers have had a certain investment in finding a modern "skepticism" toward established truths and received ideas in ancient authors, perhaps especially ancient poets. But "skepticism" depends on "belief," and thanks to work like Feeney's it is no longer a certainty that the skepticism of, say, Cicero in his letters and dialogues would have been felt by their author or audience as flying in the face of the *mos maiorum*

---

[105] Interesting, especially in light of the earlier discussion of Perloff (1985), to compare Foucault (1970) 44 (= [1966] 59) : "In the modern age, literature is that which compensates for (and not that which confirms) the signifying function of language."

[106] Feeney (1998) 12–46 on "belief," drawing upon Sperber (1975) and Veyne (1988b). A strain of Romanticism of course read pre-Christian Roman culture as languishing in the exhaustion of its own forms and so groping toward an unknown new (Christian) order: popular portrayals of Rome along these lines included Pater's *Marius the Epicurean* and Sienkiewicz's *Quo Vadis*. Fitzgerald (1995) 125–7 identifies a similar sentiment in Granarolo's (1967) characterization of Catullus.

(just as a kind of "skepticism" seems to have been "traditional" during many centuries of European Catholicism).[107] The same applies, of course, to social norms conceived of as a "belief system." When we use, for instance, the term "adultery" in discussions of Catullus, it is easy (if not unavoidable) to lose sight at some point of what by now everyone knows: the fact that, in a tradition with no decalogue and no post-Kantian "personhood," the native Roman term will have had a radically different construction from the modern one.[108]

The Modernist critical construction of Catullus here outlined owes its most powerful and influential expression, at least in English, and owes even most of what might be called its invention, to the work of a Catullan scholar-critic whose name it has been difficult to hold at a distance until now in the discussion. Throughout the second half of the twentieth century, Kenneth Quinn represented the "traditional," received view of Catullus' poetic achievement and place in literary history, a *communis opinio* that Quinn himself had in considerable measure brought into being through a 1972 full-length study, through a 1970 commentary on all the poems, and perhaps most influentially through a 1959 monograph that proclaimed, as it launched, *The Catullan Revolution*.[109] One brilliant young man's poetic manifesto about another, this slender volume by its provocative title held out a Yeatsian promise to vindicate an ancient poet against the generations of "bald heads forgetful of their sins" and so give back to the world Catullus in all his fresh and dazzling power.

"Manifesto" is a word chosen advisedly. Quinn's critical bombshell (whose fallout we still breathe) has more than a tenuous generic affinity with the innumerable manifestoes produced by Modernist literary and artistic movements of the early and middle twentieth century. The book's central thrust may be characterized, I hope without unfair oversimplification, as a modernizing or updating of Catullus. This was to be accomplished by applying

---

[107] Feeney (1998) 16–17 and 80–3 on Cicero and "brain-balkanisation." On Catholicism and the difficulty of finding a historical "age of faith," Greeley (1995).

[108] On adultery in Roman law, Edwards (1993) 34–62. It seems important to remark here that such a recognition neither bars nor excuses the reader from making moral judgments. See Richlin (1992) xxiii on this point, and Fitzgerald (1995) 212–235 well documents a long misogynist tradition of occluding the reprehensible qualities of the speaker of Catullus' poems.

[109] Quinn (1959), (1970), (1972).

recent (in 1959) literary critical principles to a reading of the poems in such a way as to bring out Catullus' own revolutionary modernness. In Quinn's words:

The poetry [Catullus] wrote is close in form, style and spirit to much of our own contemporary poetry and, like our own poetry, it differs sharply in form, style and spirit from the poetry it largely superseded. It is this up-to-dateness that makes Catullus popular with us and causes us to regard him as important. Because of it we approach the study of his poetry with a sympathy that his interpreters in the nineteenth century seem not always to have possessed. On the other hand, the shape and nature of the revolution in Roman poetry that Catullus represents tend to be concealed from us by this very up-to-dateness, in circumstances that should instead heighten our interest in their analysis.[110]

Broadly, *The Catullan Revolution*'s aim was to correct two sets of views within Catullan criticism that Quinn found unsatisfactory: first, a set of gushingly moist Romantic notions about poetic creation and the nature of "poetic genius"; and second, a set of dry-as-dust philological opinions about Catullus' indebtedness and close ties to Greek, especially Hellenistic, poetic traditions. The generation before Quinn had given strong expression to both these sets of views, in the respective works of Eric Havelock and A. L. Wheeler (predecessors whom Quinn treats with exemplary respect even as he argues against their conclusions).[111] In place of Havelock's Romanticism, Quinn put forward a model of poetic creation informed by his own enthusiastic reading of Modernist poets and critics.

Havelock's notion of "lyric genius," old-fashioned at the time of Havelock's writing, was by 1959 easy to dismiss out of hand, along with the "cant of romantic criticism" represented in the assumption that "the true lyric poet, like Shelley's skylark, pours his full heart in profuse strains of unpremeditated art."[112] Quinn eloquently made the point that even a poem like the couplet beginning *odi et amo* ("I hate and I love," Poem 85) was not a spontaneous cry of the heart, as it might appear taken in isolation, but rather an instance of the "quickening introspection and the subtleties of self-analysis that Catullus learned to express more and more perfectly."[113] The Romantic paradigm of poet as "genius," a sincere, authentic songbird with nature his only tutor, is

---

[110] Quinn (1959) 3.   [111] Havelock (1939), Wheeler (1934).
[112] Quinn (1959) 30.   [113] Quinn (1959) 41.

here replaced with the high Modernist model of poetry as the locus of a different kind of sincerity, one of "introspection" and "self-analysis." Quinn's invocations of Romantic poets are not confined to negative contexts. But when they are named with approval, their conjuring is effected once again in a high Modernist mode. The following instance appears in a discussion of Catullus' "personal" use of mythology in Poem 64 (as against the "impersonal" use of mythology made by Hellenistic poets):

> Catullus, like Keats, was a barbarian who so transformed the raw material of his own life in his poetry that it attained heroic stature, and who contrariwise experienced the excitement of personal involvement in recreating what a modern poet has called – approvingly
>
> > *legends that strut in verses out of the past,*
>
> because the stuff of legend has an organized tension about it that the rawer material of contemporary life seems to the poet to lack.[114]

Keats stands as the first term in an almost Emersonian chain of approbation that includes "barbarian," "heroic," "personal," and "organized tension." Catullus' miniature epic on the wedding of Peleus and Thetis, a poem bristling with hermetic difficulty and Hellenistic learning, is thus recharacterized as just the sort of thing that a barbarian like Romantic Keats or any "modern" poet ought to love to throw his vibrantly heroic personality into.[115] We are of course here already in the thick of the second part of Quinn's project, the more difficult one with the higher stakes, namely his attempt to overturn the view, then best represented by Wheeler, of Catullus as a poet steeped in a continuous poetic tradition that included Hellenistic poetry.

Earlier criticism's formulation of two Catulluses – one a "lyric genius" or, as Kroll had put it, a "spontaneous, primitive child of nature," the other "Alexandrian" and therefore negligible – had made matters more difficult for Quinn here, at least to the extent that he hoped to rehabilitate such Catullan poems as the miniature epic without giving way on his contempt (the word is not too strong) for Hellenistic poetry.[116] Throughout his work, Quinn is at

---

[114] Quinn (1959) 51. The line of poetry quoted is identified in a footnote as belonging to "Through Literature to Life," by L. D. Lerner. "I quote this poem," Quinn adds, "because Mr Lerner's reaction to life and literature seems to me thoroughly Catullan."

[115] And Quinn was in large measure successful: the decades to come produced a series of readings of Poem 64 as "personal poetry," of which notable examples include Putnam (1961) and Daniels [Kuntz] (1967).

[116] Kroll (1968) vii (first published in 1922), cited in Quinn (1959) 30.

pains to demonstrate that "wrongheadedness" and "formalism" are at the root of the view then prevalent among classicists concerning Catullus' relation to his poetic tradition, a view that Quinn sets forth in these terms: "The common view may be summarized briefly. Firstly, Catullus' "models" (as classical criticism likes to call the writers who shape the poetry even of a genuinely creative poet) are Greek, and in particular Alexandrian, not Roman."[117] Note that the word "model" provokes a parenthetic defense of Catullus against the philologists in the name of a Romantic (high Romantic this time, rather than neo-Romantic Modernist) notion of "originality" and a distaste for allusivity and "secondariness."[118]

Quinn's aim of driving a wedge between living, modern (Roman) Catullus and dead, rotting ("Alexandrian") poetic tradition required nothing less than a recasting of the history of ancient literature according to Modernist paradigms. This he carried out with quiet authority in his first two chapters, "Background" and "The Tradition Re-Shaped." A first gesture, after the characterization of "the Hellenistic background" as a time when chance had "silenced the voice of poetry," was to separate Catullus from poetry of *craft*.[119] The epic-tragic tradition, vehicle of most serious Roman poetry before Catullus, was a style "shaped by craftsmen, often foreigners, good at their trade, but not pretending to any insight into the world about them deeper than that needed to manipulate stock types."[120] Catullus and his generation represented a new kind of poet. The phenomenon that produced them was "perhaps primarily a social one"; a combination of independent social status and disaffection for contemporary political ideals led the new poets to turn (like Symbolists and other *fin-de-siècle* poets) away from "the service of the community" to a "more esoteric, more purely poetic kind of poetry."[121] The historical and political upheavals of Catullus' time, which Quinn explicitly compares to

---

[117] Quinn (1959) 19.

[118] On Roman "secondariness" and its aesthetic, Bryson (1990) 53 and Fitzgerald (1995) 167–8; on its woes, Habinek (1992).

[119] Quinn (1959) 5. Strange to consider that these words were written four years after Pfeiffer (1955) had given voice to an enthusiastic optimism (justified in the event) concerning "the future of studies in the field of Hellenistic poetry."

[120] Quinn (1959) 9.

[121] Quinn (1959) 24, 26. "Esoteric" of course invokes Yeats, but also the Symbolists (*Axel's Castle* and the like); "more purely poetic" is reminiscent not only of Mallarmé (Quinn speaks often of *littérature pure*) but also of Palgrave's introduction.

those of the early twentieth century, had produced a "new spiritual atmosphere" (Quinn uses this phrase more than once) which in turn pervades Catullus' poetry of *personality*.[122]

The theories of poetic composition that Quinn favors are taken, again, from Modernist sources. Citing T. S. Eliot and Robert Graves, he espouses a model of poetry as something between religious epiphany and autopsychotherapy. While in the throes of writing – of writing poetry that is neither "instructive," "dramatic" or "narrative" (meditative lyric, then) – the poet, in Eliot's words, is "oppressed by a burden which he must bring to birth in order to obtain relief." Graves is called in for corroboration, with his formulation of a "pathology of poetic composition" in which the work of writing a poem begins when "a poet finds himself caught in some baffling emotional problem, which is of such urgency that it sends him into a sort of trance." The poem is either a solution or at least a clear statement of that problem. Graves explains: "Some poets are more plagued than others with emotional problems, and more conscientious in working out the poems which arise from them – that is to say more attentive in their service to the Muse."[123]

It is clear enough from the above that the poet – the *true* poet – was to be, in Quinn's view (and perhaps in the view of most Catullan critics for the rest of the century), not a playful, performative and technically brilliant wordsmith in the manner of a Pope or a Pound, but rather an intensely personal maker of new meaning in the manner of Wordsworth and Stevens. The writing of genuine poetry, under this model, had to be a matter of deep, often painful involvement of the poet's own personality rather than a matter of erudition, painstaking craft and intellectual delight. It is equally clear that Catullus' age, in Quinn's narrative of it, was an age of despair, full of the upheaval that is productive of personal crisis – the *good* kind of personal crisis, that is, the kind experienced by Roman neoterics and twentieth-century Modernists. Both of these healthy "modern" despairs, one contemporary and one ancient, were to be sharply distinguished from the "disease" whose symptoms were the poetic productions of Hellenistic Alexandria and whose causes lay in "a more complete despair of society and a more passive escapism than the social upheavals of

---

[122] Quinn (1959) 23, 47.   [123] Quinn (1959) 92.

the last century of the Republic, which aroused stronger, less decadent emotions, emotions more useful to poetry."[124]

While Catullan scholarship has done anything but stand still since *The Catullan Revolution*, Quinn's Modernist paradigm of Catullan poetics has continued to be one of the most pervasive influences in subsequent literary study of the poet. This is so, I think, partly because of the very high quality of Quinn's critical writing (and if I have been somewhat harsh toward him here, it was precisely in an effort to counteract at least some of the powerful charm of his words); partly because of the persistence of a kind of vernacularized "Modernism of accommodation" at most levels of both scholarly and public discourse about poetry, with the result that an occluded high Modernism comes to stand in the place of ahistorical *truth* about poetics; and partly because of a tendency (related to the invisibility of a vernacular Modernism) among latter-day Catullan scholars to continue to write against the same Romantic critical baggage ("biographical criticism," "poetry as cry of the heart") that early twentieth-century scholars had already cast over their shoulders, while Modernist critical tenets, closer to home, go largely unquestioned.

Quinn's association of Catullus with "the beginnings of modern lyric" is still central to Catullan criticism, and even his notion of different "levels of intent," though somewhat discredited in those specific terms, perhaps still has its reflex in a continued tendency (a tendency older than Quinn's work, certainly) to go about reading Catullus by focusing the attention upon the "important" (read "Lesbia") poems of the collection.[125] Finally, Quinn's distaste for Hellenistic poetry in general and Callimachus in particular (that name never appears in *The Catullan Revolution*; the later *Catullus: An Interpretation* mentions it a few times, grudgingly and disapprovingly) is probably a major factor in the continued reluctance of recent literary studies to treat the intertextual presence of Callimachus' poetry in the Catullan corpus as a profound and enlivening influence.

---

[124] Quinn (1959) 26, also 59–60. [125] Quinn (1959) 27–43, 85–100.

CHAPTER 2

A postmodern Catullus?

MAKE IT NEW.
Ezra Pound

MAKE CATULLUS NEW

Everyone knows that "the Romans," though perhaps closer to us
than "the Greeks," still were not like us, and that Catullus lived in
"a world not ours."[1] Further, most professional readers of literature both ancient and modern have been persuaded by some version of the argument that a text is never fully extricable from its
reception history, and that new critical attempts to get at ancient
texts "as they really are" will consequently either introduce new
critical misprisions or, more likely, recapitulate old ones. "All the
new thinking," precisely because it is "about loss" – about our
irretrievable distance from the texts to whose study we are drawn
by love, desire, nostalgia (but also by curiosity, appetite, delight) –
inevitably in some measure "resembles the old thinking."[2]

Then again, it may be that the passing from one set of critical
preconceptions to another, the superimposing of one paradigmatic grid over another, represents a privileged moment, one
that offers us the clearest view we can hope to get, through the two
competing trellises that almost cancel each other out, of the thing
itself. If that insight, from *The Order of Things*, has any validity on
the grand historical scale of Foucault's subject, then perhaps a
somewhat new misreading of Catullus' poetry has the possibility
of saying something right about it, at least in the way that a *mot
juste* or a *callida iunctura* manages to say something right.[3] Since the

---

[1] Wiseman (1985) 1–14.
[2] On love and the study of ancient literature, Most (1998).
[3] Foucault (1970) xix–xxi (= [1966] 11–13).

discussion has thus far been framed in the globalizing and generalizing terms of literary historical periodization (terms whose problems are evident enough), I may as well here explicitly characterize my project as an attempt to approach a premodern and preromantic Catullus by reading a postmodern Catullus. By that epithet I intend a set of notions that are both precisely definable and rather different from its now most common associations. The previous chapter has hinted at what a postmodern Catullus might look like, and why a classicist might find interest and utility in the sight. The present one will spell out the interpretive gain I seek in pursuing this avenue of approach, and how such a framework will interact with my reading of the poems.

"Postmodern" is a contested, even a contentious term, whose problems go well beyond those of historical periodization.[4] It would be surprising if all readers greeted its presence here with eagerness. Nor is all resistance to the term (and its referent) based on uninformed prejudice or unthinking reaction. At the broadest and most general level, any observer could be pardoned for concluding that while postmodernism may have had a valuable lesson to teach, academic culture and the culture at large have conned that lesson patiently and long since learned it thoroughly, so much so that further repetition can only have the perverse effect of emphasizing the movement's most negative aspect: the false irony and facile cynicism of the know-it-all hipster *poseur*. Postmodernism on this view (to adopt for a moment some of its own ready-to-wear wit) would appear to be a word with a bright future behind it, a mode that, before it had a chance to amass a history, *was* history.[5]

At the level of our own specialty discipline, one still encounters the opinion, and not just among older scholars, that "being postmodern" for a classicist amounts in practice to a glittering distraction from the hard (and real) work of philology ("the art of

---

[4] Two central theoretical enunciations of the postmodern are Lyotard (1984) and Jameson (1991). See also Vattimo (1985) and Harvey (1989). More to my own purposes are its earlier literary enunciations, chief among them Antin's (1972) essay on modernism and postmodernism in American poetry. See also Calinescu's (1987) survey of modernism and postmodernism read as two "faces of modernity" (alongside the avant-garde, decadence and kitsch). Simpson (1995) reads the "academic postmodern" as a triumph of "the literary," in the sense that terms and approaches derived from the study of (largely Romantic) literature are applied by postmodern academics to non-literary disciplines.

[5] Perloff (1999) remarks on postmodernism's apparent obsolescence in the 1990s.

reading slowly") and an arrogation of the noble dignity of philosophy (without the inconvenient labor of formally studying philosophy) to what is a respectable but ultimately far humbler pursuit.[6] This latter set of objections to the postmodern is not to be dismissed out of hand, but rather engaged in meaningful debate. If those objections are to be answered and their proponents' minds altered, what will convince, ultimately, is not so much counterargument as counterexamples. Of these there is an increasing supply, in the form of work that, through critical and judicious application of theoretical concepts and frameworks to a painstaking and rigorous control of ancient source material, advances knowledge and understanding in ways that situate themselves recognizably within the aims of the discipline of classical scholarship. Such work often simultaneously makes important contributions to other fields, including critical theory itself. Catullan criticism has already benefited from work of this nature, of which several examples have been mentioned here.

While the present reading of Catullus aligns itself with certain aspects of postmodern critical theory and makes grateful use of the theoretical alignments of recent Catullan scholarship, my own invocation of the postmodern aims principally at recuperating an earlier moment in the word's history, prior to its academic appropriation as a mode of discourse and prior to the vernacularization of Anglophone deconstructionism as a mode of universal debunking.[7] I am less interested, for present purposes, in postmodern theory than in postmodern *poetics*. It bears pointing out that the earliest articulations of the postmodern belong historically not to European theorists but rather to American poets.[8] The word's first certain attestation is often credited to the poet Charles Olson. Writing in North Carolina in 1950, Olson proclaimed himself an "archaeologist of the morning" who celebrated "the post-modern, the post-humanist, the post-historical, the going live present, the

---

[6] On this definition of philology, attributed to Roman Jakobson, Watkins (1990) 25; also see de Man (1986) 23–4 on Reuben Brower's "reading in slow motion."

[7] On "deconstruction" in American journalism, Johnson (1994) 23–7.

[8] The point is worth stressing in the particular case of Foucault. While American postmodernists, especially in the plastic arts, have often invoked him as a founding hero, postmodernism was "a label he famously derided thus shortly before his death: 'What is it that they mean by postmodernity? *Je ne suis pas au courant.*'" Recounted by Bourdieu (1999) 76.

'Beautiful Thing.'"[9] Marjorie Perloff has described a number of the characteristics that distinguish postmodernist poets from their Modernist and Romantic predecessors, and these have been sketched earlier: a preference for the performative and ludic over the sincere and introspective; for emotional volatility over emotional intensity; for erudition, verbal wit, invention and allusivity over immediacy and "originality"; for encyclopedic collage over meditative lyric.[10] Another recent critic of postmodern poetry, Joseph Conte, locates the central achievement of these middle and late twentieth-century poets, and their crucial break with such Modernist poets as Pound, in the discovery of a new formalism, an exercise of "that new perception of form which is essential in any poetry of distinction."[11] This new sense of form, for Conte, is most powerfully instantiated in the postmodern "long poem," of which the chief examples include Olson's *Maximus Poems*, William Carlos Williams' *Paterson*, and – the most eccentric, difficult, and in many ways the most interesting of the three – Louis Zukofsky's *"A"*.[12]

Zukofsky's long poem (just over eight hundred pages), written in twenty-four sections according to a plan conceived by the poet in his youth, represents the systematic work of half a century.[13] *A-1* was written in 1928; *A-24* was completed in 1978, the year of Zukofsky's death. A rate of composition that a Roman poet, and Catullus in particular, would have respected and admired (though Catullus admittedly might have judged the single volume far too fat), and a methodical manner of poetic creation that fits ill with both Romantic (Shelley, Keats) and Modernist (Eliot, Graves) paradigms of poetry as shaggy outburst or introspective meditation. Both during his life and since his death, Zukofsky has remained very much a "poet's poet." Despite some important critical essays on his achievement (Davenport, Taggart) and the recent appearance of a number of scholarly monographs, Zukofsky's

---

[9] Olson (1974) 40, cited in J. Conte (1991) 6. "Beautiful thing" is a recurring phrase from William Carlos Williams' *Paterson*. On Olson's relation to Williams (and Pound) and his "anti-symbolism," von Hallberg (1978) 44–81.

[10] See 24–6 above.

[11] J. Conte (1991) 5.

[12] Olson (1983), Williams (1992), Zukofsky (1993).

[13] The earliest sketch for *"A"*, conceived already as a long poem in twenty-four parts, dates from 1927–8 and still exists, on a single creased page. Ahearn (1983) 38. See also Scroggins (1998) 24.

work and even his name are still all but unknown outside the specialty field of twentieth-century avant-garde American poetry.[14] Catullan scholars are of course the exception here. A Zukofskian "translation" of the entire Catullan corpus appeared in 1969, the product of a spousal collaboration between Celia and Louis Zukofsky (as are parts of *"A"*). Thanks to this work, any Catullan specialist can be presumed to know at least the name of Zukofsky and probably to have glanced into the 1969 volume – and perhaps thereupon to have resolved never to think of it again. There are very few things in literature to prepare a reader for the Zukofskys' Catullan renderings (certainly not Pound's comparatively sober and decorous Modernist version of Propertius).[15] As a sample of this work at its most extreme, here is the first stanza of Poem 51, in Catullus' Latin translation of Sappho 31, and in the Zukofskys' version. This latter is a piece that Louis Zukofsky had already incorporated, collage-style, alongside some of his own earlier writing and some correspondence with W. C. Williams, into the end of *A-17*, composed in 1963:[16]

Ille mi par esse deo videtur,	He'll hie me, par *is* he? the God divide her,
Ille, si fas est, superare divos,	he'll hie, see fastest, superior deity,
qui sedens adversus identidem te	quiz – sitting adverse identity – mate,
spectat et audit.	inspect it and audit –

Zukofsky's stated aim – "to breath the 'literal' meaning with [Catullus]" – is here realized in a poetic utterance that conspicuously places the sound of the source text on a par with its sense, rendering now the one, now the other, juxtaposing them without choosing between them, and consequently baffling the reader who searches for a hierarchical signifying relation between word and meaning at the level of language, or between form and content at the level of poetry.[17] Bafflement is perhaps too mild a

---

[14] Essays: Davenport (1981), Creeley (1989) Taggart (1994), and now a collection edited by Scroggins (1997). Monographs: Ahearn (1983), Stanley (1994), Scroggins (1998).

[15] On Pound's Propertius, Sullivan (1964).

[16] Zukofsky and Zukofsky (1969), Zukofsky (1978) 388.

[17] On Zukofskian "translation," Scroggins (1998) 275–7. Interesting to note that Porter (1995) has discerned a similar baffling of the form/content binarism in the poetic theory of Catullus' exact contemporary Philodemus.

word: Zukofskian "translation" seems almost engineered to provoke fright and outrage. Not the least frightening thing about this production is its sheer quantity. Apart from the complete Catullus in a separate volume, *"A"* features scattered snippets from Greek and other Roman authors, a long passage from the Hebrew of the Book of Job opens *A-15*, and *A-21* is a line for line version of the entire text of Plautus' *Rudens*. All of these are done in a manner whose effect suggests that of being half asleep while hearing a radio broadcast in a foreign language and construing native sense out of foreign speech sounds. Or again, the words of the translation proceed like a running gag, a (bad) punning answer to the question "What does this text say?" The joke is at least as old as Plautus' *Poenulus*, in which a character claims to understand Punic, but in fact simply interprets every Punic phrase he hears as the sense equivalent of a Latin phrase that it resembles in sound.[18] Unlike Plautus' Milphio, however, the Zukofskian translator in fact has (or has cribbed) a competent knowledge of the lexical and "literal" meaning of the source language. It is simply that, instead of choosing only among synonyms (as a "sensible," "reasonable" translator does), Zukofsky throws phonetic homonymy with the original utterance into the mix together with lexical synonymy, juxtaposing them along the same axis of selection and giving them fully equal priority, fully equal likelihood of being selected at each decision-making moment in the process of translating.[19]

Zukofsky's "translation" method vexes and problematizes the sets of binary oppositions around which the act of reading and the act of linguistic communication itself are figured, at least in ordinary understanding: sound/sense, form/content, exterior/interior and – the binarism that would appear to define the act of translation – foreign/native. While Zukofsky's renderings of foreign poetry into English are hardly comparable to Catullus' (or any premodern poet's) poetic translations, at least one instance of Catullus translating foreign sound into native sense has recently been suggested. It appears, startlingly enough, in the text that so many readers of Catullus have taken as most defining of his lyricism

---

[18] Plautus, *Poenulus* 961–1030.
[19] On linguistic axes of selection, Jakobson (1987). In the Zukofskys' translation of the Catullus stanza above, not only phonetic but also graphic similarity goes into the mix: note, for example, that "mate" represents *[identide]m te*, as though a letter had fallen out of the printer's plate.

(or personality) and his sincere anguish (or meditative introspection): when Catullus sings "I hate and I love" (85.1), it may be that the sounds from his lips are engineered to echo, in reverse, the end of the first verse of a thematically similar epigram by Philodemus: "[Xanthippe's] harp playing, her speech, her speaking eyes and voice" (Phil. *Epigr.* 1 Sider [=*AP* 5.131] 1: ψαλμὸς καὶ λαλίη καὶ κωτίλον ὄμμα καὶ ῷδή; cf. 85.1: *odi et amo*).[20] In any event, the foreign/native binarism lights up an interesting and important point of affinity between the two poets. Both Catullus and Zukofsky stood in a problematic and paradoxical relation to the "inside" and "outside" of their cultural contexts and poetic traditions. Zukofsky spent his childhood and youth in Manhattan's Lower East Side. He grew up at least bilingual, in Yiddish and English, with a thorough grounding in Hebrew. His first encounter with the high culture of "Western literature" was through theatrical productions of Shakespeare in Yiddish translation, though he went on later (at age eleven, his biographers tell us) to read all of Shakespeare in English. Entering Columbia at age sixteen, with John Erskine and John Dewey among his teachers and Mortimer Adler among his classmates, Zukofsky belonged to the first class of undergraduates to be trained under Erskine's newly conceived "Great Books" curriculum. Among the fruits of that education was an easy, almost aristocratic familiarity with central artifacts (e.g. Aristotle, Spinoza, Shakespeare, Bach) of this new American humanist vision of "Western culture," a familiarity bewrayed by the encyclopedic allusivity of nearly every page of *"A"*.[21] Yet his acquisition of the symbolic capital of high culture and a prestigious university degree, though it gave him a position and livelihood (as a college English instructor), never fully removed Zukofsky from the status of outsider, either in the public context of his career as a poet and his relations with readers, critics and fellow poets, or in the private context of the subjective experience represented in his poetry.[22]

What we can gather of Catullus' life and career, both from his

[20] Sider (1997) 64.
[21] Ahearn (1983) 11, 19–26.
[22] On "symbolic capital," Bourdieu (1972). A chief factor in Zukofsky's outsider status was of course anti-Semitism, of which Pound delivered some particularly monstrous expressions in Zukofsky's regard. On the relations between the two poets, Stanley (1994) 71–108.

poetry and by induction from external evidence, suggests an interestingly similar and similarly paradoxical status within his culture
and society. The site of Catullus' birth, and probably of more
than half his life, was the middle northern Italian city of Verona.
That city and its surrounding region were in Catullus' lifetime
only fairly recently, and thus only incompletely, romanized. Verona was however long since hellenized, long since a participant in
what was still very much the prestige culture of the entire Mediterranean basin. Verona's hellenization at the time, through commerce of every kind, may thus have been more profound than that
of Rome.[23] If the young Catullus came to his *grammaticus* at Verona already speaking Greek, then he will have acquired the literary versions of that language and its high culture literary artifacts
at a significantly lower cognitive cost than many of the elite Romans who were later to become his fellow poets, his audience, and
his friends and enemies.[24] That is of course speculative. What is
certain, however, is that Catullus' exquisite and sensitive renderings of Sappho (Poem 51) and Callimachus (Poem 66), as well as
the pervasive intertextual presence of Greek literature throughout
the Catullan corpus, bespeak a thorough knowledge of the Greek
language and a very high degree of the sense of ownership of that
language's culture. Even more telling is the fact that Catullus' poetry, so rich in Greek elements, nowhere explicitly articulates the
simultaneous admiration and suspicion, the cognitive division and
anxiety *vis-à-vis* the foreignness of a foreign tongue more culturally
prestigious (and so more "expressive" than one's own) that we find
loudly voiced in the writings of Cicero and Lucretius, Catullus'
exact contemporaries.[25]

It is certain that Catullus' first language, the dialect he grew up
speaking in Verona and to which he perhaps reverted on visits
home, though probably a dialect of Latin, was not identical to the
prestige dialect of Rome. It is likewise all but certain that by the
time of his mature poetic production, Catullus had acquired a full
mastery of standard Roman Latin. Catullus was a master player

---

[23] On the hellenization of central Italy: Coarelli (1976) 337–9 and (1983), also Zanker
(1983), both cited in Wiseman (1985) 94 n. 6, 93 n. 3. On Catullus' bilingual culture:
Horsfall (1979), also Wiseman (1979) 167–71 and (1985) 94, 110.

[24] Though Crassus' spoken Greek, for example, was said to be so good that listeners took
him for a native speaker (Cic. *de Orat.* 2.2).

[25] On Roman bilingualism and its anxieties, Dubuisson (1981) and MacMullen (1991), also
Veyne (1979).

(perhaps *the* master player, but we lack the records of his opponents' performances) at the high stakes game of invective verse. It is hard to believe that Catullus would have so fiercely ridiculed Arrius' "hypercorrect" misplaced aspirates (Poem 84) if he had left himself open to easy retaliation in kind on the basis of Veronese dialect features that he had failed to eradicate from his own Latin speech.[26] But however correct his spoken Latin and thorough his Hellenistic culture, however exquisite his poetry and sparkling his *urbanitas*, it remained that Catullus at Rome could never lay full claim to the status of native *urbanus*, nor even to the *nomen Latinum*, at least not without the reservation of a divided loyalty.[27]

The point deserves emphasis, if for no other reason than the fact that we are still coming off a long stretch of reception history during which the Veronese Catullus, like the Mantuan Virgil, was classed as a "Roman poet" plain and simple, with no problematic attached to the epithet.[28] It is not hard to discern, beneath the laughter, seamlines of specifically Italic anxiety and resentment along the fabric of represented subjectivity performed by the speaker of Catullus' poems. In addition to an ear hyperattuned to dialect formations, there are such moments as the comic confusion (Poem 44.1–5) over the geographic attribution of some farmland owned by Catullus' family (those who don't want to offend Catullus call it Tiburtine; those who do are ready to swear by anything that it's Sabine). Then there is the loud protestation, made during a visit home to Verona, that *Rome* is the poet's true home and seat, and that being held back at Verona is not only a negative status mark (*turpe*, 68.27) but a positive torment (*miserum*, 68.30). And Catullus' taunting cries of raw invective, made in the context of political satire and aimed (probably) at Pompey in the person of Rome's founding culture hero (*cinaede Romule, haec uidebis et feres?* "Romulus you faggot, are you going to look at this and just take it?" 29.5,9), point silently to the fact that the voice uttering those cries belongs to no scion of Romulus. The same is true of Catullus' sarcastic praise of Cicero (who, though not born at Rome, was

---

[26] On Poem 84, Vandiver (1990).
[27] The same, of course, can be said of all the great poets of the next generation, though the construction of *Romanitas* had arguably become a different thing by this point.
[28] Exceptions to the general response have included those for whom cultural, social and political affiliations conflicted in a comparable way: e.g. in the seventeenth century, the Catholic Dryden, and in the twentieth, Allen Tate and the other American Southerners of the Fugitive movement.

every bit a Latin and the voice of a new construction of *Romanitas*)
as "the most eloquent of Romulus' descendants" (49.1).[29] It is perhaps even truer of his indignant and disgusted description of the
men "shucked" by Lesbia in alleyways and crossroads as "descendants of great-hearted Remus" (58.5).[30]

Catullus thus appears in his poems as an imperfectly colonized
Italian subject of Rome and of a Roman discourse that he possesses fully by mastery, but never fully owns by membership. This
simultaneous presence, at the level of represented subjectivity, of
a sense of superiority, through possession of the symbolic capital
of prestigious "high culture," and a sense of inferiority, through a
problematically partial outsider status with respect to the surrounding culture (in the other sense), makes an interesting and
potentially fruitful point of comparison between Catullus and
Zukofsky. That comparison is one aspect of a wider application of
postmodern poetics to a reading of premodern Catullus, which I
shall now delineate broadly under the rubrics of the next three sections: intertextuality; the notion of a poetry collection; and, what
is for my reading the most pervasive and important, performance.

INTERTEXTUALITY

Under this wide and now widely used term I include the appropriation of poetic texts alongside that of other non-poetic and
even non-literary "speech genres" such as legal or military diction.[31] A given instance may take the form of, or be most usefully
classified as, "poetic reference," citationality (including intratextual self-citation), translation (whether "literal" or "free"), or
"allusion" in one of several senses of the term.[32] Precisely what
aspect or feature of an intertext is being appropriated into a text
in a given occurrence varies widely, and arriving at the answer to

---

[29] Of course, the poem is open to two mutually contradictory readings (as "sincere" or
"ironic"). Critics have ranged on both sides, and the text of the poem itself refuses to
pronounce: Selden (1992) 464–7. On the politics of Poem 49, Tatum (1988).

[30] Adams (1982) 168 on *glubo* ("strip of its bark").

[31] On "speech genres," Bakhtin (1986). Among writings on intertextuality outside of classics, I have benefited particularly from Still and Worton (1990) and Genette (1982).
Within Roman literature, see especially Barchiesi (1984), Conte (1986), Farrell (1991) and
Hinds (1998). On "explicit" and "implicit" intertextuality, Jenny (1976). Also see Riffaterre (1980a) on intertextuality as an instance of "syllepsis."

[32] It is chiefly thanks to the work of Hinds (1998) that the divergent discourses represented
by these terms are now in dialogue within the study of Latin literature.

that implied question is part of the reader's act of interpretation.[33] The intertext's presence within a text may point primarily, for example, to the intertext's author, who is thus put forward as an admired (or reviled) predecessor or as the representative of a genre, a style or a theory of poetic composition (Conte's "code model").[34] Conversely, the intertext's importance may lie chiefly in the area of narrative content or structure, as for example in the sustained presence of both the *Iliad* and Apollonius' *Argonautica* (alongside other Greek and Roman intertexts) in Poem 64.[35] The intertext may emphasize and intensify the text's surface meaning. It may instead contradict, problematize, or force a radical reinterpretation of that text, sometimes in a manner that refuses to adjudicate among these readerly choices.

Examples of all these versions of intertextuality are easily found in the poetry books of both Zukofsky and Catullus, but with an important difference. In the case of Zukofsky, most of the intertexts are easily accessible to the reader; their "tracks" are easily traceable.[36] They are, after all, drawn in large measure from "Great Books" and from other intact and familiar artifacts of high culture such as the music of Bach and Handel. Zukofsky's *"A"* does not yet have a commentary to answer C. F. Terrell's on Pound's *Cantos*.[37] Nonetheless, many of Zukofsky's most ephemeral and "personal" intertexts are now available through critical articles and monographs, all of them far more reader-friendly and immediately accessible than Zukofsky's own poetic text. The exact opposite is true for Catullus. Our interpretation of Catullan intertextuality is necessarily controlled by the loss of much, indeed most, of what Catullus read. To that extent, Catullan intertextuality is of necessity often more "readerly" than "writerly." Sometimes we have occasion to prove Michael Riffaterre's point: the competent reader can "sniff" the presence of intertextuality

---

[33] No particular reason, then, to avoid the rhetoric of intentionality. Interpretation consists precisely in construing "meaning," which is nothing other than a readerly account of what is "intended" by the text's words. On the act of reading, Fish (1980) esp. 21–67 and Iser (1978).

[34] On *modello-codice*: Conte (1986) 31; on its near equivalent, *modello-genere*, Barchiesi (1984) 91–122.

[35] On Poem 64: Thomas (1982) on its "polemics of poetic reference," Clare (1996) on the intertextual presence of Apollonius, and Stoevesandt (1995) on the poem's relation (as prequel) to the *Iliad*.

[36] Riffaterre (1980b), Barchiesi (1984).

[37] Terrell (1980).

without having precise knowledge of the intertext.[38] Our ignorance, our lack of full "readerly competence" as readers of Catullus is forced upon us by historical accident.[39] Sometimes we have
only a fragment of the intertext, as in the case of Poem 40, or the
anonymous (to us, not to Catullus or Cicero) Hellenistic hexameter verse preserved by Cicero (and chance) whose literal translation makes a bizarre (to us) appearance in Catullus' epyllion
(64.111).[40] Undoubtedly there are many other intertexts present in
the Catullan corpus of whose existence every external trace has
been lost.

The paradox is strange. Zukofsky's often impenetrably hermetic
text gestures toward intertexts that are themselves both traceable
and readable. The text of Catullus, conversely, gives an impression of searing immediacy that wins it passionate partisans in
every generation, and yet the reader wishing to trace its tradition
is immediately confronted with a body of material quite indigestible to anyone without a philologist's formation, temperament and
"cult of the fragment." In this light, it is not difficult to understand
why twentieth-century poetic translators of Catullus have tended
to ignore scholarship's increased focus upon the allusive, the
learned, the performative and even the hermetic in Catullus' verse
diction and poetic craft, continuing instead to give us an Englished
Catullus rhyming out words "in love's despair" for young lovers
"tossing in their beds."[41] Recent poetic translators of Catullus, in
other words, have for the most part chosen to engage neither contemporary Catullan scholarship nor contemporary poetics (the
Zukofskys' "translation" being the most notable exception to the
latter). Even within classical scholarship, the importance and centrality of Catullan *arte allusiva* to Catullan poetics is a contested
issue, with new enunciations of the Catullan poetics of allusivity
still resisted in some quarters as "revivals" of that same "Alexandrian Catullus" that Quinn had found so distasteful in Wheeler.[42]

---

[38] Riffaterre (1990).
[39] On readerly "competence," Culler (1981) 50–3.
[40] On Archilochus, 178–9 below. The underlying Greek hexameter verse is preserved at
Cic. *Att.*8.5.1. See Fordyce (1961) and Thomson (1997) ad loc.; both suspect Callimachean
authorship for the line.
[41] The observation about translations of Catullus has recently been made by Vandiver
(1999).
[42] See, for example, Nappa (forthcoming), who is less than enthusiastic about Thomson's
(1997) emphasis, throughout his commentary, upon the "Alexandrian" in Catullus.

Applying a postmodern poetics to Catullan intertextuality will not grind us a more powerful lens through which to go "allusion hunting," nor will it lessen the complexity of the philological apparatus that must be brought to bear in analyzing the fragmentary evidence of a given poetic reference. What it can offer specifically to Catullan criticism is a way toward a fuller and more satisfying *aesthetic* account of Catullus' poetics of intertextuality. Within both ancient and modern literary studies, intertextuality, for all the "literature" it has produced in the last few decades, still labors, I think, under a vague sense of bad faith, even of bad conscience. A kind of aesthetic scandal attaches to it, and this is not the case merely among those who regard "doing intertextuality," like "doing theory," as a distraction from the scholar-critic-reader's real work. Certainly part of the problem lies in a vernacularized and modernized version of Romanticism's cult of "poetic genius" and its authenticity of "originality."[43] But that cause alone seems only partly to account for critical anxiety in the face of the difficulty of distinguishing between "exemplar models" and "code models," and between direct reference ("explicit" intertextuality) and a *topos*. Stephen Hinds suggests that if we push hard enough, the distinction eventually gives way in every case.[44] The fragmentary state of our evidence is obviously a factor, but even when we possess both text and intertext intact and entire, our tendency as readers has long been to reduce one of the two to a fragmentary state through "detextualizing." So, for example, until recently, in critical accounts of the intertextual presence of Apollonius' *Argonautica* in the *Aeneid*, the prestige of the (central) Virgilian text in large measure overpowered the (extracanonical) Apollonian intertext, disintegrating it into fragments placed in *Aeneid* commentaries.

Hinds' astute observations, and the corollaries derivable from it, point toward what is fundamentally an aesthetic problem, one that has an interesting counterpart in the criticism of twentieth-century collage art. When newspaper fragments appear in a Picasso collage, or when Joseph Cornell wraps boxes in pages from the *Fables* of La Fontaine, are the fragments to be registered by the viewer simply as "printed text," or does it matter what that text says? The answer to that question, twentieth-century artists and critics have suggested, is simultaneously "Yes-and-No not either-or" to both

---

[43] Meltzer (1994).   [44] Hinds (1998) 34–47.

parts of it.[45] A similar aesthetic of simultaneity and juxtaposition obtains in such postmodern long poems as *"A"* and *Paterson*, where newspaper articles, personal letters and postcards, snippets of performances, advertisements and celebrated remarks of the day take their place alongside poetic allusivity and "lyric" expressivity, in a manner that refuses to point the reader toward a hierarchical or syntactical relation between the two. Reading Catullus in this light, I suggest, stands to enrich critical understanding and appreciation of Catullan intertextuality.

Alongside the older resistance to the intertextual, in Catullus and elsewhere, deriving from a Romantic authenticity of original genius, we can also discern a subtler resistance in the name of a Modernist authenticity of earnest sincerity. The scandal of intertextuality, for many twentieth-century readers, has been not only aesthetic but to a certain degree also ethical, an issue not so much of theft as of decorum. Richard Thomas' well-known rejection of the term "allusion" as too ludic a name for serious business was not for nothing.[46] The instinct behind that gesture is a sure one. If the sensibility of a late twentieth-century reader of Latin poetry was made uncomfortable by its relentless "poetic reference," the discomfort arguably more often stemmed not from a high Romantic revolt against the erudition embodied in those references, but rather from a high Modernist sense of scandal at their insolently playful frivolousness. (Eliot's *The Waste Land*, after all, had shown just how serious, how Modernist, allusivity could be made to be, in the right hands.)

Here again comparison with the postmodern may recuperate an aesthetic valorization of the "Alexandrian" poetics of intertextuality that has troubled the reception of Roman and Hellenistic poets. Here is a passage from one of the earliest sections of Zukofsky's *"A"*:

> *At eventide, cool hour*
> Your dead mouth singing,
>   Ricky,
>
> Automobiles speed
> Past the cemetery,

---

[45] Cage (1967) 79, cited in Perloff (1985) 183.
[46] Thomas (1986), discussed by Hinds (1998) 21–5.

> No meter turns.
> Sleep,
>
> With an open gas range
> Beneath for a pillow.[47]

Most readers will agree that these lucid and simple verses embody a "lyric" intensity, an elegiac sorrow and a narrative situation of the highest ethical seriousness. "Ricky" was the nickname of a younger brother of a close friend of Zukofsky who had in fact recently committed suicide.[48] It seems fair to make the comparison to some of Catullus' powerfully moving verses on his own brother's death (in Poems 68 and 101). The Zukofskian passage's first verse, however, contains a remarkable surprise. The italics (present in the original text) make it immediately clear to the attentive reader of the previous sections of *"A"* that this line alludes explicitly to the text of Bach's *St. Matthew Passion*, since all words in italics up to this point in *"A"* have belonged to that same intertext. The exact reference is easily locatable as the first line of a bass recitative near the end of the work, marking the moment when Christ's body is handed over for burial. The German text reads: *Am Abend, wo es kühle war* ("at evening, when it was calm"). Reading that intertext aloud (with a bad American accent) gives the reader who has tracked it down the sudden and startling realization that Zukofsky's "cool hour," which seemed at first a simple "mistranslation" of the German adjective, is in fact a sonic approximation of the underlying phrase: *kühle war*. This is an early instance, then, of that bilingual punning that Zukofsky's later "translations" were to practice on a grander and far more relentless scale.

The aesthetic question immediately implies an ethical one. How, as readers, are we to interpret the presence of this unquestionably ludic moment of performative verbal wit alongside the intense seriousness of both text (Ricky's suicide) and intertext (Christ's burial)? Surely not as an instance of New Criticism's "aesthetic distance" or Eliot's "objective correlative."[49] If any-

---

[47] *A-3*, Zukofsky (1993) 9.

[48] Richard Godfrey Chambers, the younger brother of Whittaker Chambers, committed suicide in 1926. Ahearn (1983) 66–8, also 50–1 on *A-3*.

[49] Eliot (1975) 48 (originally published in 1919). On Eliot's "objective correlative" as the clearing of an affective space in which to live out his personal "crisis," see Miller (1977). Its best known application to Roman poetry is Williams (1980) 31–3, 46–7 and passim.

thing, the sonic syllepsis gives the feel of an intensification, a "going live present" that allows the poet, through verbal play, to impersonate, "breathe with," both the dead young man and the bass soloist in the Bach *Passion*. What registered on first reading as a jarring breach of poetic decorum comes, on further reflection and reinterpretation, to suggest that the fault in my initial judgment lay instead with my own readerly notion of decorum.

Two ludic moments of Catullan intertextuality in the face of death have operated similarly upon the sensibilities of at least some twentieth-century readers. The elegiac farewell to his dead brother cleverly echoes the proem of the *Odyssey*:

πολλῶν δ' ἀνθρώπων ἴδεν ἄστεα καὶ νόον ἔγνω,
πολλὰ δ' ὅ γ' ἐν πόντῳ πάθεν ἄλγεα ὃν κατὰ θυμόν
(*Od.* 1.3–4)

and he saw many cities of men and learned how they
    thought,
and he suffered many pains on the sea, pains within his heart

Multas per gentes et multa per aequora uectus
    aduenio has miseras, frater, ad inferias   (101.1–2)

After traveling through many countries and many seas,
    here I am, brother, I've come to your sad remains.

And perhaps even more remarkably, the elegiac consolation to Calvus on the death of his beloved enters into dialogue with a line of Calvus' own poetry, echoing it, responding to it and – a gesture we have learned to associate with Hellenistic poetics – "correcting" it, though the point here in dispute is something very far from the name of a river in Asia or the kind of wood used to make oars for the *Argo*:[50]

---

[50] Thomas (1986) 185: "Perhaps the quintessentially Alexandrian type of reference is what I would call **correction**, Giangrande's *oppositio in imitando*. This type, more than any other, demonstrates the scholarly aspect of the poet, and reveals the polemical attitudes that lie close beneath the surface of much of the best poetry of Rome" (boldface original).

... forsitan hoc etiam gaudeat ipsa cinis
                        (Calvus 15–16 Courtney)

... who knows? maybe her ashes are even getting some
enjoyment from this

certe non tanto mors immatura dolori est
    Quintiliae, quantum gaudet amore tuo.   (96.5–6)

Of this much I'm sure: her early death does not give
Quintilia as much pain as your love gives her enjoyment.

The fragment of Calvus is a pentameter verse in elegiac distich.
Catullus has thus placed his indicative certainty (*gaudet* – not without a wink in the direction of the erotic) in the precise metrical
position of Calvus' subjunctive tentativeness (*gaudeat*). Gian Biagio
Conte, who has shed light on the intertextual presences in these
two poems of Catullus, has remarked, I think rightly, that both of
them are likely to seem jarring and even contextually inappropriate to modern readers.[51] The fault, again, would seem to lie in our
own sense of poetic decorum, the result of Modernist and neo-
Romantic formations. Performative verbal wit in the face of death
and grief did not seem any more out of place to Catullus than it
had to his Hellenistic predecessors.[52] Nor did it seem so to Zukofsky, or for that matter to Milton (*Lycidas*), poets who seem to have
shared with Catullus a conviction that the "cry of the heart" need
not silence the play of the mind. The postmodern, with its aesthetic of simultaneity and juxtaposition, finds itself again in league
with the time "before the flood" of Romanticism.[53] The former
stands to offer the "modern" reader's sensibility a path back to the
latter.

---

[51] On Poem 101 and the opening of the *Odyssey*, see Conte (1986) 32–3. On Poem 96 and
Calvus fr. 15–16 Courtney, Conte (1994) 136 writes tellingly: "The sophisticated habit of
allusion is so innate to this poetics that it makes an appearance even where the emotional
circumstances must have been so strong as to make it seem almost out of place."
[52] On aspects of wit and the performative in the Hellenistic sepulchral epigram, Lattimore
(1962), Thomas (1998), Gutzwiller (1998) 11–12 and passim.
[53] Bloom (1973) 11.

COLLECTION

Did the manuscript that turned up at Verona during Dante's life-time reflect, in whole or part, an ordering of Catullus' poems done by the poet himself? The "Catullan question" is still with us, and not likely to disappear soon. All the surviving major Latin poetry of the generation after Catullus – Virgil, Horace, the elegists – has come to us grouped in collections whose authorial integrity as poetry books is for the most part both clear from the books them-selves and guaranteed by external evidence. Catullus' ancient re-ception points to the plausibility of a collection of poems under his name known as the *Sparrow* (*passer*).[54] *Passer* is the first word of Poem 2 (Poem 1 is a prefatory dedication), and ancient poetry books were sometimes known by their first words (e.g. Propertius' *Cynthia*). There is room, then, to build a tolerable argument for the poet's own hand in the arrangement of at least the polymetric poems (Poems 1–60).[55] As for arguments for authorial arrange-ment of the entire corpus, these are for the most part based on the internal evidence of thematic and formal structure, at orders of magnitude ranging from pairs and triplets of individual poems to schemes taking in all the poems of the corpus.[56] Neither the inge-nuity nor the complexity of such arguments is necessarily a strike against them. Poem 64, for example (the prime example, but many shorter poems can be compared as well), is clearly the work of a poet in love with structure and the complex interplay of sym-metry and asymmetry.[57]

And yet it has to be admitted that if even part of what we pos-sess of Catullus is a series of poems ordered by their author, it is a strange sort of collection, one whose principle of organization is

[54] The case is argued vigorously by Skinner (1981) for the polymetrics and (1988) for the entire corpus. Quinn (1972) 9–53 is crucially important as well. The arguments for a posthumous editor are given their strongest statement by Hubbard (1983).

[55] Many a clever scheme has been devised. See most recently Jocelyn (1999), who argues against reading Poems 1–60 as "polymetrics," contending instead that Poems 1–61 constitute an authorially designed unit consisting of three types of poetry: "Phalaecian" ἐπιγράμματα, ἴαμβοι and μέλη.

[56] Wiseman (1969) sketches such a scheme. More recent and far more elaborate, both structurally and biographically, is Dettmer (1997). Important to note that "in antiquity, the standard edition of Lucilius, which dated from republican times, consisted of three rolls, arranged according to metre": Rudd (1986) 82.

[57] On the "passionate virtuosity" of Poem 64's concentric arrangement, notable is Martin (1992) 151–71. Bardon (1943) remains classic on the structure of many shorter poems.

not readily apparent. Throughout the corpus there reigns an astonishing heterogeneity of thematic content, poetic diction, implied occasion or context, tone and "speech genre." Even more disconcerting than the diversity of the poems is the effect of their ordering. No surviving ancient Latin poetry collection even approximates the kaleidoscopic diversity of the Catullan corpus.[58] The frequent juxtaposition of starkly contrasting poems is itself a tolerable argument for the likelihood of authorial arrangement: it is not impossible to imagine a posthumous editor of Catullus' *Collected Poems* so laborious (and so self-confident) as to strive for the bold avant-garde effect in arrangement, but it is certainly easier to imagine the poet himself doing so. This is particularly true in the several cases of triplets formed by two poems of similar theme and diction making bookends around a jarringly different piece in the middle.[59]

From whatever angle viewed and at whatever scope, the "Catullan question" is ultimately inseparable from an aesthetic question: namely, "what should a poetry collection look like?" Assume for a moment that we had established conclusively that the received corpus faithfully reflects a single literary artifact conceived by the poet and executed as three bookrolls to be kept together in a single *scrinium* (book crate).[60] Even in that case, as critics we would still have before us the task of giving a viable aesthetic account of that work of literary art in the face of its considerable distance both from Augustan poetry collections and from the expectations of many modern readers of ancient poetry. It is precisely here that the work, and the poetics, of such postmodernist poets as W. C. Williams and Louis Zukofsky may offer a new angle of approach toward positive aesthetic valuation of those Catullan poems, and those qualities of Catullus' poetic output as a whole, that have most resisted critical interpretation. From Schwabe to the end of the twentieth century, the best and most sensitive critical accounts of the corpus as a whole have largely been informed by some version of Romantic (or Modern-

---

[58] Certainly not that of Martial, whose collections contain many imitations of Catullan *nugae* ("trifles"), but nothing of Catullus' lyric intensity. On Catullus and Martial, Newman (1990) 75–103.

[59] Most recently, Jocelyn (1999) focuses on the "triplet" made by Poems 10 through 12.

[60] On the material experience of reading an ancient bookroll, Van Sickle (1980). On reading culture at Rome, Dupont (1994) and Fantham (1996).

ist) plenitude and cohesion, whether in the guise of autobiographical narrative, lyric intensity, Coleridgian "organicism" or
meditative consciousness.[61] While many of Catullus' individual
poems have sparkled brilliantly under the light shed by these critical accounts, the collection as a whole (even in the hands of critics
who argued strongly for unity) has tended to take on the look of a
truncated statue or ruined temple upon which the viewer is invited
to gaze with a Winckelmannian nostalgia. Postmodernist poetics
reminds us that "whole" need not mean "organic." Those same
qualities that give the Catullan corpus the look of a "shattered
lamp" (Janan) may, when regarded with a different set of appetites than those of narrative desire, look instead like a delightfully
tessellated surface of a thousand facets.[62] Alongside a "will to narrative" (Miller) instantiated in Catullus' poetry book, might we not
also posit something of the "will to absolute play" that Greenblatt
discerns in Marlowe, and if not that then at least a positive will to
farrago?[63] This last suggestion is not out of keeping with what we
know or can surmise about the aesthetic values both of Catullus'
poetic traditions (Lucilian *farrago*, Hellenistic *poikilia*) and of his
contemporary "low culture" entertainments (mime).[64] Our own
culture offers us access to what is in many ways a comparable sensibility, both through the mediatic discourses of television and
hypertext and also through such literary works as *"A"* and *Paterson*,
works which, like the Catullan corpus, present narrative and lyric
elements bafflingly juxtaposed with elements of radically different
speech registers. The example of Quinn's work is at hand to demonstrate how much we may hope to gain by continuing to do what
Catullan scholarship can by now claim as a tradition: to supple-
ment philological slow-motion reading of the text with a poetic
sensibility formed by the bravest poetry of every age.

PERFORMANCE

In the face of an ancient or postmodern serial poetic collection's
"dispersal of the speaking subject," performativity itself can often

[61] J. Conte (1991) 27–35 on Coleridge and "organic form."
[62] Janan (1994). See 14–16 above.
[63] Miller (1994) 57 and 12–14 above. On Marlowe's "will to absolute play" (read as darkly
 sinister), Greenblatt (1980) 193–221. For an alternate (though still politically aware) reading of Marlovian exuberance, see Heaney (1995).
[64] On mime and Roman literature, Fantham (1989).

be seen as the unifying and driving force shaping a book's form and providing its generic identity.[65] Several recent studies have highlighted the specific importance of the performative, and possibly of actual performance, to Catullus' poetry and poetics. Under the rubric of literal performance, T. P. Wiseman has suggested that the hymn to Diana (Poem 34) and the Attis narrative (Poem 63) may each represent the text of an actual performance given at a specific occasion.[66] Similar theories had of course long since been put forward about the two wedding poems (Poems 61 and 62), and many scholars had of course long since dismissed these theories out of hand.[67] Here again it is possible to discern the operation of (unstated) normative, aesthetic axioms about what poetry fundamentally is ("a world apart"), how it ought to function in a society, and by whom and under what circumstances it ought to be consumed.

Wiseman's speculative identification of Catullus *mimographus* (whose existence is not speculative but well attested) with our poet also deserves mention here, as does his further suggestion about the final verse of the corpus: *at fixus nostris tu dabis supplicium* ("but *you*, run through by *my* missiles, will get summary punishment" 116.8). The line's prosody has a final sibilant (in *dabis*) failing to "make position" (i.e., lengthen its syllable) when followed by a word beginning with a consonant (*supplicium*). Common in older poetry of both high (Ennius) and low (Plautus) register, the feature was by Catullus' time a mark of archaizing or otherwise looser diction (it is common, for example, in Lucretius). Aside from this parting shot at the end of Poem 116, no other instance of it occurs in Catullus' poetry. To these facts Wiseman added the observation that this same verse may possibly contain what I would call a metrical pun. The verse scans fully correctly as a pentameter (apart from the admission of a metrical feature elsewhere disallowed by Catullus) and so properly fulfills the formal constraints of the elegiac couplet. At the same time, thanks to its exceptional prosody, the same verse can also be scanned as an iambic line of a type ap-

---

[65] Gold (1999) has recently suggested something along these lines in the case of Juvenal.

[66] Wiseman (1985) 92–101, 198–206, though in the latter case Wiseman concludes with the certainty that "the *Attis* brought to the stage a drama whose origins lay deep in its author's psychological experience" (206).

[67] On context and possible performance of Catullus' "wedding poems," Fedeli (1972) and Thomsen (1992).

propriate to comedy and, it seems, to mime. For Wiseman, the "pun" is a possible wink to the audience signaling Catullus' career change, now that his collection is done, to full-time mimographer.[68] If there is anything to this intriguing observation, it offers a view of Catullus ending his poetry book by cracking open its own dictional decorum and the constraints of its own genre(s), as if to burst out of the bookroll onto the boards. A further comparison to Zukofsky's poetry book suggests itself here. The final section of *"A"* also presses the performative beyond the generic limits of its own collection and into the area of literal performance, though it does so on a scale as sustained (nearly 250 pages) and outrageous as Catullus' is momentary and subtle. *A-24* is a kind of sonic collage constructed by Celia Zukofsky under the title *L. Z. Masque*. What appears at the end of *"A"* is thus, on one reading, not the artifact itself but rather the script, or better, the score of an actual performance piece consisting of four separate voices simultaneously reciting four different poetic texts by Louis Zukofsky, to the accompaniment of harpsichord suites by Handel. Catullus' fleeting gesture at the end of his book may possibly have signaled a comparable blurring of generic boundaries in the name of performance.[69]

Quite apart from the arguments for Catullus as a composer of any number of pieces for actual dramatic or choral performance, recent Catullan critics have highlighted various aspects of the performative within the poems themselves. J. K. Newman, applying models derived chiefly from Russian formalism, has read the entire corpus as the iambic-satiric performance of a carnival "grotesque."[70] William Fitzgerald has read Catullan lyric and its modulations as a "drama of positionality."[71] Still more recently, Brian Krostenko's semantic study of approbative adjectives such as *bellus* and *uenustus* – dubbed "côterie" epithets by earlier scholarship – has given new insights on how those terms had been coopted first as evaluative terms of rhetorical art and then, in the last generation or two of the republic, as markers of a very specific

---

[68] Wiseman (1985) 188–9. This suggestion has not been greeted with enthusiasm, but it bears underscoring that in any case the existence of a writer for the stage called Catullus – and never distinguished from the poet – is securely attested by both Martial (5.30.1–4, 12.83) and Juvenal (12.110–1, 7.185–8).

[69] I suggest another possibility about this metrical effect in Poem 116 at 188–9 below.

[70] Newman (1990) 198–200, 256–58 and passim.

[71] Fitzgerald (1995) 1–4 and passim.

brand of Hellenized Roman performative excellence whose context, and whose performance, seem to have come to an abrupt end with the generation that witnessed the rise of the principate.[72]

The word "performative," applied to Catullan poetics, raises the question "performative of what?" My answer to that question gives this study both its title and its central focus on Catullus' poetry as a multifaceted and complex performance of "Roman manhood," the literary reflection of a social and cultural construction of manhood that obtained among elite males at Rome during the lifetimes of Caesar, Cicero and Catullus. That construction's broadest contours are of course not specific to the particular time and place in which Catullus wrote. Recent work in anthropology and sociology has made it increasingly possible (and meaningful) to speak of a continuous "ancient Mediterranean" or even simply a "Mediterranean" manhood, though the specificity of a given point along that continuum is not to be elided.[73] The specific moment within which history situated Catullus appears to have witnessed a new intensity in the Hellenization of the Roman elite, through increased access to Greek luxury goods and high culture artifacts of every kind, and owing perhaps even more to the increased presence at Rome of purveyors of Greek literary culture who had immigrated or been brought as captives.[74] That moment reached its terminus with the "cultural revolution" that (whether as symptom, as cause or as co-constituted event) accompanied the passage from republic to principate, a revolution that appears to have radically transformed the cultural context and social constraints within which individual excellence could be performed.[75] In any case, as Krostenko's work suggests, the approbative lexicon with which the republic's last generations had evaluated social performance seems to have lost its semantic context and function in the first generation of the principate. An important aspect of that social performance (with a longstanding Roman tradition of *dicacitas* behind it) had been the relatively free exchange of spoken

---

[72] Krostenko (2001).
[73] Herzfeld (1985), Gilmore (1990), Bourdieu (1972) and (1998). Stewart (1994) 75–8 is justifiably skeptical about the broad application of the term "Mediterranean culture," but his objections are focused chiefly on the inclusion of Arabic-speaking societies in a Mediterranean continuum.
[74] On republican Rome's Hellenism, see for example Gruen (1990) and (1992) 223–71. On the importance of Greek-speaking slaves as educators at Rome, Rawson (1985) 66–79.
[75] Wallace-Hadrill (1997) 3–11.

and written invective, a lively commerce of wit that, if it did not set all its players on a precisely equal footing, had at least emboldened Catullus to direct some of his most scathing barbs against Caesar's favorites, and Caesar's own person.[76] How radically the events of the three decades after Catullus' death had altered the constraints of social performance may be judged from a remark of Asinius Pollio. When asked why a man of his reputation for wit had failed to respond in kind to a satiric invective poem directed at him by Augustus, Pollio responded: "it's hard to write a poem against a man who can write your death warrant."[77] No comparable consideration ever stayed Catullus' hand. Julius Caesar is said to have responded to Catullus' invective smear campaign with neither retaliation in kind nor threats of a direr vengeance, but rather with an attempt at personal and familial reconciliation.[78]

The extent to which the elite Roman man's manhood was an acutely performative business, and carried out under the constraint of constant surveillance, has been highlighted by such work as Catharine Edwards'.[79] A toga hiked up too high and tight marked the man inside it a bumpkin (*subrusticus*). Draped too low, its flowing folds presented to the observer an irrefutably obvious metonym and metaphor (with all the "obviousness" of every cultural construct) of the softness and looseness of its wearer's effeminacy.[80] The sight of the young Julius Caesar in a tunic with a loose belt drooped fetchingly about the hips is said to have so excited the hypermasculine ire of Sulla that the conquering general had to be held back from fatally bashing the youth who would

---

[76] Esp. Poems 29 and 93.

[77] *non est facile in eum scribere qui potest proscribere* (Macrob. *Sat.* 2.4.21). An understandable reticence – Pollio's own father-in-law, L. Quinctius, had been proscribed (Appian, *BC* 4.27.114) – but note that Pollio's response performatively assured the interlocutor that his famed wit had suffered no diminution.

[78] Suetonius, *Jul.* 73. None of this is to suggest that public life under the empire was less a theatrical matter, or manhood a less performative one. The contrary seems to be true. See, on imperial theatricality and manly performance respectively, Bartsch (1994) and Gleason (1995).

[79] Edwards (1993), esp. 63–97.

[80] Cicero accuses Catiline's followers of, among other traditional marks of effeminacy, wearing "sails not togas" (*Cat.*2.10.22). And a young man doing his internship in the forum (*tirocinium fori*) was required to wear his toga in such a manner that its upper folds constrained his arms from broad gesticulation: a way, presumably, of protecting a freeborn Roman youth from exposing the delicate boyishness of his movements to the desirous or contemptuous (or both) eyes of Roman men. Austin (1960) ad Cic. *Pro Caelio* 11.

one day give his name to the emperors of Rome; Cicero, for his part, claimed to have judged that the state would have nothing to fear from Caesar after he had seen the latter scratch his head with a single finger.[81] A disproportionate number of similar contemporary animadversions on effeminacy attach themselves to the name of Caesar, but then Caesar was the most conspicuous and for a time the most powerful man of his day. There is no reason to think that any elite Roman male was exempted from observations on his social performance, and conclusions about his manhood, of the type that Catullus claims in Poem 16 to have received from Furius and Aurelius. Even Cicero, for all the manly *grauitas* and all the intolerance of everything effeminate that his forensic speeches seem to embody, came under criticism for a certain looseness in the hips (*elumbis*) and perhaps an unseemly rhetorical overuse of the higher registers of his tenor voice.[82] Attention to the external performance of manliness operated at a level of intensity that, in a modern context, would likely be attributed to a given individual's obsessional pathology. In Catullus' Rome it was rather the norm of social interaction among men. Individual performance of manhood, for an elite Roman male, was thus both compelled and constrained. Keen competition for distinction necessitated constant and conspicuous public social performance. At the same time, every semiotic element of that performance, in dress, comportment and speech, was subject at every moment to ideological evaluation along the binary spectrum of virility/effeminacy, an evaluation whose vigilance made no allowances or exceptions.

Recent work in cultural anthropology offers instructive comparisons to this agonistic and performative construction of manhood as well as a useful vocabulary for describing it. Michael Herzfeld's *The Poetics of Manhood*, a study of social interaction among men in a Cretan village, theorizes social performance as embodying a "rhetoric of the self." Drawing on sociologist Erving Goffman's *Presentation of the Self in Everyday Life* as well as Roman Jakobson's structuralist definition of the "poetic function in language" as a

---

[81] Dio 43.43.1–4 and Plutarch *Caes.* 4.4, cited at Edwards (1993) 90, 63. An epigram of Calvus (fr. 18 Courtney = Schol. Juv. 9.133) comments similarly on Pompey's effeminate head-scratching technique.

[82] Calvus again (interesting that Catullus' friend seems to have set himself up as something of an arbiter of virility). He is said to have pronounced Cicero "limp and flaccid" (*solutus et eneruis*). Brutus was still harsher, calling Cicero "emasculated and loose in the hips" (*fractus atque elumbis*). Tacitus, *Dial.* 18.5.

foregrounding of the *message* itself and a concomitant back-grounding of that message's referent, Herzfeld characterized the self-presentation and interactional strategies he witnessed among Cretan village men as "performances of selfhood":

[T]he successful performance of selfhood depends on an ability to iden-tify the self with larger categories of identity. In any encounter, the skilled actor alludes to ideological propositions and historical antecedents, but takes care to suppress the sense of incongruity inevitably created by such grandiose implications; as with virtually any trope, the projection of the self as a metonymical encapsulation of some more inclusive entity rests on the violation of ordinariness. A successful performance of per-sonal identity concentrates the audience's attention on the performance itself: the implicit claims are accepted because their very outrageousness carries a revelatory kind of conviction. It is in this self-allusiveness of social performances, and in the concomitant backgrounding of everyday considerations, that we can discern a poetics of social interaction. The self is not presented within everyday life so much as in front of it.[83]

In Glendiot men's creations of "meaning" (*simasia*) through outra-geous tales of animal theft – acts sometimes vaunted as feats of macho bravado and *eghoismos*, at other times justified as motivated by hunger, and at still other times described as carried out for the purpose of "making friends" – Herzfeld discerned the operation of "a rhetoric of self-justification balanced against self-recognition," which in turn reflected an "imbalance between center and peri-phery" at the heart of the speaker's self-identification.[84] The Glendiot man's manhood is thus defined and evaluated in terms far more aesthetic and poetic than characterological and ethical:

In Glendiot idiom, there is less focus on "being a good man" than on "being good at being a man" – a stance that stresses *performative excellence*, the ability to foreground manhood by means of deeds that strikingly "speak for themselves." Actions that occur at a conventional pace are not noticeable: everyone works hard, most adult males dance elegantly enough, any shepherd can steal a sheep on some occasion or other. What counts is ... effective *movement* – a sense of shifting the ordinary and ev-eryday into a context where the very change of context itself serves to invest it with sudden significance. Thus, instead of noticing *what* men do, Glendiots focus their attention on *how* the act is performed. There must be an *acceleration* or *stylistic transfiguration* of action; the work must be done

---

[83] Herzfeld (1985) 10–11. Also Goffman (1959), Jakobson (1987).
[84] Herzfeld (1985) 23.

with flair; the dance executed with new embellishments that do not disrupt the basic step of the other dancers; and the theft must be performed in such a manner that it serves immediate notice on the victim of the perpetrator's skill: as he is good at stealing, so, too, he will be good at being your enemy or your ally – so choose! Both the act of theft and the narration that follows it focus on the act itself. They announce the quality of the theft, the skill with which it has been performed and recounted, as primary components of the author's claim to a manly selfhood that captures the essence of Glendiot, Cretan, and Greek identity all at the same time. To the extent that they succeed, they are said to have *simasia*, meaning.[85]

How directly applicable is a Herzfeldian "poetics of manhood" to the poetry of Catullus? Even at their most universalizing, Herzfeld's formulations are obviously oriented toward the description of social interaction within the specific community that was the object of his study. Work in cultural anthropology since Herzfeld has continued to corroborate a constructionist view, at least of a sort, of gender and more specifically of manhood. If most societies (though, interestingly, not all) evince a discourse and an ideology of manhood as a fragile and elusive possession to be earned, won and carefully guarded, the ways in which that manhood is defined and evaluated show the widest imaginable diversity from culture to culture.[86] The two passages cited above suffice to make it clear that Herzfeld's Cretan villagers construe not only manliness and unmanliness along significantly different gridlines from those inscribed in the text of Catullus' poems, but also such factors as the relation to property (theft, work, wealth and scarcity) and to food (hunger, satiety, gluttony).[87] Differences in cultural context, social position, and a host of other considerations make for radically different discourses of selfhood, of excellence and of manhood.

These qualifications, I think, are unobjectionable and obvious. But the same qualifications apply equally well to the differences between the cultural constructs informing Catullus' poems and those of all his modern readers, and it is precisely these differences that the act, and the pleasure, of reading Catullus tend all too easily to elide, however critically and historically informed the reader – indeed, sometimes as a result precisely of the reader's

---

[85] Herzfeld (1985) 17–18.
[86] Surveyed in Gilmore (1990).
[87] On "systems of food imagery" in Catullus, Richlin (1988).

sympathetic and richly imaginative critical tact. Hence the possibility of an interpretive gain through triangulation, the possibility that introducing a third term between text and reader may relax the insistence, if only momentarily, of those binarisms that haunt the criticism of literature, and haunt all the more insistently the criticism of a text that we receive already under the looming power of its constructed author's personality: likeness and difference, attraction and aversion, celebration and resentment, excusing and "deconstructing." In the first part of this study, where the focus has been on Catullan reception, I have attempted to hold up such a third term primarily through explicit invocation of a poetics of the postmodern as elaborated by its poets and critics. In what follows, where the focus will be on reading the Catullan collection and individual poems, a further point of reference, an alternate third point of the triangle, will be sought in a Herzfeldian performative poetics of manhood.

CHAPTER 3

Manhood and Lesbia in the shorter poems

ἀνώνυμος τυγχάνει οὖσα μέχρι τοῦ νῦν

Aristotle, *Poetics* 1449b

("[The object of poetics] remains nameless to date.")

THE OBJECT OF CATULLAN POETICS

It still remains to show in what sense Catullus' text embodies a Herzfeldian "poetics of manhood." We might begin with its unmistakably positive aesthetic valuation of the extraordinary and the conspicuous as evidenced in hyperbolic claims whose "very outrageousness carries a revelatory kind of conviction."[1] Performatively outrageous claims about self and other could plausibly be called a defining feature of the poems. Most of these claims are centered around the appetites and senses of the speaker or interlocutor's body.[2] At times the object of performance is a refined aesthetic connoisseurship, as when Catullus pronounces an ointment's fragrance so fine that it will make Fabullus wish himself "all nose" (Poem 13), or complains that his life is in danger from the effect of a book of bad poems he has received as a Saturnalia gag gift from Calvus (Poem 14). Elsewhere it is the Catullan speaker's own insatiable appetites, whether oral (as in Poem 7's self-avowedly "mad" hunger for a series of infinitudes of kisses) or genital (as in Poem 32's notice served on Ipsitilla that she prepare herself for nine copulations without a pause). Even the frustration or mortification of an appetite is thrown into the relief of performative excess, as when Catullus, having stolen a single kiss from the boy Juventius, describes himself "hung high upon a cross for more than a whole hour" (99.3–4), weeping and pleading while

---

[1] Herzfeld (1985) 11. See 60–2 above.   [2] Richlin (1988).

the boy washes Catullus' kiss off his lips as though it were the "foul spittle of a wolf that smelled of piss" (99.10). Two classes of hyperbolic claim, however, outstrip the rest for unforgettable insistence: first, a series of violently obscene invective threats and insults of every kind scattered throughout the corpus; and second, a series of declarations of passionate and faithful love. Neither of these classes of Catullan performance has its match for expressive force elsewhere in the surviving literature of the language. The first has been a scandal and an embarrassment for most of Catullus' modern reception history. And it is the claims of the second kind, in the "Lesbia poems," many of them so close on their face to expressions of modern "romantic" love, that have given their poet his uniquely favored status as the "tenderest of Roman poets," the "lyric darling," "*ce vivant*," and even, like Virgil (a poet more revered but less beloved), an *anima naturaliter cristiana*.[3]

If the rhetoric of Catullan self-representation depends in large measure on the staking of outrageous claims, the articulation of those claims lends itself easily enough to description in Herzfeld's poetic and rhetorical terms. Catullus' allusivity "to ideological propositions and historical antecedents" was sketched in the earlier section on intertextuality, and this aspect of his poetry will structure the final chapter in which a pair of "character intertexts" will be read as "code models" of a manhood performed through oscillatory modulations of fierce aggression and exquisite delicacy. Further, Catullus' relentless "self-allusivity," in Herzfeld's Jakobsonian sense of a poetic foregrounding of the performance act itself through its "stylistic transfiguration," is precisely what the previous chapter attempted to articulate by foregrounding Catullan wit and invention over the qualities of originality, sincerity, intensity and introspection that centuries of readers have celebrated in their Catullus.

What of Herzfeld's suggestion that the "skilled actor" of a performed selfhood "takes care to suppress the sense of incongruity inevitably created" by his "grandiose claims"? The question is subtler than the previous ones. Its answer in Catullus' case, I think, is complicated precisely by Catullus' reception history. On my own reading, the poems hardly urge a characterization of their speaker as highly effective at suppressing incongruity, and I should

---

[3] *ce vivant*: Granarolo (1957).

be very surprised if many readers were awaiting an elaborate demonstration of that assertion. It seems frankly impossible to sustain credence in the piety, chastity and fidelity to which the speaker of the "Lesbia poems" lays claim in a series of sublime declarations of love tenderly offered and tragically spurned. It is not so much the illicit, adulterous status of the union so envisaged that sticks in the craw (on that count it has long been easy to build a cohesive and even satisfying reading of the poems as the cry of a Hegelian beautiful soul in revolt against a sick society).[4] It is rather the cynical and even brutal connoisseurship of the objectified bodies of women and boys in other poems, and the violent misogyny of those "Lesbia poems" in the mode of rejected despondence, that has led most of us, the current "interpretive community" of Catullus' readers, to doubt the validity and even the seriousness of Catullus' claims to *pietas* and *fides* in Lesbia's regard. And to the extent that we take the Catullan corpus to be a collection organized by its author, the stridently dissonant juxtapositions of its arrangement only serve to throw its speaker's self-contradiction into sharper focus.

If this reading represents the majority opinion of current Catullan scholarship, it is important to remember that we possess its vantage point only because we stand on the shoulders of the great Catullan "skeptical readers" of the late twentieth century.[5] For most of his (long) modern reception history, Catullus was indeed a "skilled actor," so skilled in the art to conceal art that readers were quick to come to his aid, excusing what they could and simply editing out of the discussion (or the school text) what they could not. The poet's skill was of course not the only factor at work. As William Fitzgerald has pointed out, many of Catullus' earlier modern readers have had an investment in maintaining the assignment of an ahistorical truth value to ideological propositions about culture and society that were identical or close to the propositions embodied and personated by the Catullan speaking subject.[6] Losing sight of this, by eliding reception history and

---

[4] Perhaps the strongest reading of Catullus as poetry of social commentary is Konstan (1977) on Poem 64. See also Petrini (1997). If Lesbia was Clodia Metelli, she may have been widowed at the time of Catullus' writing. In any case, Poem 83 seems to depict Lesbia talking to her husband.

[5] Along with Skinner, other important skeptical readers of Catullus include Selden (1992), Richlin (1992), Fitzgerald (1995), Hallett (1996) and Greene (1998).

[6] Fitzgerald (1995) 212–35.

proceeding directly to an "ethical" reading, runs the risk of trivializing the important work in Catullan scholarship that made such a reading possible. Each age has its own morality and its own hypocrisies. Catullus' poems present a persona that manages to run afoul of those of his own historical moment as well as ours. It is hard to say which is the greater danger at the current juncture: to condemn Catullus too hastily on the grounds that he ought to have conformed to a modern liberal ethics of human rights and personhood, or to excuse him too hastily by the strategem of positing, just behind the persona, the presence of a "poet" who *did* conform to it.

Finally, what I take to be the central feature of Herzfeld's "poetics of manhood" seems not only present but pervasive through the Catullan corpus: a prioritizing of the performative over the ethical, so that "there is less focus on 'being a good man' than on 'being good at being a man.'" A Catullan poem, on this reading, is above all a *captatio* (a "play" for approbation), a *lacessatio* ("challenge"), a performance of excellence. "Being good at," through a *uis* and *uenustas* ("force" and "wit") that leave the interlocutor gasping for breath, is the answer I propose to the question "what are Catullus' poems about?"[7] Their contexts are indeed political and social, but they participate in those contexts as performances in front of them rather than as critiques from without. They are spoken on a stage. Theirs is a poetics and even a politics of performance rather than a Stevensian "life lived apart from politics," and the performative excellence for which they strive belongs, in the first instance, to the social ("homosocial") interaction among Roman elite males.[8] It is in this sense that it is both possible and appropriate, I think, to speak of a poetics of manhood in Catullus, and even to suggest that, setting aside for a moment the Lesbia poems, the object of Catullan poetics – his "politics of rhythm" – consists in the performance of manly excellence.[9] In fact, as this chapter will suggest, even many of the

---

[7] Cicero, recounting in a letter his public standoff with Clodius (*Att.* 1.16.8), tells Atticus that he will not give a play by play account of the verbal exchange, since outside the performance context of the contest itself (ἀγών) they retain neither their "force" nor their "wit" (*neque uim neque uenustatem*). This paragraph has benefited from discussion with Eleanor Leach.

[8] Coined by Sedgwick (1985).

[9] "Politics of rhythm": Meschonnic (1995).

poems featuring Lesbia are similarly "homosocial," and similarly motivated and informed by a Catullan poetics of manhood.

MAN TO MAN (THE POLYMETRIC POEMS)

Poems in their Place: The Intertextuality and Order of Poetic Collections is a 1986 volume of essays devoted chiefly to English and American poetry collections from early modernity (Sidney and Jonson) to the twentieth century (Plath). Ancient poets and their collections are represented by some remarks in an introductory essay and by W. S. Anderson's chapter on "The Theory and Practice of Poetic Arrangement from Vergil to Ovid." Catullus thus misses the book's purview by a generation, but a single mention in the editor's introduction presents an instructive long-range snapshot of the majority opinion on his place in the history of the poetic collection. We read: "Centuries before Petrarch and Dante, Horace – and his predecessor Catullus – had shown how a recognizable narrative of love could emerge from a collection of discrete lyrics arranged in temporal sequence." A footnote elaborates:

The Catullan corpus begins with a sequence of poems (2–11) designed to trace the progression and final dissolution of a love affair ... We cannot be sure, however, that Catullus arranged his corpus as we now know it.[10]

"Lyric," "narrative," "love affair" and "temporal sequence": the defining preoccupations of so much twentieth-century Catullan criticism. A new reader of Catullus' poetry who had seen this remark would, I think, reasonably expect to find there, after the dedicatory Poem 1, a series of discrete lyrics in temporal sequence relating the narrative of a love affair. And what would she actually find?

First, the two sparrow poems, one (Poem 2) addressed to "my girl's sparrow" and steamily erotic whether or not it encodes a penis joke, the other (Poem 3) and containing a witty lament on the sparrow's death (a Hellenistic *topos*, and again quite possibly a penis joke).[11] Next, Poem 4, recounting to an audience of "guests"

---

[10] Fraistat (1986) 4, 15 (n. 12). Obvious that the characterization of Horace given here would be even harder to sustain upon close reading of the Odes.

[11] For the cause of decency, Jocelyn (1980); for that of ribaldry, in a learned Hellenistic vein, Thomas (1993).

in a breezily aristocratic tone the career of a small boat (*phaselus*) in the manner of Hellenistic epigrams on pets or, for example, conch shells. Then the first kiss poem (Poem 5), addressed to Lesbia, mad and giddy and full of *carpe diem* (before Horace) and thousands of kisses. Then Poem 6, in which Catullus upbraids, or teases, a man named Flavius in an attempt to make him reveal the identity of his female lover; Catullus proffers the opinion that, since Flavius won't say who she is, she must be a "diseased whore." Then a second kiss poem (Poem 7) addressed to Lesbia, this one full of infinitudes (sands of the desert, stars of the sky) and containing a riddling reference to Callimachus. Then Poem 8, in which Catullus addresses first himself and then the *puella* ("girl"), seeming to try to convince them both (whether slyly or no) that he is saying goodbye for good, since she no longer wants him. Then an outburst of unadulterated joy (Poem 9) at the news of the return from Spain of a friend named Veranius; Catullus looks forward to hugging Veranius' neck, kissing his mouth and eyes, and drinking in his traveler's tales.[12] Then Poem 10, in which a friend named Varus takes Catullus out of the forum to meet Varus' new girlfriend ("not a charmless little whore" is how Catullus first sizes her up, at 10.3–4); Catullus fakes ownership of a friend's parked sedan chair with its team of bearers and is embarrassed when the woman calls his bluff. And finally Poem 11, addressed to Furius and Aurelius, to whom, after a geographical excursus upon the ends of the earth to which they would follow their friend, Catullus entrusts a brief message of farewell to "my girl": words of violent obscenity (directed toward the woman and her other lovers) and delicately compassionate tenderness (directed toward Catullus himself).

Of the ten poems, two are addressed to Lesbia by name (Poems 5 and 7), and another addresses her as *puella* (Poem 8). Three more refer to her, again as *puella*, describing her desire or sorrow (Poems 2 and 3) and, in the last poem, sending her a nasty message (Poem 11). The remaining four poems (Poems 4, 6, 9 and 10) have no connection with Lesbia, at least none that emerges from either the text of these ten poems or the rest of the collection. It is difficult to imagine that a reader innocent of Catullan criticism who put down the book at this point would come away with the impression

----

[12] On Veranius, see Syme (1956) 129–34.

of having read the narrative of a love affair's progress and dissolution, even in a jumbled or fragmentary version. One might
object that continued reading and rereading of the entire corpus
would eventually throw the opening sequence into a different
light. It is certainly true that the collection both invites and
rewards continued rereading in all directions.[13] Lesbia's presence
in Poems 2 through 11 carries more poignancy and import, certainly, for a reader who comes back to them after having read all
the epigrams. But it is less certain that a reading of all the poems
would necessarily bring the nonspecialist reader to the conclusion
that the "Lesbia poems" dominate the collection (they do not do
so numerically, in any case), and even less certain that she would
characterize this poetry book as the production of an emotionally
intense (or "lyric") individual subjectivity whom we "overhear"
(Mill) "talking to himself, or to no one at all" (Eliot).[14]

But let us continue the experiment of a Winklerian "first reading" of Catullus – though it will almost immediately break down
before the collection's insistence on being read in several directions at once.[15] Pushing on through the corpus after Poem 11, the
reader next encounters thirty-seven poems of which the vast
majority (twenty-nine by my count, just over three quarters) are
addressed to, or take as their subject, a man or pair of men,
almost always called by name.[16] None of these thirty-seven poems
is addressed to Lesbia. Her name makes only one appearance
among them, and that in an unsavory context. Poem 43 is
addressed to "the *amica* ('girlfriend,' but not a nice word for it) of a
decoctor from Formia" generally identified with Julius Caesar's

---

[13] Miller (1994) 56–7, 75–6. Also Wiseman (1985) 137.
[14] Mill (1976) 12, cited in Batstone (1993) 143; Eliot (1961) 105–6.
[15] Winkler (1985).
[16] The 37 poems are those numbered 12 through 50, counting 14b as a separate poem, with
    no poems between 17 and 21. The 29 poems to males or about males are: Poems 12 (to
    Asinius Marrucinus), 13 (to Fabullus), 14 (to Calvus), 15 (to Aurelius), 16 (to Aurelius and
    Furius), 17 (on an unnamed cuckolded husband from the region around Verona), 21 (to
    Aurelius), 22 (to Varus, on Suffenus the poetaster), 23 (to Furius), 24 (to Juventius), 25 (to
    Thallus), 26 (to Furius), 27 (to his wine steward slave), 28 (to Veranius and Fabullus), 29
    (to "Romulus the *cinaedus*," on Mamurra, Caesar and Pompey), 30 (to Alfenus), 33 (to
    Vibennius and his *cinaedus* son), 35 (to Caecilius, by way of an apostrophized papyrus let-
    ter), 36 (on Volusius, addressed to his *Annales*), 37 (to the patrons of a tavern and in par-
    ticular to Egnatius), 38 (to Cornificius), 39 (on Egnatius), 40 (to Ravidus), 44 (addressed
    to Catullus' farm, but aimed at the poetaster Sestius), 46 (a farewell to his provincial co-
    hort), 47 (to *Porcius* and *Socration* ["Piggy" and "Little Socrates"]), 48 (to Juventius, a kiss
    poem), 49 (to Cicero) and 50 (to Calvus).

friend Mamurra, whom Poem 29 had already lambasted.[17] Catullus first greets the woman and then proceeds to inventory her body parts: nose, feet, eyes, fingers, mouth, tongue.[18] Finding them all lacking in beauty, he expresses his indignation at a "tasteless, witless age" that dares compare this woman to his Lesbia:

> te provincia narrat esse bellum?
> tecum Lesbia nostra comparetur?
> o saeclum insapiens et infacetum!   (43.6–8)

> The province tells the tale that *you*'re a beauty?
> My Lesbia's, then, to be compared to *you*?
> O age without a drop of taste or wit!

In Poem 41, on the same woman, Catullus had expressed a mock concern for her sanity after she had proposed to him the price of ten thousand sesterces.[19] Commentators, ever quick to excuse Catullus, have tended to read Poem 43 (like the similar Poem 86, on Quintia) as a backhanded but gallant compliment to Lesbia, whose beauty is here deemed a peerless standard.[20] Surely Poems 41 and 43 are at least open to a different interpretation, as a bit of very forehanded invective – sexual, financial and even political – directed principally at the "*decoctor* from Formia." The pair of poems serves notice (1) that Mamurra's *amica* has tried to prostitute herself to Catullus, (2) that she has asked him for an exorbitant sum, presumably because Mamurra hasn't an *as* to spend on her and she knows that Catullus, unlike Mamurra, is not only richly propertied but also solvent, (3) that Catullus' Lesbia is far more desirable than Mamurra's *amica*, and finally (4) that

---

[17] Crook (1967) 371: "Decoction, then, in Republican times, was declared or adjudged insolvency, and it was in all circumstances infaming, though it was admitted that some people were unlucky."

[18] The *blason anatomique* was a topos of Hellenistic poetry, on which see Sider (1997) on Philodemus *Epigr.* 7 (= *AP* 5.132).

[19] She is apparently called by name here – something like "Ameana," but the text is corrupt beyond sure repair.

[20] But as Ferguson (1985) 125 remarks, "we cannot disassociate the attack on Ameana's looks and the attack on Mamurra's politics." Papanghelis (1991) closes a programmatic and Callimachean reading of Poem 86 with the suggestion that Poem 43 may encode a similar statement. I agree with Skinner (1979) 114 that Poems 41 and 43 are "expert variations on a satiric theme," but I am less confident that reading the poems in that light will "temper their personal acerbity" or give them the viewpoint of "the man of refinement."

Mamurra's *amica* is being praised extravagantly by a generation of Veronese provincials low on connoisseurship of feminine charms – and perhaps more to the point, a generation eager to flatter an associate of Caesar by making his *amica* out to be a great beauty.[21] On this reading, of course, both Mamurra's *amica* and Lesbia are commodified, made into units of enjoyment and exchange, while the real players, the subjectivities, are the two men involved: Catullus, the message's sender, and Mamurra, its ultimate addressee.

In addition to that single mention of Lesbia's name in the thirty-seven poems between 11 and 51, there are three references to a *puella* almost universally identified by readers as Lesbia (the logic of the collection again seems to insist upon the identification, and to argue otherwise seems again perverse). All three of these references appear in poems addressed to or aimed at men: Poem 13 (to Fabullus), Poem 36 (to Volusius' *Annales*) and Poem 37 (to the "sleazy bar and its sleazy barflies"). In Poem 13, Catullus invites his friend Fabullus to come to dinner – and to bring the dinner along, not without a *candida puella* (13.4, "sparkling girl"). Pleading a purse full of nothing but cobwebs, Catullus offers instead to repay Fabullus for the dinner with a remarkable gift:

> sed contra accipies meros amores
> seu quid suauius elegantiusue est:
> nam unguentum dabo, quod meae puellae
> donarunt Veneres Cupidinesque,
> quod tu cum olfacies, deos rogabis,
> totum ut te faciant, Fabulle nasum.   (13.9–14)

> But in return you'll get the very stuff of love,
> or something – if there be such – sweeter, finer:
> I'll give to you a scent that all the gods
> and goddesses of love gave to my girl.
> And when you take a whiff, my dear Fabullus,
> you'll pray the gods to make you nothing but nose.

Whatever interpretation is put on the scent promised to Fabullus by Catullus, it seems a simple statement of fact to say that the *puella* in this poem serves as a coin of exchange passed between the

---

[21] Maselli (1994) 49–51 on this poem.

sender and receiver of the poem, both adult males, this time in a friendly rather than a (serious or mock) hostile relation.[22]

The next twenty poems or so (Poems 14–35) feature no *puella* susceptible of identification as Lesbia. The erotic life of Catullus, however, is here represented as anything but inactive in Lesbia's absence. One of these poems takes the form of a message on a tablet (*tabellam*, 32.5) addressed to "my sweet Ipsitilla, my darling, my delight" (*mea dulcis Ipsitilla,* | *meae deliciae, mei lepores*, 32.1–2), asking her to invite him over at midday and to be ready for "nine fuckerations in a row" (*nouuem continuas fututiones* 32.8) because Catullus has had his lunch, is lying on his back, and has a bulge bursting through his tunic and cloak.[23] Three of the same twenty poems mention the boy Juventius. In a pair of invective poems to Aurelius, one of two rivals for the boy's attention, Catullus refers (apparently) to Juventius twice as "my loves" (15.1, 21.4). A third poem is addressed to the boy as "little flower of the Juventii" (*flosculus ... Iuventiorum*, 24.1), urging him not to respond to the advances of the other rival who, though *bellus* ("nice-looking"), possesses – Catullus says it three times – "neither slave nor money-chest" (24.5, 8, 10).[24] The identification of that rival will have been made clear by the previous poem as one Furius (identified by some scholars with the poet Furius Bibaculus).[25] Poem 23 had begun "Furius, you who possess neither slave nor money chest" (*Furi, cui*

---

[22] Very full discussion of the poem and its scholarship in Gowers (1993) 229–44. The two most arresting suggestions (neither out of keeping with Catullus' self-presentation) as to what is meant by the *unguentum* belong to Littman (1977) (the *puella*'s vaginal secretions) and Hallett (1978) (an anal lubricant). Witke (1980) has (over)argued against both. Still, I am inclined to take the ointment as chiefly (not exclusively) representing poetry itself. Philodemus asks a woman for a song with the words "strum me some myrrh with your delicate hands" (ψῆλόν μοι χερσὶ δροσιναῖς μύρον, *Epigr.* 3 Sider [= *AP* 9.570] 3), and Poem 13 closely resembles Philodemus *Epigr.* 27 Sider (= *AP* 11.44), in which Piso is invited to the Epicureans' monthly celebration of their founder. Sider suggests, ad loc., that the "Latin invitation poem" (Edmunds 1982) may thus reflect not "Roman social conventions" but rather Epicurean ones.

[23] Here again it is possible to read Catullus performing a dialogue with Philodemus, who complains thus of his diminished sexual powers: "O Aphrodite! I who formerly (did) five (acts) and even *nine*, now scarcely (do) one from dusk to dawn" (ὁ πρὶν ἐγὼ καὶ πέντε καὶ ἐννέα, νῦν, Ἀφροδίτη, | ἐν μόλις ἐκ πρώτης νυκτὸς ἐς ἥλιον *Epigr.* 19 Sider (*AP* 11.30) 1–2).

[24] Beck (1996) 275–288 has argued that the Juventius poems constitute a separate cycle and were even published as a separate "Furius and Aurelius *libellus*" consisting of Poems 14a–26.

[25] See e.g. Paratore (1950) 219. If the identification is correct, then the date of his birth in Jerome (103 BCE) is too early.

neque seruus est neque arca, 23.1), "nor bedbug nor spider nor fire,"
and had gone on to urge Furius to count his blessings (I para-
phrase literally): a father and a stepmother whose teeth can eat
flint; an excellent digestive system; no fear of fire, crumbling
buildings, crime or poison (the reason, we are to understand, is
that he owns nothing); a body dryer than horn, without sweat,
saliva, snot or phlegm; and something even purer than all this
purity, an asshole cleaner than a salt-dish. Furius doesn't shit ten
times a year, and when he does, what comes out is harder than
beans or pebbles. You can rub it between your fingers without
getting them dirty.

What can be the point of this stream of fierce invective poured
out with Rabelaisian gusto upon Furius' dryness? The final lines of
the poem, linking back to the opening, give the answer:

> haec tu commoda tam beata, Furi,
> noli spernere nec putare parui,
> et sestertia quae soles precari
> centum desine: nam sat es beatus.   (23.24–27)

> Such advantages, Furius, such good fortune:
> these are not things to scorn or undervalue.
> And as for the sesterces you keep begging for –
> the hundred – give it up. You're well enough off already.

The dryness of Furius' body is both metaphor and metonym of his
financial distress.[26] This pair of poems (23 and 24) responds on
several levels to comparison with the pair on Mamurra's *amica* (41
and 43). Both pairs have their members linked by a scorchingly
scornful, memorably snappy invective formula directed by Catullus at another man: "neither slave nor money-chest," referring to
Furius in Poems 23 and 24; "*decoctor* from Formia," referring to
Mamurra in Poems 41 and 43. In both instances, the brunt of the
scorn is financial. Both pairs feature a "love" object, whether
woman or boy, whose function in the text is primarily as a contested property and a coin of invective exchange. The invective

---

[26] In Poem 26 we learn that Furius' small villa (*uillula*, 26.1) is "set against" (*opposita*, 26.1,
but the word is also a financial technical term meaning "mortgaged against": Maselli
[1994] 16–7) a horrible and pestilential wind: neither North, South, East nor West, but
rather 15,200 sesterces.

message in both cases is sent by a solvent Catullus to a bankrupt (or at least insolvent) male enemy.

A PRETTY PAIR OF DIRTY "LESBIA POEMS"

The two remaining references to Lesbia (called *puella* rather than by name) between Poems 11 and 51 come in Poems 36 and 37, both of which bear comparison to the invective pairs just discussed. As individual pieces and as a pair, these two poems are as carefully constructed as anything in the corpus, though it would be difficult to argue (as twentieth-century critics have often done for other Catullan poems) that their intricacy of form functions primarily as a vessel for intensity of feeling. Each poem consists of exactly twenty verses (Phalaecians or "hendecasyllabics" in 36, scazons or "choliambics" in 37), and each is divided into precisely equal halves by a strong paragraph break coming at the exact midpoint. The *puella*, entering both poems in a causal clause (*nam*, "for": 36.3, 37.11), appears as a character only in the first ten lines of Poem 36, and only in the last ten lines of Poem 37. Lexical and structural parallelisms make both poems into rings. Each poem features a striking intratextual citation from a jarringly different context within the Catullan collection. Each poem is an invective message directed at a named individual male enemy and, in what is perhaps the most insolently Rabelaisian (though by no means the most obscene) touch of the entire corpus, each poem is situated under the sign of a ruling excretory "element": Poem 36 is a shit poem aimed at Volusius, Poem 37 a piss poem aimed at Egnatius.[27]

Poem 36 is addressed to the "annals of Volusius, sheet after sheet of shit,"[28] called upon to fulfill a vow for "my girl." Its pictured scene is the moment before Volusius' poetry is thrown into the fire. After the opening apostrophe to the doomed bookrolls, the first ten lines analeptically give the narrative background:

> Annales Volusi, cacata carta,
> uotum soluite pro mea puella.
> nam sanctae Veneri Cupidinique

---

[27] On "obscenity" Roman and Catullan: Lateiner (1977), Richlin (1992) 1–31 and 144–63, Skinner (1992), Barton (1993) and Fitzgerald (1995) 59–86.

[28] This inspired translation is Krostenko's (2001).

uouit, si sibi restitutus essem
desissemque truces uibrare iambos,
electissima pessimi poetae
scripta tardipedi deo daturam
infelicibus ustulanda lignis.
et hoc pessima se puella uidit
iocose lepide uouere diuis.   (36.1–10)

Annals by Volusius, sheet after sheet of shit,
time to pay the vow now for my girl.
You see, she made a vow to Venus and to Cupid,
that if I would be reconciled to her
and leave off hurling sharp invective iambs,
she would offer in turn to the limping fire-god
the writings – the choicest – of the worst of poets,
giving them over to kindle unlucky logs.
And it seemed to her, it seemed to that worst of girls,
that the vow that she vowed to the gods was a charm of a
     joke.[29]

The narrator-poet recounts that this "worst of girls" (*pessima
puella*, 36.9) vowed to Venus and the Cupids – thinking her vow
clever and witty (*iocose lepide*, 36.10) – that if Catullus be reconciled
to her and stop brandishing his fierce iambs, she would in turn
consign to the flames the "choicest writings of the worst poet"
(*electissima pessimi poetae* | *scripta* 36.6). The "worst poet," in Catul-
lus' *style indirect libre* recounting of the *puella*'s words, is implicitly
understood to be Catullus himself. A nice symmetry of focaliza-
tion seems to obtain at this point: Lesbia (in her words as recounted by Catullus) has described Catullus as *pessimus poeta*, and
Catullus seems to have retaliated in kind by referring to Lesbia as
pessima puella. *Pessimus*, in both instances, appears to have an ethical, characterological meaning: each of the two quarreling lovers
attributes "meanness," "nastiness" to the other.

   The second half of the poem takes place in the narrative present, as Catullus first acquits himself of an astonishing mock-
sacrificial prayer to Venus whose diction and line length swell the
hendecasyllable's slender sails to unparalleled epic-hymnic proportions, and then ends the poem with an envoi to Volusius'

---

[29] Buchheit (1959), still the fullest reading of the poem, takes it as chiefly a piece of poetic
program. See also Clausen (1987) 7.

poetry, closing the poem's ring with a final verse identical to the initial one:

> nunc o caeruleo creata ponto,
> quae sanctum Idalium Vriosque apertos
> quaeque Ancona Cnidumque harundinosum
> colis quaeque Amathunta quaeque Golgos
> quaeque Durrachium Hadriae tabernam,
> acceptum face redditumque uotum,
> si non illepidum neque inuenustum est.
> at uos interea uenite in ignem,
> pleni ruris et inficetiarum
> annales Volusi, cacata carta.   (36.11–20)

> But now, o goddess of wine-dark sea's conception,
> thou of Idalium's peak, of Uria's open sky,
> thou who by Ancon's reef, by Cnidus' reedy banks
> dwellest, thou of Amathus and Golgi,
> thou of Durrachium, tavern of the Adriatic,
> pray count this vow as tendered, paid in full,
> if there by any charm in it, any grace.
> And as for you, then, into the fire with you
> and the witless redneck platitudes you're stuffed with:
> *Annals* by Volusius, sheet after sheet of shit.

The four hymnic verses (36.12–15) are a dazzling display of Hellenistic erudition, both by the hermetic exoticism of their geography and also by the symmetry of their arrangement and construction: note especially the "cletic" anaphora of the relative pronoun in each line, the perfect distribution of two place names per line, and the main verb (*colis* ["dwellest"], 36.14) lodged like a pearl at the opening of the third verse, the inventory's precise midpoint. This is a poet's programmatic announcement of his ability to do *anything* – in any metre and in any context. Even in Phalaecians, Catullus can show Volusius how hexameter poetry ought to sound; and how it ought to sound, according to Catullus, is like Callimachus, Theocritus, Apollonius and, of course, like Catullus himself when he writes hexameters. His miniature epic similarly addresses Venus as *quaeque regis Golgos quaeque Idalium frondosum* ("you who rule Golgi and leafy Idalium," 64.96; cf. 36.12, 14). It is quite impossible to say which of these two Catullan poems is intratextually citing the other, which passage has been cut and which one pasted.

The line at Poem 64 is probably a direct rendering of the first verse of a female singer's hymn to Aphrodite at Theocritus *Idyll* 15.100: Δέσποιν', ἃ Γολγώς τε καὶ Ἰδάλιον ἐφίλησας ("Lady who lovest Golgi and Idalium"). In the face of this Theocritean intertext, it is all the more dangerous even to speculate as to the order in which Catullus composed the two passages, since if Poem 36's cultic epithets are burlesque in tone, they may just as well be a burlesque of Theocritus' poem as of Catullus' own miniature epic. It is however interesting and perhaps significant that *Idyll* 15 and Poem 36 both prominently feature female speakers as connoisseurs passing aesthetic judgment in specialized terms of approbation: Catullus' *puella* thinks her own vow to have been vowed *lepide* and *iocose*; in Theocritus, Gorgo admires the palace's tapestries with a pair of "Alexandrian" terms of art expressed in a Homeric tag (λεπτὰ καὶ ὡς χαρίεντα ["light and so lovely"], *Id.* 15.79) that Catullus would have recognized (and of which his *iocose lepide* may just possibly be a reflex). Theocritus' second lady, the unsophisticated Praxinoa, remarks instead on the artists' "exact lines" (τἀκριβέα γράμματα, 81) and marvels at the lifelike realism of the figures with a naïve outburst worthy of Monsieur Jourdain: "What a clever thing is man!" (σοφόν τι χρῆμ' ἄνθρωπος, 83).[30] Just as the *puella*'s self-congratulating *iocose lepide* is immediately followed by Catullus' own hymnic performance, so the Theocritean ladies' remarks are followed nearly immediately – a brief comic scene intervenes when a bystander asks the women to stop chattering in their Doric accent – by the beginning of the hymn on Adonis that opens with the two cultic epithets in a single line cited above. If we are willing to entertain the possibility that Catullus at Poem 36 had in mind the entire context of the Theocritean poem, and not just the "fragment" cited in our commentaries, then the intertext might seem here to reinforce Catullus' implied dig at the *puella*: she may think herself to have pulled off an urbane and charming performance of wit, but in fact her wit is as urbane as Praxinoa's broad Doric vowels and as charming as Volusius' fat annals.

The identification of Poem 36's *puella* as Lesbia seems inevitable. The vow to "Venus and Cupid" recalls both the second sparrow poem and the invitation to Fabullus (*Veneres Cupidinesque*, 3.1

---

[30] Hunter (1996) 116, conversely, takes it that the two women share a single register of admiration.

and 13.12). Further, once the epigrams have been read, the mention of Catullus reconciled to Lesbia (*restitutus essem*, 36.4) seems to point to Poem 107, where Catullus emits a cry of joy in the opposite situation: Lesbia has been reconciled to him. But the present poem hardly bears witness to erotic obsession, or even *amour-passion*. The second half of the poem subverts, supplants and almost preempts the *puella*'s utterance as reported in the first half. By the poem's end, the speaker has established first that the *pessimus poeta* is not Catullus but Volusius, and second that the epithet *pessimus* is to be taken performatively, of poetic or rhetorical excellence, rather than ethically, of character or "personality." *Pessima puella*, on the other hand, now seems to signify in both senses. Lesbia's nasty attempt at wit (nasty to Catullus, that is), of which she was proud, has been shown up by Catullus to be just as lacking in taste as her literary judgment. Catullus, not Lesbia, is the one who knows what is *lepidum* ("charming") and *uenustum* ("nicely put together," an adjectival form from *uenus*), and it is consequently Catullus (by an etymological figure) who has an ear with the goddess herself: his prayer has been heard, he has paid and canceled the vow made by Lesbia, precisely by the superior force of his own poetic power.[31] There is even an implicit threat: if Lesbia persists witlessly in a war of wits with Catullus, he always has his sharp iambs at hand to hurl in her direction. Everything in Catullus' stance here bespeaks a hypermasculine, aggressive mastery – a mastery that expresses itself both in scatological *convicium* ("verbal abuse") against Volusius and in the performance of verbal wit and exquisite poetic form.

Poem 36 is one of seven in the corpus containing attacks by Catullus on the poetic production of other poets. The other six are Poem 14 (against Caesius, Suffenus and Aquinus, along with any others contained in the book given to Catullus by Calvus), Poem 22 (against Suffenus), Poem 44 (against Sestius), Poem 95 (against Volusius again, in the context of praising Cinna's *Zmyrna*), Poem 95b (against the Hellenistic poet Antimachus) and Poem 105 (against Mamurra under the pseudonym *Mentula* ["prick"]). Poem 36 is the only such programmatic attack to feature any connection to a *puella*. There is no indication anywhere in the corpus that Volusius, or any of the other poets whom Catullus attacks *qua*

---

[31] Krostenko (2001) on *uenustus*, also Seager (1974).

poets, was a rival in love.[32] To judge from the rest of the collection, then, Lesbia's role in Poem 36 would seem to be at best that
of a minor character, and at worst that of a (secondary) co-victim
with Volusius, making a pair of targets for Catullus to strike with
one invective stone.

It is of course always possible to argue that the open hostility of
Catullus' stance toward Lesbia in Poem 36 represents the tragic
result of an impassioned and possessive lover's long anguish suffered at the hands of a fickle, promiscuous woman, a "worthless
mistress." The misogynist "guess" or "conjecture," as Janan
reminds us, emerges from "resentment at the impossibility of the
sexual relation relegated to Woman's side of the equation, as fan-
tasized whore, castrating bitch, and the like."[33] Courtly love is the
conjecture at the opposite end of the spectrum from misogyny,
and both those conjectures are easy enough to tease out of the
Catullan corpus through critical interpretation.[34] On that level,
Poem 37, the last "Lesbia poem" before Poem 51, almost seems –
by its text and by its connections to other poems in the collection –
to invite a reading as an exposure of the absurdity of both those
conjectures, in a raucous farce that spares none of its players, least
of all its speaker:

> Salax taberna uosque contubernales,
> a pilleatis nona fratribus pila,
> solis putatis esse mentulas uobis,
> solis licere, quidquid est puellarum,
> confutuere et putare ceteros hircos?
> an, continenter quod sedetis insulsi
> centum an ducenti, non putatis ausurum
> me una ducentos irrumare sessores?
> atqui putate: namque totius uobis
> frontem tabernae sopionibus scribam.
> puella nam mi, quae meo sinu fugit,
> amata tantum quantum amabitur nulla,
> pro qua mihi sunt magna bella pugnata,
> consedit istic. hanc boni beatique
> omnes amatis, et quidem, quod indignum est,

---

[32] Gellius seems to be a rival (Poem 91), presumably for Lesbia, and also a poet (Poem 116),
but Catullus never attacks Gellius as a *poet*. On the Gellius poems, see 186–9 below.

[33] Janan (1994) 71.

[34] On "Woman as Thing," Lacan (1986) 253–6, Zizek (1994).

omnes pusilli et semitarii moechi;
tu praeter omnes une de capillatis,
cuniculosae Celtiberiae fili,
Egnati, opaca quem bonum facit barba
et dens Hibera defricatus urina.   (Poem 37)

Sleazy bar, and you, its sleazy barflies –
column number nine from the Twins in caps –
you think you own the only pricks in the world?
You think you get to gangfuck every girl
there is, and say that other guys are billygoats?
Just because there are a hundred or two of you
losers sitting there, you think I won't dare
to facefuck all two hundred in your seats?
Think again: I'm going to give your bar
a paint job. Pricks all over the front.
It's because my girl, who's run from my lap,
more loved than any girl will ever be,
the girl I fought for, fought great wars for her,
has taken a seat at the bar. You're loving her, too,
all of you so fine and happy and – the worst of it –
all of you such puny little streetscum fuckers.
Especially you, Egnatius, one of the hairy ones,
scion of rabbit-ridden Celtiberia,
with that swarthy beard that makes you look so fine
and those teeth: your Spanish piss-paste makes them shine.

This masterpiece of comic writing, a brilliant mime in miniature, is both shockingly violent and at the same time an exquisitely crafted poetic composition. Note the anaphora of *solis* (3,4), answered symmetrically in form and sense by the anaphora of *omnes* (15,16); also the sputtering repetition of the prefix in *contubernales* (1), *confutuere* (5), *continenter* (6) and climaxing, as the *puella*'s presence in the bar is revealed, in *consedit* (14). The repetition of *taberna(e)* (1,10) frames the first half, and perhaps connects the poem to the other member of the pair it forms (see 36.15). The *puella* (11) first enters the poem's narrative at the very opening of the second half. The motion of the piece starts with the collectivity of the tavern crowd and ends by zeroing in on its Celtiberian victim.[35]

---

[35] Egnatius is to be attacked a second time in Poem 39, on the same charge of using urine for dentifrice, though without any mention there of the *puella*.

Poem 37 recalls at least two poems from earlier in the collection. Like the more famous Poem 16, this one contains a Priapic threat of violent sexual retaliation (*irrumare*, 37.8) against a group of men who are said to have impugned the speaker's manhood. Just as Poem 16's Furius and Aurelius had thought Catullus "insufficiently *pudicus*" (16.4) and "hardly a man" (*male marem*, 16.13), so the "barflies" of Poem 37 seem to think that they are the only men, the only ones with penises.[36] There Catullus had promised to irrumate and pedicate Furius and Aurelius; here he threatens to irrumate all two hundred of the tavern's patrons and then come back (if we understand the Latin correctly) to paint obscene graffiti on the tavern's outside wall as a public advertisement of his perfect squelch.[37] Taken literally, Catullus' threat to perform oral rape on a group of two hundred men is wild hyperbole; the "barflies" would of course kill or at least incapacitate Catullus – if not at once by retaliatory assault (the more likely), then at length by exhaustion. The threat is either absurd bluster or else figurative, meaning that Catullus will irrumate the *sessores*, "fuck them over," precisely by painting penises all over the front of the bar, or perhaps (performatively) by the writing of this poem itself.[38] In any event, this Priapic threat is unique in the Catullan corpus in being physically impossible of literal realization.

Poem 37, like Poem 36, also features a close verbal link to another poem in the collection, this time a central "Lesbia poem" on which critical attention has been lavished:

> fulsere quondam candidi tibi soles,
> cum uentitabas quo puella ducebat,
> amata nobis quantum amabitur nulla.   (8.3–5)

> There was a time when suns shone bright on you,
> when you would go wherever the girl would lead,
> the girl I loved more than any will ever be loved.

---

[36] "You think you're the only one ..." seems to be a topos of republican Latin verbal abuse. Compare Cicero fr. 21 Crawford (to Clodius): *tu solus urbanus*.

[37] We have examples of such graffiti from Pompeii, as *CIL* 4.4977: *Quintio hic futuit ceuentes et uidit qui doluit*. Adams (1982) 119, and see Williams (1999) 326 n. 3 on the interpretation of *futuit* and *ceuentes*.

[38] Other examples of Pompeian graffiti similarly "pedicate" the reader performatively. Adams (1982) 124–5.

puella nam mi, quae meo sinu fugit,
amata tantum quantum amabitur nulla,
pro qua mihi sunt magna bella pugnata,
consedit istic.   (37.11–14)

It's because my girl, who's run from my lap,
more loved than any girl will ever be,
the girl I fought for, fought great wars to win her,
has taken a seat at the bar.

This instance of intratextual citation would perhaps have been a scandal for the Romanticizing (and neo-Romantic Modernizing) strand of interpretation of Poem 8, had that strand of interpretation paid much attention to Poem 37. The modern reception of Poem 8 suggests that its text permits or even invites (in Daniel Selden's tight formulation) "two equally coherent, yet simultaneously incompatible understandings of the poem": Poem 8's speaker is either tragically sincere (and Macaulay's tears were not shed in vain) or else comically ironic, but he cannot be both.[39] The best arguments against the "sincerity" of Poem 8 have been, as is often the case, intertextual ones: Richard Thomas and Marilyn Skinner have pointed to affinities between Poem 8's diction and the language of comic lovers in Hellenistic New Comedy as preserved (for the most part) in Menander, and in Plautus' adaptations of that comic theatre to the Roman stage.[40]

And what of Poem 37? Does it, like Poem 8, generate a pair of "equally coherent, yet simultaneously incompatible" readings? It is certainly true that this poem has been conscripted into service as a (minor) moment in the tale of impassioned anguish that is the Lesbia novel; but I think it fair to say that the small critical attention paid to the "sleazy bar" has had a greater investment of interest in preserving the integrity of the Lesbia novel than in reading Poem 37 as a poem. One detail in particular has resisted interpretation: the speaker claims to have fought "great wars" (*magna bella*, 37.13) for the woman inside the bar. Earlier commentators tended to brush this verse aside, to explain it away rather

---

[39] Selden (1992) 470. On Macaulay, Fordyce ad loc.
[40] Skinner (1971), Thomas (1984).

than explicate it.[41] Quinn, after characterizing this poem (rightly, I think) as "important and exciting," recognizing it as a "lampoon" and calling its opening verse "rollicking," gives an account of the *magna bella* that folds itself seamlessly back into the narrative of poor Catullus and wicked, wicked Lesbia:[42]

We are not told what the many battles were, here or anywhere else in the collection. But they are part of the hypothesis of Poem 37; they help to narrow the context, to set that context somewhere down the long line of descent from the fading illusions of Poem 8 toward the dull anger and disgust of final dismissal of Poem 11.[43]

The Lesbia novel is taken as a narrative already fixed, tragically preordained. Minor poems like 37, however "exciting," are not allowed to alter or edit that narrative, and Catullus' stance as victim (in poems other than 37) is taken in full seriousness and applied throughout the corpus.[44] The Catullus of Poem 37, however, seems to be as much at pains to paint himself as a comically absurd blusterer as many readers have been at pains to give him back his high moral seriousness and his *simpatico* as a tender lover roughly wronged.

Nothing in the rest of the corpus affords an explicit context for the "great wars" Catullus claims in Poem 37 to have fought. Something in the poem itself, however, does. Though my translation has obscured it, the first two lines of Poem 37 play on military language. The "barflies" of 37.1 are *contubernales*, "comrades-in-arms" or more literally "tent-mates," a term applied to soldiers who shared a single tent (*taberna*) – ten men and their captain to a tent – and applied more broadly to those who served in the military together.[45] The etymological pun in 37.1 is in fact treble, since

---

[41] E.g. Merrill (1893) 68: "probably referring only in general to the great difficulties accompanying a successful *liaison* with a married woman, and one of Lesbia's social position"; Kroll (1968) 71: "Die *bella* sind natürlich in übertragenem Sinne zu verstehen und beziehen sich auf die Überlistung des Gatten und die Überwindung der Nebenbuhler." A recent exception: M. Johnson (1999) takes the *magna bella* as a reference to the Trojan War, with Catullus as Menelaus and Lesbia as Helen (Lesbia is thus "Other" in the Lacanian sense). Johnson concludes on a strongly modernist characterization of the poem as one of "mixed, complex emotions," giving "insight into [Catullus'] inner world and the crumbling world outside" (95).

[42] "Rollicking": Quinn (1972) 40, 96; two of no fewer than thirty references to Poem 37 in this work.

[43] Quinn (1972) 97.

[44] On Catullus' stance as victim, Fitzgerald (1995) 114–39.

[45] Noted by Johnson (1999) 86, also Thomson (1997) ad loc. The word *taberna*, it bears noting, appears in the Catullan corpus only in Poems 36 and 37.

contubernalis has the additional meaning of "sexual partner," said (often scornfully) of slaves, who were barred legally from contracting marriage (*conubium*) and so joined in unions of cohabitation (*contubernium*).[46] The sexual connotation is of course activated by the poem's first word: the *taberna* is *salax* ("randy") because its *contubernales* are so.[47] The military context and the etymological punning both continue into the second verse: "from the cap-wearing (*pilleatis*) brothers the ninth column (*pila*)." The pun is based on a false etymology this time (not that it matters – and Catullus may have thought it a true one). Its point has never been satisfactorily explained.[48] The brothers are Castor and Pollux, the reference is to their temple in the Roman forum, and the epithet pictures them wearing a cap known as the *pilleus* (or *pilleum*). This felt cap was worn at festivals such as the Saturnalia and by recently manumitted slaves (the origin of the French Revolution's "Phrygian cap").[49] Neither of these uses explain the cap's connection to the Dioscuri, but a later grammarian's gloss does: "the ancients gave Castor and Pollux felt caps (*pillea*) because they were Laconian (Spartan), and the Laconians have the custom of fighting in felt caps (*pugnare mos est pilleatis*)."[50] To call the Dioscuri *pilleati fratres* is thus to picture them in military uniform.

Let us return to Catullus' "great wars." Given that this poem opens by setting a burlesque, even carnivalesque context through a pair of puns involving military imagery, given that the characterization of the "barflies" as *contubernales* reads both as playful fiction (since they are no soldiers) and as bawdy comedic gag (by the sexual reference pitched at the lowest social register), and given that Catullus' Priapic threat to irrumate two hundred men is on its face a venting of wildly absurd braggadocio, it seems at least worth suggesting that the claim to have "fought great wars" for the *puella* be taken not as a veiled reference to be fitted by the

---

[46] Bradley (1994) 50, Treggiari (1991) 52–4.

[47] *Salax*: a term applied, for example, to roosters, rams and Priapus (see *OCD* s.v.), and so fairly equivalent to its Elizabethan derivative "saucy." *Contubernalis*: Plautine comedy had already played bawdily upon the word in the context of a grisly joke. At *Mil.* 184 the crucifixion of slaves is described as their "being given in *contubernium* to crosses" (*crucibus contubernalis dari*).

[48] Herescu (1960) 435 calls the pun *pilleatis-pila* "évident mais mystérieux (pour nous)."

[49] At Plaut. *Am.* 462, a slave looks forward to the day he will shave his head and put on the *pilleus*.

[50] Fest. 207, cited by Kroll (1968) ad loc.

reader into the collection's novelistic narrative, but rather as a line spoken "in character," as an instance of Catullus "getting into" the ridiculous stock role of *miles gloriosus* ("Braggart Soldier") in which his miniature mime has cast him. On that reading, the *puella* is cast in a role rather different from that of a goddess turned whore. She reads more like an *amica* from Plautine comedy, perhaps even a captive slave who has run away. The words *quae meo sinu fugit* ("who has run from my embrace") are often compared to Poem 8's *nec quae fugit sectare* (8.10, "and don't chase after her who runs from you"), with the difference in tense taken to indicate that Catullus' sick and dying hope of Poem 8 has now slid further down the "long line of descent" to disillusioned despair. It is at least worth pointing out that *fugit*, in the perfect tense, is what Latin says of a runaway slave, and that *sinus* ("lap") is open to a bawdily sexual interpretation.[51]

Magna bella pugnata ("great wars fought"), too, is open to a sexual interpretation in a comic-satiric vein: a grammarian's gloss cites a passage from Lucilius in which *pugna* ("a fight") is used figuratively for illicit sex (*stuprum*).[52] *Amare* is no less susceptible to a sexual interpretation – made more likely by the words *omnes amatis* (37.15, "you're all 'loving' her") spoken to the *contubernales* later in the same poem – which raises at least the possibility that the line cut from Poem 8 has been pasted into a context where it reads less like an anguished lover's proclamation of a love that will go down in history, and more like a smuttily hypermasculine boast in the manner of Henry Miller, or of Catullus' note to Ipsitilla (Poem 32).[53]

To the extent that we allow this reading of Poem 37 as a performance, a "personation," with Catullus as Pyrgopolynices (or a burlesque Achilles) and the *puella* as his runaway *amica*, it becomes difficult to sustain broad claims for "social comment" or intensity

---

[51] *Sinus* in the sexual sense is more often (though not exclusively) used of a woman: possibly an indication that the speaker experiences being bested by his amorous rivals as feminization. Compare Philod. *Epigr.* 23 Sider (= *AP* 5.107) 8: ἡμεῖς δ' ἐν κόλποις ἥμεθα Ναϊά-δος ("but I sit in the lap of Naias"). *Sedere* probably has a similarly erotic sense in Poem 37: Herescu (1959).

[52] Lucilius 1323 M, Donatus (ad Ter. *Eun.* 5.2.60), cited by Newman (1990) 188, who takes Catullus' *bella pugnata* as a surprise variant on the expected *bella gesta*. The *para prosdokian*, on this reading, foregrounds the ambiguous word.

[53] For a contemporary use of *amare* and *amor* in a purely sexual sense, Cicero *Cat.* 2.8: "*alios ipse amabat turpissime, aliorum amori flagitiosissime seruiebat,*" cited in Adams (1982) 188.

of (represented) introspection attached to this poem. Those things, or something like them, are of course present in the corpus; to argue otherwise would be pointless. But not all the poems in the collection are spoken from the same stance, and not even all the "Lesbia poems" tell the same Lesbia story. It is perhaps important in this regard to note that Poem 37 contains no explicit or even implied moral condemnation of the *puella*. Indeed, there is simply no question of her subjectivity. The speaker does not wonder how she could have been so cruelly unfeeling, nor does he offer a picture of his own suffering for love. The exchange or message, as in the poems discussed above, is "homosocial": an affair between men, between Catullus and the *contubernales*, and ultimately between Catullus and Egnatius. What the Catullus of Poem 37 has lost is chiefly *existimatio* ("face") and only secondarily the *puella*; his manhood has been impugned, and it is for that reason that the loss of the *puella* smarts. The *contubernales* now think themselves the only ones with penises; Catullus reasserts his own Priapic manhood against the collective through the threat of irrumation and painting the tavern's front with penises, and against Egnatius by portraying him with a mouth befouled with his own urine – a kind of displaced irrumation.

On this reading, neither "courtly love" nor even "misogyny" functions in the represented interiority of the poem's speaker. And this is so not because he has followed the Epicurean advice of Catullus' contemporary, Lucretius, and reached a point "beyond obsession and disgust," but rather because he occupies a stance conceptually anterior to any notion of a "sexual relationship" between a man and a woman whose (Lacanian) impossibility would drive him to oscillate between divinization and demonization, those two versions of Woman as Thing.[54] But the woman of Poem 37 hardly seems to occupy in the speaker's interiority the status of Lacan's "object raised to the dignity of the Thing." If she is fetishized here, the position she occupies, on the reading I have proposed, is far more that of a Marxian commodity – a prize, like Briseis to Achilles (whose "relationships" were with other men, as friends or enemies) – than that of a "traumatic kernel."[55]

---

[54] Nussbaum (1994) 140–91, and discussion in Janan (1994) 166 n. 21.
[55] On the Lacanian Thing (called *das Ding* by Zizek) as "traumatic kernel," Zizek (1989) 132 and passim.

PASSING NOTES

After the pair formed by Poems 36 and 37, the polymetric poems
feature three further mentions of Lesbia, all of them by name.
The first of these, Poem 43, on Mamurra's *amica*, has already been
discussed.[56] The third, Poem 58, addressed to Caelius, complains
that Lesbia, whom Catullus loves more than himself and all his
people, is now "shucking" the descendants of Remus in crossroads
and alleys. The second occurrence of the name comes in Poem 51:

> Ille mi par esse deo uidetur,
> ille, si fas est, superare diuos,
> qui sedens aduersus identidem te
>   spectat et audit
>
> dulce ridentem, misero quod omnis
> eripit sensus mihi, nam simul te
> Lesbia, aspexi, nihil est super mi
>   .   .   .
> lingua sed torpet, tenuis sub artus
> flamma demanat, sonitu suopte
> tintinant aures, gemina teguntur
>   lumina nocte.
>
> otium, Catulle, tibi molestum est:
> otio exsultas nimiumque gestis:
> otium et reges prius et beatas
>   perdidit urbes.

> That man there I say is a god on earth. No:
> That man (dare I say it?) is more than godhead.
> He's the man who sits there beside you, sits there,
>   looks at you, hears you
>
> Gently laughing, laughter that takes my senses
> out with pain whenever I hear you laughing.
> Just one look at Lesbia: all my senses
>   register nothing,
>
> but my tongue is frozen, a red-hot wire is
> subtly introduced in my veins, my ears make
> music all their own, and then night comes, night comes
>   putting my lights out.

[56] See 70–2 above.

> Too much time's your problem, Catullus. That's it:
> too much time. You loll in a bath of too much
> time, and time brings death to a king, they say, and
> death to a kingdom.

Irresistible to scholars, critics and translators alike, this version of Sappho competes with the sparrows (Poems 2 and 3) and kisses (Poems 5 and 7) for the distinction of being the best known and loved of Catullus' "lyrics." More than that, it resides at the center of a long-standing critical construction of the speaking subject behind this parcel of poems, a subjectivity all of passionate fire and "feminine" tenderness. Critical shift from a Romantic model of poetry as sincere outburst to a Modernist one of poetry as meditative introspection has done little to alter the contours and coloration of that subjectivity. So much is this the case that it might still seem nothing short of impertinence to speak of this poem as an embodiment of Catullan "poetics of manhood," except perhaps insofar as the poem's speaker manifests passionate jealousy in the face of a male rival enjoying the privilege of speaking to the woman called Lesbia.[57]

Many readers of Catullus have been drawn to take Poem 51 as the beginning of an autobiographical narrative of the poet's affair with Clodia Metelli, with Poem 11, the corpus' only other poem in Sapphic strophes, bringing a symmetrical end to the story by its dire leavetaking addressed to Lesbia in care of Furius and Aurelius. This theory exercises its appeal even over readers who have left Romantic biographical criticism far behind.[58] It may well be correct. The pseudonym Lesbia ("woman of Lesbos") can easily be thought to have its motivation and origin in this Catullan translation from the Greek poet of Lesbos. That consideration is still

---

[57] The rival, *ille*, is often taken to be Metellus Celer, Clodia's husband. (Wilamowitz [1913] 56–61 had thought Sappho 31's occasion a wedding; Wiseman [1985] 153 thinks this likely.) But Metellus Celer died in 59 BCE: an early date for the composition of Poem 51, and impossible if we take Poem 51 to refer (metrically and symmetrically) back to Poem 11 (composed no earlier than 55 BCE). Shipton (1980) has proposed an intriguing alternative: take *ille* instead as P. Clodius Pulcher, Clodia's brother, and Poem 51 thus becomes a devilish bit of invective against brother and sister along the same lines as Cicero's *Pro Caelio*.

[58] Schwabe (1862) 98 had surmised that Poem 51 was written about the same time as the kisses and sparrows. Quinn's (1972) 56 opinion that "the name Lesbia seems to have been invented for poem 51" is now very widely shared: see e.g. Miller (1994) 62 and Thomson (1997) 327.

often taken as an argument for placing the poem first in the chronology of the "love affair," though the fact that the poem appears to motivate the pseudonym could just as easily lead, under a different set of presuppositions, to the suggestion that Catullus did the translation, and came up with the name Lesbia, before he had ever met Clodia, and only subsequently had the idea of applying the poetic name to the biographical beloved. If that purely hypothetical, and probably to many readers unappealing, suggestion were to be entertained, it would of course leave open the question of the identity of the addressee whose name was encoded in Poem 51 at the time of its composition. One possible, though again hypothetical, answer to that question is that Catullus has here framed his translation as a love poem to the "woman of Lesbos": Sappho herself. The conceit, a performatively outrageous and simultaneously delicate one, would be quite in keeping with the traditions of Hellenistic epigram, which favored laudatory interpellation of dead poets.

In any case, three well-known considerations about this remarkable piece complicate and problematize the application of Romantic or Modernist poetic paradigms to a reading of it. The first and most obvious of these is the fact that the poem is not an "original" work but a translation from Sappho's Greek, albeit a translation strikingly refracted and personalized by the insertion of the names Lesbia and Catullus into the poem.[59] Critics – those, that is, who have resisted a straightforward and transparent attribution of Sappho's sentiments and even Sappho's symptoms to Catullus – have negotiated the poem's status as a translation in variously ingenious ways, suggesting for instance that literary translation was a perfect vehicle for Catullus' first tentative declaration of a love still uncertain of requital: if he had revealed too much too soon, he could always explain the words away as a mere literary exercise.[60] Two assumptions can be seen at work here: (1)

---

[59] See the powerful arguments for a difference between the (lyric) subjectivity embodied in Catullus' translation and Sappho's original in Miller (1994) 106–7 and passim. See also Greene (1999). For Miller, the chief difference lies in the fact that Poem 51 interacts with the other poems in the Catullan collection. One might respond that Catullus read his Sappho just as we read our Catullus: in a poetry collection. (He may have suspected that Sappho had no hand in the ordering of that collection. But then, our reading of our Catullus labors under a comparable difficulty.) On Sappho and Sapphic subjectivity, Stehle (1990) and duBois (1995).

[60] First suggested by Wilkinson, in discussion following a conference paper: Bayet (1956) 47–8. Adopted and elaborated by Quinn (1970) 271 and (1972) 57–60.

that the poet who proudly applied the word *nugae* ("trifles," 1.4) to his poetic productions would have recognized the implicit dichotomy between a literary exercise and a genuine (because "lyrically" sincere or intense) poem, and (2) that Catullus in fact sent, as a love letter, a copy of Poem 51 to the woman he called Lesbia (perhaps even substituting the name Clodia for the metrically equivalent pseudonym).[61]

Catullus' translation has rather more of the ludic and performative than it is sometimes given credit for.[62] Sappho's poem had begun with the following strophe:

> φαίνεταί μοι κῆνος ἴσος θέοισιν
> ἔμμεν' ὤνηρ, ὄττις ἐνάντιός τοι
> ἰσδάνει καὶ πλάσιον ἆδυ φωνεί-
> σας ὑπακούει   Sappho 31.1–4

> He seems to me to match the gods,
> that man, the one who sits before
> your face and hears, up close, the sweet
> sound of your voice ...

It is often remarked that the simple declarative assertion of Sappho's first verse ("I think him the equal of gods") is in Catullus' version first literally rendered in the opening verse, only to be answered in the second verse by a hyperbolic outbidding ("I think he *surpasses* the gods") which is itself qualified by a loudly pious apology ("if it be right to say it"). Neither the stakes-raising claim nor the apotropaic piety drawing attention to it reflects anything in the Sapphic original, and many have pointed to this second verse as an instance of Catullus' "Roman" sensibility deflecting and modulating the stark simplicity of Sappho's archaic Greek.[63] It is true that a similar gesture, in a similar context, is to be found in one of the few surviving pieces of Roman erotic epigram predating Catullus, but it should be kept in mind that that earlier epigram is itself profoundly Hellenistic in sensibility and sentiment,

---

[61] A suggestion as old as Page (1896) ad Hor. *Carm.* 2.12.13. More recent enunciations by Williams (1968) 304–5, 549–56 and Lyne (1978) 179. Overview of the question in Randall (1979). Miller (1994) 102 and Greene (1999) 3 both favor the hypothesis.

[62] Sensitive appreciation of Catullus' achievement in translating Sappho in Ferguson (1985) 147–50.

[63] Ferrari (1938) 59, also Fordyce (1961) and Quinn (1970) ad loc. For Quinn, however, the diction expresses not Catullus' Romanness but rather his "intensity of feeling."

and that the "loudly pious" protestation was in fact a common enough feature of Hellenistic poetry in more than one genre.[64]

Still, unless we are content to say that Catullus had managed to render into the terser Latin all or enough of the Greek of Sappho's first strophe in the three other lines and so added the second verse simply as a *cheville*, there ought to be some aesthetic account for it. At least part of that account, I suggest, may reside in the sonic play of the two Catullan verses. They feature, remarkably, perfect assonance in their first five syllables: *ille mi par es(se)* (51.1) is echoed by *ille si fas est* (51.2) The effect might be compared to the practice of later Roman poets such as Ovid, who made the first verse of his first elegy assonate with the opening of the *Aeneid*.[65] It might even be compared to Louis Zukofsky's "translation" technique, though what Catullus' second verse "breathes with" is not Sappho's original but rather Catullus' own first verse, as if to throw a spotlight on both original's and translation's *incipit* by a delayed, recapitulated, stuttered beginning. A further sonic effect: the pronominal beginnings of the first strophe's first three verses form an assonating (and grammatical) triplet – *ille* (51.1), *ille* (51.2), *qui se(dens)* (51.3) – that finds its symmetrical answer in the final strophe's triple anaphora of the word *otium* ("leisure," 51.13–15).

Catullus' last strophe appears not to be a direct translation of anything in the Sappho, though the fragmented state of the original renders this uncertain.[66] In any case, the second problematizing consideration in interpreting the poem is precisely this abrupt change of tone, theme and sentiment in its closing stanza. The previous strophes, following Sappho's Greek fairly closely, had shown the Catullan speaker not only rendered powerless by love and so by the logic of binary gender ideology "feminized," but also speaking words of love originally framed and authored by a

---

[64] Q. Lutatius Catulus 2.3–4 Courtney: *Pace mihi liceat, caelestes, dicere uestra:* | *mortalis uisus pulchrior esse deo* ("Grant me your leave, heavenly powers, to say it: the mortal [a beautiful boy] looked fairer than the god [the rising sun]"). On the "loudly pious" apotropaic gesture in Apollonius of Rhodes, Hunter (1993) 101–29, also Wray (forthcoming).

[65] McKeown (1987) ad Ov. *Am.* 1.1.1.

[66] Sappho fr. 31 contains a fourth strophe, which Catullus seems not to have translated (on this see Vine [1992]), and the (corrupt) opening verse of a fifth. Wilkinson (in Bayet [1956] 47–8) argued that Catullus' poem ended at the third strophe. Fordyce (1961) agreed, though without going so far as to orphan the final strophe in his printed text. Thomson (1997) ad loc. withholds judgment but provides a rich bibliography.

woman poet.[67] The final strophe, in sharp contrast, seems to turn away from the feminine and from the erotic, personating instead a most masculine concern for wealth and power, the lessons of history, the proper use of free time, and the bland moral maxims of the "reality principle." It is from this that so many readers of the poem conclude that at the end of his Greek translation exercise Catullus, like Shakespeare's Antony, has suddenly had a Roman thought.[68]

Lament, however, and in particular erotic complaint, veering off at the end into the gnomic is a common enough feature of Greek literature. A Hellenistic example of specifically erotic context, one we can expect Catullus to have had in memory or at his fingertips, appears in Theocritus' idyll on the Cyclops. Bringing himself up abruptly at the end of a lengthy and somewhat comical Lover's Complaint, Polyphemus, like the Catullan speaker of Poem 51, closes his poem-within-the-poem with an address to himself and a call from the world of love's idleness back to the routine of work:

> ὦ Κύκλωψ Κύκλωψ, πᾷ τὰς φρένας ἐκπεπότασαι;
> αἴ κ' ἐνθὼν ταλάρως τε πλέκοις καὶ θαλλὸν ἀμάσας
> ταῖς ἄρνεσσι φέροις, τάχα κα πολὺ μᾶλλον ἔχοις νῶν.
> τὰν παρεοῖσαν ἄμελγε· τί τὸν φεύγοντα διώκεις;
> εὑρησεῖς Γαλάτειαν ἴσως καὶ καλλίον' ἄλλαν.
> πολλαὶ συμπαίσδεν με κόραι τὰν νύκτα κέλονται,

---

[67] Janan (1994) 71–6 compellingly reads Catullus' Sappho translation alongside Lacan's reading of St. Teresa of Avila to show Poem 51's speaker oscillating between the "erotic takeover" of "the persistent skepticism of *jouissance féminine*" and the masculine "certainty of the idiot's *jouissance*." Indeed, the Catullan speaker's gender seems *at issue* in a way quite unlike anything in Sappho. Note that in Poem 51, the speaker's masculine gender is loudly announced at the opening of the second strophe (*misero*, 51.5, reflecting nothing in Sappho's Greek, as noted by Thomson [1997] ad loc.), and only subsequently is the addressee's gender revealed (*Lesbia*, 51.7). In the Sappho, conversely, the addressee's feminine gender is clear from the opening strophe, while that of the speaker remains ambiguous until the fourth strophe (χλωροτέρα, Sappho 31.14).

[68] Poem 51's closing "*otium* strophe" may however be more Sapphic than critics generally allow. Passerini (1934) 52–6 and Fraenkel (1957) 211–13 saw that under Catullus' *otium* lies a set of Hellenistic notions connected with the term τρυφή ("decadence", not attested in archaic Greek). But the surviving line of Sappho's last strophe (ἀλλὰ πᾶν τόλματον ἐπεὶ ..., "but everything is (to be) endured, since ...") does seem to introduce a gnomic consolation (Lattimore [1944]), and as Knox (1984) argues, that consolation may have been framed around the term ἀβροσύνα, a near synonym of τρυφή/*otium*, and attested in Sappho.

κιχλίζοντι δὲ πᾶσαι, ἐπεί κ' αὐταῖς ὑπακούσω,
δῆλον ὅτ' ἐν τᾷ γᾷ κήγών τις φαίνομαι ἦμεν.

(Theoc. Id. 11.72–9)

O Cyclops, Cyclops, where have you wandered in your wits?
If you would go plait cheese-crates and gather greens
to take to your lambs, you'd show more sense by far.
Milk the one that's at hand; why chase the one that runs
   away?
Maybe you'll find another Galatea, a better one, too.
A lot of girls are asking me to play with them all night long,
and they all giggle whenever I listen to them.
It's clear that on land, at least, even I am somebody.

The Theocritean Cyclops' closing moment of self-interpellation (famously imitated by Virgil) might seem on its face to belong to a very different register from that of Poem 51's Catullus.[69] On a wider view of the two contexts the comparison begins to seem apter. *Idyll* 11 opens in its poet's own voice, with a witty gnomic statement addressed to a physician friend (and fellow poet) followed by an announcement of the poem's burden:

Οὐδὲν ποττὸν ἔρωτα πεφύκει φάρμακον ἄλλο,
Νικία, οὔτ' ἔγχριστον, ἐμὶν δοκεῖ, οὔτ' ἐπίπαστον,
ἢ ταὶ Πιερίδες· κοῦφον δέ τι τοῦτο καὶ ἁδύ
γίνετ' ἐπ' ἀνθρώποις, εὑρεῖν δ' οὐ ῥᾴδιόν ἐστι.
γινώσκειν δ' οἶμαί τυ καλῶς ἰατρὸν ἐόντα
καὶ ταῖς ἐννέα δὴ πεφιλημένον ἔξοχα Μοίσαις.
οὕτω γοῦν ῥᾷστα διᾶγ' ὁ Κύκλωψ ὁ παρ' ἁμῖν,
ὡρχαῖος Πολύφαμος, ὅκ' ἤρατο τᾶς Γαλατείας,
ἄρτι γενειάσδων περὶ τὸ στόμα τὼς κροτάφως τε.
ἤρατο δ' οὐ μάλοις οὐδὲ ῥόδῳ οὐδὲ κικίννοις,
ἀλλ' ὀρθαῖς μανίαις, ἁγεῖτο δὲ πάντα πάρεργα.

(Theoc. Id. 11.1–11)

There is no remedy for love, Nicias – no ointment,
I think, no cream – other than the Muses. A painless one
for mortals. Pleasurable, even. But not an easy one to find.
But I think you know that well, being a doctor,
and being a beloved favorite of the Muses nine.
And yet the Cyclops, you know, my countryman of ancient
   times,

---

[69] *Ecl.* 2.69: *a, Corydon, Corydon, quae te dementia cepit?*

Polyphemus – he managed quite easily, when he loved
  Galatea,
as he was sprouting his first downy whiskers about the mouth
and cheeks. And he loved, not with apples, or roses, or
  ringlets,
but with out and out madness, counting everything else
  worthless.

Polyphemus, for all the Colin Clout burlesque of his performance
within the poem, is set forth in the poem's opening frame as an
exemplum of a specific medical problem.[70] The patient's complaint
is precisely that erotic madness whose symptoms Sappho's poem
had described so unforgettably.[71] Its only relief, Theocritus claims,
is to be sought in the arts not of doctors but of poets. Polyphemus'
abrupt and impatient self-address at the end of his song (*Id.* 11.72–
9, cited above) thus represents, on one reading, the process of his
poetic therapy arriving at the resolution of a cure. The Theocritean speaker returns in the final two verses to make this explicit,
echoing the words of the poem's opening and getting in one last
gleeful dig at his well-heeled doctor-poet addressee:

οὕτω τοι Πολύφαμος ἐποίμαινεν τὸν ἔρωτα
μουσίσδων, ῥᾷον δὲ διᾶγ' ἢ εἰ χρυσὸν ἔδωκεν.
(Theoc. *Id.* 11.80–1)

And so, you see, Polyphemus corralled his passion by making
  it
music. And he managed more easily than if he'd spent his
  money.

Catullus' poetic performance, like Theocritus', appears to feature
poetry as a therapy, or at least a response, a "working through," in
the face of a passion whose symptoms are portrayed in a language
close to clinical symptomatology. It also features a poem sur-
rounded by a frame addressed to a fellow poet and whose two
ends echo each other verbally. It does so, that is, if we take Catullus' performance unit to consist not in Poem 51 by itself but in

[70] On exemplarity and framing in *Idyll* 11, and on the doubtful success of Polyphemus'
poetic cure, Goldhill (1991) 249–61.
[71] Devereux (1970) went so far as to render an "expert medical" diagnosis of Sappho's
"seizure" and, even more regrettably, a characterization of the underlying psycho-
physiological pathology ("inversion") evidenced by it.

the pair formed by reading it together with the poem immediately before it in the collection:

> Hesterno, Licini, die otiosi
> multum lusimus in meis tabellis,
> ut conuenerat esse delicatos:
> scribens uersiculos uterque nostrum
> ludebat numero modo hoc modo illoc,
> reddens mutua per iocum atque uinum.
> atque illinc abii tuo lepore
> incensus, Licini, facetiisque,
> ut nec me miserum cibus iuuaret
> nec somnus tegeret quiete ocellos,
> sed toto indomitus furore lecto
> uersarer, cupiens uidere lucem,
> ut tecum loquerer simulque ut essem.
> at defessa labore membra postquam
> semimortua lectulo iacebant,
> hoc, iucunde, tibi poema feci,
> ex quo perspiceres meum dolorem.
> nunc audax caue sis, precesque nostras,
> oramus, caue despuas, ocelle,
> ne poenas Nemesis reposcat a te.
> est uemens dea: laedere hanc caueto.   (Poem 50)

> Yesterday, Licinius, while we were at leisure,
> we played at length upon my tablets.
> (We had made an agreement to be *delicati*.)
> Scribbling out verses, each of us
> would play now in this mode, now in that,
> rendering like for like in wit and wine.
> And I went away, Licinius, so
> enflamed by your charm and your jokes
> that food could give no pleasure in my pain
> and sleep refused to put my poor eyes to rest.
> Instead, wild with utter madness, I tossed
> in bed, kept waiting for the daylight
> to talk to you and be with you again.
> But when my limbs, exhausted from their struggle,
> were lying, nearly dead, on the mattress,
> I made you this poem, my dear,
> so you could see from it the extent of my pain.
> Now, don't you dare be brazen, my darling,
> and don't you dare reject my prayers,
> or Payback might just come around and get you.
> She's one wild goddess: do not dare offend her.

Cast as a letter from Catullus to C. Licinius Calvus, fellow poet and friend (the two names are very often paired in Catullus' ancient reception), Poem 50's narrative of a day spent with Calvus in poetic improvisation turns to a self-depiction of its speaker in the throes of erotic madness.[72] An enumeration of symptoms concludes with a petulant plea cast in the traditional language of an abandoned lover. With Poems 50 and 51 taken as a pair, their progression is remarkably similar to that of Theocritus' idyll on the Cyclops, the chief difference being that Catullus assumes the speaking role in both frame (Poem 50 and the last stanza of Poem 51) and internal poem (the first three stanzas of Poem 50). Just as the Theocritean frame is foregrounded by verbal repetition – that the Cyclops "managed easily" thanks to his poetic therapy is announced first proleptically in the opening address to Nicias (7) and then analeptically in the closing verse (81) of the idyll – so Poem 50's initial opening of a poetic and affective space in the name of "leisure" (*otiosi*, 50.1) is answered and closed by the abrupt self-assessment and moralizing warning on the dangers of *otium* that ends Poem 51 (13–16).[73]

To compare this Catullan pair to Theocritus' eleventh idyll – not as an explicit intertext or a model directly alluded to, but rather as a structurally and thematically similar example that Catullus is certain to have known – is, so far as I know, to say a new thing about it. Continued resistance to finding still more "Alexandrian" elements in Catullus is almost certainly a factor here, especially where it is a question of Catullus not only at his most lyrical but also basking in the archaic light of burning Sappho.[74] On the other hand, to take Poems 50 and 51 as a pair, and even to read Poem 50 as the "cover letter" to the Sappho translation, is a suggestion now several decades old, cited often enough and probably known to anyone writing on Catullus, but one that seems not to have resonated with the best recent literary treatments of Poem 51.[75] The possibility of reading these two poems as

---

[72] Important discussions of this poem include Pucci (1961), Segal (1970), Burgess (1986) and Williams (1988).

[73] On Catullus' announcement of *otium* as the programmatic opening of a poetic space (Blanchot's "*espace littéraire*"), see Platter (1995) 218–19. On the ambivalence of *otium* and the resulting "semiotic slippage" embodied in Catullus' deployment of the term, Miller (1994) 137–8. On *otium* in Roman thought, André (1966).

[74] A resistance most recently expressed in regard to Poem 51 by Vine (1992) n. 23.

[75] The notion of Poem 50 as the "*lettre d'envoi*" to Poem 51 was first suggested in print by Lavency (1965), who attributes the idea of reading the poems as a pair to an unpublished suggestion of J. Mogenet. See also Clack (1976).

a pair is the third and last of the problematizing considerations to be taken into account, and it is here that there emerges, through comparison with a number of other poems in the corpus, the possibility of reading Poem 51, this central "Lesbia poem," as a further instance of an intensely performative Catullan poetics of manhood.

The argument for reading Poems 50 and 51 as a pair, based on evidence in the text of the two poems, in the text of the corpus and in the wider context of Roman epistolary practice, is rather more compelling than might seem at first glance, perhaps even more compelling than it has seemed to those who have put it forward. In addition to the framing programmatic announcement of *otium* that opens Poem 50 and closes Poem 51 (taken as significant even by critics who reject the suggestion of Poem 50 as a covering letter), there is the strikingly similar description in both poems of erotic distress, elaborated in physical and almost clinical terms. Both poems' speakers portray the pleasure of merely conversing with the beloved (Calvus in Poem 50, Lesbia in Poem 51) as a blissful attainment, and their deprivation of that pleasure as the root cause of their symptoms. More specific, and still more striking, is the fact that Poem 50's speaker begins the enumeration of symptoms, the revelation of his illness, by calling himself *miserum* ("wretched," 50.9). Poem 51's speaker describes himself with the same word (*misero*, 51.5), and the epithet there is a purely Catullan addition to the poem, reflecting nothing in Sappho's original. The announcement that he is "miserable" thus stands in each poem as the first indication of its speaker's erotic suffering. Further, in Poem 51, the appearance of the word is the only moment, apart from the poet's own name in the final strophe, in which the speaker's gender is indicated. It is here that the reader first becomes aware that Poem 51 is not so much a translation, one might say, as a performed imitation of Sappho's original poem, an appropriation or ventriloquizing of her words in the male (Catullan) speaker's own voice.

If the two pieces stand as a single epistolary missive, then the deictic pronoun at 50.16 – *hoc, iucunde, tibi poema feci* ("I made you this poem, delightful man") – will refer not to the poem containing it but to the translation following it. The bilingual etymological figure in *poema ... feci*, if it refers to Catullus' Latin version of Sappho's Greek, does more than take on special appropriateness in this context.[76] It flashes off the page as a moment of performative wit throwing a foregrounding spotlight onto the virtuoso performance about to come in the form of the Sappho rendition.[77] This demonstrative pronoun within a prelude poem referring to the subsequent poem, as others have already noted, has an exact parallel in the covering letter to the only other full-scale translation within the corpus.[78] Poem 66 is Catullus' translation of a long passage from Callimachus' *Aetia* on a lock of hair sacrificed by Berenice, Ptolemy III Euergetes' queen. Immediately preceding the translation is a dedicatory epistle in which Catullus protests that grief over his brother's death has kept him from poetic composition, but not so completely as to keep him from fulfilling a poetic duty to a friend:

> sed tamen in tantis maeroribus, Ortale, mitto
>   haec expressa tibi carmina Battiadae,
> ne tua dicta uagis nequiquam credita uentis
>   effluxisse meo forte putes animo   (65.15–18)

> But even in so great a grief, Ortalus, I am sending you
>   these pressed out (i.e., translated) verses of Battus' son,
> so that you won't think your words, without effect, entrusted
>   for safekeeping to roving winds, to have wafted from my
>   mind.

"These verses" (65.16) belong not to Poem 65 but rather, unambiguously, to the version of Callimachus that constitutes the following poem (Poem 66) in the collection.[79] The passage cited here is preceded and followed by similes of exquisite delicacy, both of them putting Catullus implicitly in a feminine role.[80] The tone is wheedling, delicately petulant: very close, in other words, to the tone adopted by Catullus in Poem 50 to Calvus.

Ortalus' "words" (*dicta*, 65.17), as Catullus' response to them

---

[76] Greek ποιῶ, root verb of ποίημα, is the equivalent of Latin *facio*, so that the words *poema feci* mean "I composed a composition."

[77] On Catullan "virtuosity," Fitzgerald (1995) 151 and passim.

[78] Lavency (1965) 179.

[79] Poem 1 features a further Catullan instance of a deictic pronoun referring not to the poem in which it sits but rather to what follows: the dedication to Nepos offers him "this little book, such as it is, of whatever quality it may be" (*quidquid hoc libelli | qualecumque*, 1.8–9).

[80] More on this passage in Chapter 5, 197–203.

indicates, seem to have been a request, conveyed to Catullus by speech or writing, for a piece of poetry. A written request is perhaps the likelier, an epistolary "poetic challenge," a performative request for poetry that is itself a poem. The Catullan corpus contains at least one certain example of this type of poetic writing, a piece addressed to a fellow poet of whose poetic production and life we possess a few fragments:[81]

> Malest, Cornifici, tuo Catullo,
> malest, me hercule, et laboriose,
> et magis magis in dies et horas.
> quem tu, quod minimum facillimumque est,
> qua solatus es allocutione?
> irascor tibi. sic meos amores?
> paulum quid lubet allocutionis,
> maestius lacrimis Simonideis.   (Poem 38)

> Cornificius, things are bad for your friend
> Catullus. Things are bad, by God, and things are hard,
> and things are getting worse with every passing day and
>   hour.
> And *you* – it's the smallest thing, the easiest thing in the
>   world –
> what consolation have you given your friend?
> I'm angry at you. *This* is how you value my love?
> I'd like a little something in the way of consolation,
> something sadder than Simonidean tears.

The biographical or fictive experience of suffering to which this poem's speaker refers is unspecified and unrecoverable. Commentators like to speak here of "mental distress" and even "crisis of emotion," not entirely implausibly, and so leave the reader's imagination to revert to the poet's two great losses of beloved and brother.[82] On the other hand, it may be noted that the poet of these verses also wrote, for example, a poem beginning and ending with the line *Quid est, Catulle? quid moraris emori?* ("What, then,

---

[81] Q. Cornificius, quaestor in 48, mentioned by Cicero (*Fam.* 8.7.12) and Ovid (*Tr.* 2.435–6). Fragments of his poetry in Courtney. See also Fordyce (1961) 182–3.

[82] Thomson (1997) 303: "mental or, less probably, physical distress." Fordyce (1961) 182: "crisis of emotion." But Quinn (1970) 206 writes astutely: "There is a wry note in C.'s protestation of affliction which should warn us against supposing him on his deathbed, or even prostrate with overwhelming grief."

Catullus? Why not go ahead and die?" 52.1,4), and that the subject of that poem is no deeper crisis of intensely personal emotion than the speaker's dissatisfaction with two contemporary political figures. Most speakers of English (some regional dialects offer exceptions) simply have no access to a comparable native rhetorical register. This Mediterranean performative outrageousness is perhaps yet another aspect of Catullus' self-representation that "we have taken rather too much to our hearts," another place where our reading has erased Catullus' foreignness by overestimating his sincerity.[83] In any case, what can be said with certainty is that the petulantly guilt-inducing words of Poem 38, similar in some respects to the language Cicero and Pliny adopt in letters to a neglectful correspondent, explicitly request and even demand from the speaker a response in the form of a poetic performance.[84] The last verse goes so far as to throw down a glove, issuing a specific aesthetic challenge (with a Greek model as aesthetic standard) to a fellow poet: "let's see you top Simonides for sadness."[85]

Poem 30, whose addressee may possibly be identical to the (Alfenus) Varus addressed in the more famous Poem 22 on the aristocratic poetaster Suffenus, the same Varus featured as Catullus' friend and fellow *otiosus* in the still more famous Poem 10, is similarly petulant, though pitched considerably higher:[86]

> Alfene immemor atque unanimis false sodalibus,
> iam te nil miseret, dure, tui dulcis amiculi?
> iam me prodere, iam non dubitas fallere, perfide?
> nec facta impia fallacum hominum caelicolis placent.
> quae tu neglegis ac me miserum deseris in malis.
> eheu quid faciant, dic, homines cuiue habeant fidem?
> certe tute iubebas animam tradere, inique, me
> inducens in amorem, quasi tuta omnia mi forent.
> idem nunc retrahis te ac tua dicta omnia factaque
> uentos irrita ferre ac nebulas aereas sinis.
> si tu oblitus es, at di meminerunt, meminit Fides,
> quae te ut paeniteat postmodo facti faciet tui.   (Poem 30)

---

[83] Fitzgerald (1995) 235.

[84] Gunderson (1997).

[85] See Carson (1999), esp. 73–99, on Simonides' ancient reputation for τὸ συμπαθές. It bears mention that the third book of Callimachus' *Aetia* featured an episode on the tomb of Simonides (*Aet.* 3. fr. 64 Pfeiffer), spoken in the voice of the dead poet himself.

[86] On the identification of the poem's addressee, Fordyce (1961) ad loc. Wiseman (1985) 122–4 reads Poem 30 as straightforwardly sincere and so "too uncomfortably self-pitying to be an artistic success."

> Alfenus, thoughtless and false to your comrades who care for
>   you,
> have you no shred of mercy left, hard heart, for your sweet
>   little friend?
> Not a single scruple left, to betray him, faithless man, to
>   deceive him?
> But heaven does not smile on the impious deeds of men who
>   deceive.
> This truth you ignore, and abandon poor me in my pains.
> Alas! what are men to do? – tell me – in whom are they to
>   put their faith?
> You certainly kept telling me to give you my heart, you
>   traitor, you
> led me along into your love, as if all would be safe for me
>   there.
> And now you pull away, and everything you said and
>   everything you did,
> you let it all be carried away, meaningless, on the winds and
>   the mists of the air.
> If you've forgotten, the gods still remember. Faith still
>   remembers,
> and Faith will one day make you sorry for what you've done.

The saccharine self-pity and shrill self-righteousness of my translation reflect my reading of the original. The transvestite ventriloquism of this abandoned lover's complaint might seem even to
pass into something of the parodic misogyny of bad drag.[87] Commentators, working hard to help Catullus maintain his *sérieux*,
speak of bitter reproach born of melancholic distemper, of an
offense on the addressee's part more of omission than commission,
and of a certain academic stiltedness in the tone, perhaps owing to
Catullus' experimental use here – the sole instance in the corpus,
and possibly for the first time in Latin poetry – of a Greek metre
that only Horace among Latin poets ever handled with the grace
of full mastery.[88] Catullus and his contemporaries would have
associated the fiercely difficult (in Latin) "greater Asclepiadean"
metre with the Lesbian poets Sappho and Alcaeus; they would also
have known Hellenistic examples from Callimachus and Theocritus as well as the epigrammatist who gave the metre its scholarly

---

[87] On "transvestite ventriloquism," Harvey (1996).
[88] Also called "fifth Asclepiadean," this is the metre of, e.g., the *carpe diem* ode (Hor. *Carm.*
   1.11): see 10–11 above. Horace has lightened the otherwise awkward (in Latin) rhythm by
   forcing the first two choriambs' ends to coincide with word ends.

name.[89] The experimental use of a difficult metre and the wildly hyperbolic diction, I think, are keys to identifying this poem's occasional context and the type of writing to which it belongs. It seems likely that this poem's only self-revelation is precisely the "revelatory kind of conviction" that, in Herzfeld's formulation, attaches to the implicit claims of a performative outrageousness.[90] Poem 30's message, on this reading, is equivalent to that of Poem 38: it is again a request for poetic performance that itself takes the form of a poetic performance, this time a considerably more virtuosic and foregrounded performance. Alfenus' "faithlessness," then, has consisted in a lag in the epistolary exchange of poems enjoyed by the two poets, a commerce portrayed by the Catullan speaker as a love affair (in the same way that Poem 38's speaker had cried *sic meos amores?* ["*this* is how you treat my love?"], 38.6). This lover's complaint is at once a demand and a challenge, inviting its addressee to a poetically performed requital of like for like. It is significant that the climax of the Catullan speaker's guilt-inducing accusations takes the form of precisely the same charge that Poem 65's speaker assures his addressee he is at pains to avoid meriting: to lapse in the exchange of poems is to let one's own promises, and the other's pleas, be carried away on the wind (30.9–10, 68.17–18).

Poems 30 and 38 have shown Catullus offering a poetic challenge. Poem 65 has presented him on the receiving end as he responds to, or perhaps anticipates, a similar challenge. Similarly, Poem 68a, an elegy to a friend (represented as) written from Verona, refers explicitly to "this little letter composed with tears" (*conscriptum hoc lacrimis ... epistolium*, 68a.2) sent to Catullus by his addressee.[91] The friend's *epistolium*, whether in verse or prose, will

---

[89] Sappho 55 and Alcaeus 347 (Lobel Page) are notable fragmentary examples. Book 3 of the Hellenistic edition of Sappho (the "lyric collection" Catullus knew) seems to have consisted entirely of poems in this metre. Of Callimachus we have fr. 400 Pfeiffer; of Theocritus, *Idylls* 28 and 30, the latter spoken by an aging *erastes* in the throes of love-sickness for a beautiful boy, in a tone strikingly close to that of Poem 30. It begins ᾤαι τὼ χαλέπω καἰνομόρω τῶδε νοσήματος ("alas for this hard and dire-fated sickness"). Of "greater Asclepiadeans" from the hand of Asclepiades we have no surviving examples.

[90] Herzfeld (1985) 11. See 60–2 above.

[91] I take "Poem 68" as two separate poems to different addressees forming a juxtaposed pair (so Vretska [1966] 327–8). Many of the structural arguments for a unified and symmetrical "Poem 68" are strong, but they point, I suspect, to the unity of two poems as yet another Catullan pair. Thomson (1997) ad loc. for summary of arguments and bibliography.

have contained a certain amount of consolation (68a.1–4) together
with a certain amount of witty, perhaps even lightly invective, an-
imadversion on the inappropriateness of a straight-laced provincial town as a dwelling place for the young and fast-living Catullus
(68a.27–30). It will also have contained a specific request for "the
gifts of the Muses and Venus" (*munera ... Musarum ... et Veneris*,
68a.10), a request that Catullus pronounces himself at pains not to
fail to recognize, though grief keeps him from fulfilling it properly
(68a.11–12).[92]

Two more evidences of a lively epistolary commerce of poems
may be added here, one certain and one speculative. The last
poem of the corpus, addressed to the Gellius whom earlier invective epigrams have repeatedly skewered, represents a fictive or real
moment at which the Catullan speaker, having tried sending Gellius some "songs of Battus' son" (*carmina Battiadae*, 116.2, precisely
what Catullus had sent to Ortalus in Poem 66 and announced at
65.16) in hopes of inclining their recipient to friendship, sees now
that his labor (of poetic translation) has been undertaken in vain
(116.5) and that his "prayers have had no effect here" (*nec nostras hic
ualuisse preces*, 116.6).[93] The final and speculative example has already been discussed briefly in this chapter. Poem 13 is Catullus'
invitation to a house without food from a host without money.
Nearly all the poem's readers agree that this is no proper dinner
invitation.[94] Some have gone a step further and wondered how the
recipient of such a missive, even if only in the fictive logic of the
poem, could be expected to respond to it. If a poet named Catullus actually did send the poem, as it stands, to a friend named
Fabullus, the letter was almost certainly effective as a practical
joke. The poem's speaker will have awakened in Fabullus the hope
of dinner at the house of a man whose father possessed the
wherewithal to welcome the visit of Julius Caesar, only to dash
that hope with a protestation of poverty (taken seriously now by
almost no one), then to appear to offer "the essence of love" (*meros
amores*, 13.9) as a consolation prize, and finally to close with what is
perhaps an implicit unfavorable aesthetic judgment on the proportions of the addressee's physiognomy.[95] How, by the logic of

---

[92] On "Venus and the Muses," compare the anecdote recounted at 210–11 below.
[93] On the Gellius poems, 186–9 below.
[94] 73 above.
[95] On Roman mockery of individual physical peculiarities, Corbeill (1996) 14–56.

the poem, was Fabullus to respond to this porcupine of challenges tossed into his lap? Difficult to think of any way but one: to sit down with tablet and stylus and set about trying to match (outdoing seems unlikely) the outrageousness, and the high-spirited malice, of Catullus' poem. On that reading, what Poem 13 invites its addressee to enjoy with its sender is precisely a feast of words, a competitive exchange of poetic performances.

All these Catullan instances of poetic epistolarity (Poems 30, 38, 65, 66, 68, 116, and possibly 13) share two features in common.[96] First, each of them makes sense only in the form of a *poem*. They cannot be read as poetic recastings, verse transcriptions, of letters originally written in prose. Such a prose "original" would not have counted as a valid performance in the playing field of exchange: a poetic challenge, or the response to one, must itself be a performance of poetic utterance. Catullus' poetic missives differ in this way from, for example, Ovid's *Heroides*. There the elegiac form, while exerting its full pressure at the thematic and dictional levels of generic convention, is erased, rendered transparent and invisible, at the level of narrative. We do not imagine Ariadne or Penelope writing elegiac verses.[97] Catullus' letters-in-verse, conversely, stand in the collection just as if they had been pasted into the collection, or copied there verbatim from the poet's *epistolarium*. The presence of actual correspondence with other poets in the long poems of Williams and Zukofsky offers a parallel, and arguably a way toward aesthetic description and evaluation of the striking effect of cut-and-paste collage, of *farrago*, produced by the scattered presence of these poems in the Catullan corpus.[98]

The second feature common to these Catullan "letter" poems is that the epistolary commerce they represent and imply is transacted exclusively between men. In fact, setting aside Poem 51 for a moment, the only poem in the corpus that allows itself to be read as an actual letter to a female addressee is Poem 32 to Ipsitilla. And there, the speaker's request, while arguably performative of a "poetics of manhood" in the sense of embodying a hyperbolic outrageousness, issues no challenge, invites no response in kind from its addressee. Indeed, its hypermasculine boast has the look

---

[96] Poem 60 might belong to the same category, but it contains no address by name and no other mark of epistolarity.

[97] On epistolarity and performativity in the *Heroides*, Connelly (2000).

[98] 54–5 above.

of being intended more for (male) readers of the poetry collection than of representing an underlying real or fictive note to Ipsitilla.[99] The poetic epistles to men, on the other hand, all seem to invite (or constitute) a response in the form of specifically poetic performance. Further, all these poems portray the exchange of poetic letters as a kind of love relation, in terms either openly or implicitly erotic, and all of them portray their Catullan speaker in the throes of a misery whose mode ranges from the wildly histrionic (Poem 30) to the somberly sincere (Poems 65 and 68). In Poem 13 the misery portrayed is that of literal (though almost surely fictitious) poverty; in Poem 116, the misery of aggrievement at injury has turned to angry hostility.

Let us return to Poems 50 and 51. In light of the other poetic epistles in the collection, two previously mysterious aspects of the end of Catullus' letter to Calvus now admit, I think, plausible and even satisfying explanation:

> hoc, iucunde, tibi poema feci,
> ex quo perspiceres meum dolorem.
> nunc audax caue sis, precesque nostras,
> oramus, caue despuas, ocelle,
> ne poenas Nemesis reposcat a te.
> est uemens dea: laedere hanc caueto.   (50.16–21)

> I made you this poem, my dear,
> so you could see from it the extent of my pain.
> Now, don't you dare be brazen, my darling,
> and don't you dare reject my prayers,
> or Payback might just come around and get you.
> She's one wild goddess: do not dare offend her.

The nature of the speaker's "pain" is clear enough. Like the speaker of the following poem, his distress has resulted from the onslaught of erotic madness. But what of his "prayers" (*preces*, 50.18), and why the threatening invocation of the divinity of retribution (*Nemesis*, 50.20)? No explicit prayer, supplication or request has been conveyed by the poem's referential content. And if, as some critics have thought, the poem belongs to a moment early in the friendship between the two poets, it is not immediately appar-

---

[99] On Poem 32, Heath (1986).

ent why an ancient writer, any more than a modern one, would choose to signal a growing affection for a new acquaintance by threatening, even in jest, a dire retribution from heaven sure to follow upon the interlocutor's rejection of friendship.[100] But Poem 116, to Gellius, also speaks of "prayers," at a moment when those prayers have proved bootless (*nec nostras hic ualuisse preces*, 116.6), and the prayers in that instance had been accompanied by – had indeed perhaps taken the form of – translations from the Greek of Callimachus sent to a fellow poet in token of friendly feeling. The act of supplication (*preces*) described in Poem 50, I suggest, consisted precisely in producing and sending "this poem" (*hoc poema*, 50.16), namely the Sappho translation. The closing recourse to Nemesis, so undermotivated and overblown in appearance, is a feature of the same dictional register that has made Poem 50 seem tentative and a bit formal to critics. Poem 30, to Alfenus, is a more extreme example played upon this register. Its invocation of retribution in the name of personified "Fidelity" (*Fides*, 30.11) occupies the same position (the penultimate verse) in its poem and fulfils, I think, the same function as the presence of Nemesis in Poem 50.[101] Both poems adopt the stance of an abandoned lover to invoke heaven's justice, and both do so at the climax of a self-allusive and self-consciously outrageous poetic performance that issues a demand for recognition of the excellence of the man who performed it: recognition first in the form of hilarious delight and aesthetic approbation, and ultimately through the response of a competing performance in kind.[102]

Finally, a question that could only be deferred so long: what, under the present reading, becomes of Lesbia in Poem 51, this central "Lesbia poem," this incomparable lyric of the Catullan collection? The scholar who first proposed the theory of Poem 50 as the covering letter to Poem 51, and of Calvus as the recipient of

---

[100] E.g. Buchheit (1976), Quinn (1970) 236, Thomson (1997) 324–5.

[101] Catullus, again, may have associated the metre of Poem 30 specifically with Sappho. See n. 89 above.

[102] Burgess (1986), with an elucidating comparison to the reciprocal poetry contests represented in Theocr. *Idylls* 5 and 8, arrives at a similar conclusion about Poem 50 as a poetic challenge. For Burgess, however, Catullus invokes Nemesis as the underdog's champion, and so adopts a position of poetic inferiority *vis-à-vis* Calvus. The compliment seems to me so strong as to run the risk of Calvus taking it as sarcasm, and what Nemesis is being called on to guarantee is not the outcome of the contest, I think, but rather Calvus' participation in it. Reciprocal poetic competition is a phenomenon of pan-Mediterranean pervasiveness. See e.g. Dundes (1970) on Turkish boys' dueling rhymes.

both poems, expressed a hope "not to have betrayed Catullus too abundantly."[103] The concern does not seem entirely misplaced. Whatever lived experience the poet may have attached to the signifier of her name at the time of his writing, it is clear that Poem 51's Lesbia, and the Catullan speaker's stance in relation to her, belongs to an altogether different order from the farcical pair (Poems 36 and 37) examined in the previous section. This Lesbia, indeed, is something altogether Other, in the Lacanian sense. It hardly seems excessive to speak here of divinization – Catullus calls her elsewhere a "shining goddess" (*candida diua*, 68.70) – or of Lesbia as "an object raised to the dignity of the Thing" and as the "traumatic kernel" around which the symptom of Catullus' represented interiority forms itself. Recent powerful readings of Poem 51 in the lyric mode take their place in a tradition many centuries older than Romanticism, and it has not been my aim here to argue that there is vastly less to this poem than has met nearly every reader's eye.[104] Quite the contrary: I hope to have shown that the same collection that inclines the reader, through the logic of responsion (with Poem 11), to place this poem at the narrative beginning of a biographical love affair also admits and even urges the possibility, through a differently focused reading, of placing its composition in an altogether different context. Hold both readings in the mind, and the simultaneity of their juxtaposition is complete: like a fragment of newsprint in collage, the poem "reads" as coherently in the context from which it was "cut" (poems to poets) as it does in the context into which it has been "pasted" (poems to Lesbia).

Still, if Poem 51 shines with a splendor that forces us ultimately to restore to the lyric Catullus his (ultimately inalienable) lyricism, it need not be at the price of robbing the skeptical reader of her skepticism. An "object raised to the dignity of the Thing," we may point out in the name of that skepticism, is no less an object for that. If Lesbia is Catullus' *puella diuina* ("divine woman"), she is also what Cynthia would be to Propertius: his *scripta puella* ("written woman").[105] If the epiphany of her insertion into the Sappho

---

[103] Lavency (1965) 182, in a closing apotropaic gesture of piety toward the high Romantic norms of his own formation as a reader of poetry and of Catullus: "Mais cet adaptateur était un grand écrivain, tragiquement tourmenté par la passion humaine déréglée, un vrai poète aussi, que j'espère ne pas avoir trop abondamment trahi."

[104] Esp. Janan (1994) 66–76 and Miller (1994) 103–11 and passim.

[105] *puella divina*: Lieberg (1962) 82–283; *scripta puella*: Wyke (1987).

translation does indeed render present to us the moment of her first formation on Catullus' lips, if the page transcribes the name for our eyes in the place where his stylus first scraped its letters into wax by lamplight, the Lesbia whose birth we are thus privileged to witness is a creation in the image not of a woman but of a male poet's desire. And if we read the Sappho translation as here suggested, then its salutation of Lesbia as love's divinity shares more than its Sapphic metre in common with Poem 11's valediction to her as desire's demon: both poems are notes passed, quite behind her back, from one man's hand to another.

MAN TO MAN (THE EPIGRAMS)

If the epigrams did indeed follow the long poems in a published three-volume set, then the passage from Poem 68, vessel of the most intense and impassioned "personal poetry" in the long poems, to the first of the epigrams – a readerly act punctuated by putting down one roll (for a slave to rewind) and opening another – will have dealt their reader the jolt of a characteristically radical and sudden change of register. That disorienting effect is sustained through the first four epigrams by the marked dictional and thematic oscillation of their arrangement – and again the poet seems the likelier author of such an arrangement than a posthumous editor.[106] Poem 69 dilates gleefully, though with a discernible elegance and even propriety of diction, on the foul body odor that makes women refuse sex with a certain Rufus.[107] The third of the epigrams, Poem 71, appears to be directed at the same man, though in somewhat rawer diction; he is not called by name but identified only as "that rival of yours who works your love" (*aemulus iste tuus, qui uestrum exercet amorem*, 71.3).[108] Here the man in question, though now portrayed as luckier in love, suffers from gout as well as body odor, so that "whenever he fucks, he punishes both parties: he tortures *her* with his smell, and he himself all but

---

[106] The case for Catullus' own hand in arrangement has been argued less vigorously for the epigrams (Poems 69–116) than for the polymetra. But see Schmidt (1973), Wiseman (1969) 22–8 on Poems 69–92. Dettmer (1997) 171–226 argues for elaborately interlocking symmetries throughout the epigrams (and the entire corpus). Most convincing of Dettmer's charts are those highlighting localized *poikilia* of the kind that a reader could note while holding a bookroll in two hands (such as p.174, showing Poems 69–78).

[107] On the Rufus epigrams, see esp. Pedrick (1993) 173–80, whose reading however finds their diction coarser than does mine.

[108] The diction is openly sexual but probably not obscene. Similar language appears at 61.235, where the newlyweds are exhorted to "exercise" their youth (*exercete iuuentam*).

dies of the gout" (71.5–6).[109] The second and fourth epigrams, folded like fingers into the pair on Rufus, are Lesbia poems. Both complain of her fickleness: the first (Poem 70) is witty, elegant, and loosely adapted from an epigram of Callimachus (*Ep.* 25 Pfeiffer); the second (Poem 72) is more intense, or at least more insistent, and in any case admits a reading as personal and even confessional poetry.[110]

The two categories represented in the opening quartet, Lesbia poems and poems directed at men, account for all but two of the fifty epigrams.[111] It is in this section of the corpus that Catullus is often said to have articulated an uncannily modern-sounding amatory subjectivity through the vocabulary of alliance and affiliation, seeming to grope toward a place beyond the Latin lexicon in a series of impassioned pleas for mutuality and reciprocal fidelity in love whose intensity has struck nearly every reader of the short elegiac poems to Lesbia.[112] So much is this the case, and the focus of criticism has widened the skew, that a reader may easily be pardoned for remembering Lesbia as the dominant theme, in every sense, of the epigrams. At least by poem counts – admittedly a somewhat vulgar and clumsy gauge – the proportions are in fact remarkably close to those of the polymetrics: barely over a quarter of the epigrams feature Lesbia, while poems directed at men, invective for the most part, make up the other three quarters.[113]

In the thirteen "Lesbia poems" among the epigrams, her name appears eight times in as many poems; the other five either address her directly, imply her presence or, if they mention her, refer to her as *mulier* ("woman"), never *puella* ("girl").[114] Of course, the "mutuality" and "reciprocal fidelity" declared by the speaker of these poems, and celebrated as so strikingly "modern" by much

---

[109] *nam quotiens futuit, totiens ulciscitur ambos:* | *illam affligit odore, ipse perit podagra.*

[110] Poem 72 is so read by, e.g., Wiseman (1985) 165–6 and Greene (1998) 8–12.

[111] Fifty epigrams, that is, taking Poems 78b and 95b as separate poems (more out of convenience than conviction).

[112] A classic statement of this reading is Copley (1949).

[113] There is some overlap (Poems 77, 79, 82 and 83 are "Lesbia" poems directed at men), and two epigrams refer neither to Lesbia nor to any man other than the Catullan speaker (Poems 110 and 111, to Aufillena).

[114] Mentions of Lesbia by name occur at 72.2, 75.1, 79.1, 83.1, 86.5, 87.2, 92.2 and 107.4. She is called *mulier* at 70.1 and 70.3, and again implicitly at 87.1 (where she is also named in the following verse). She is addressed directly as *mea uita* ("my life") at 109.1, and simply as *tu* ("you") at 104.4 and 76.11 (later in the same poem, at 76.23, she is *illa* ["she"]). The thirteenth "Lesbia poem" is Poem 85, the famous distich beginning *odi et amo* ("I hate and I love"); no love/hate object is named or even pronominalized there, but the traditional reception of this poem seems borne out by the logic of the collection.

important middle twentieth-century scholarship (scholarship that read Catullus as groping beyond his own Romanness – toward *us*), looks rather different to the contemporary reader, and that is so thanks to recent skeptical readings of Catullus that take their place within a far broader revision of sensibilities and sensitivities in the matter of gender.[115] The master terms of Catullan love – only ideology could have obscured so obvious a point – are always subject to the definition and manipulation of the (male) Catullan speaker's mastery. The promiscuous Lesbia always manages to come out a "worthless mistress," while the promiscuous Catullus never once in the poems to Lesbia takes a step outside the stance of love's pious saint, never avers a speck on his conscience in regard to his treatment of her. It is true that Catullus' conscience does not seem entirely clear: there are intimations, and a number of critics have brought them out, that the speaker of these poems experiences the illicit nature of his relation to a Roman matron as a source of internal conflict and guilt.[116] But that is a question of the speaker's relation not to his love object but to his society, to internalized paternal prohibition, to what Lacan calls the Symbolic order. What is remarkable, and worth emphasizing again, is the Catullan speaker's complete absence of self-reproach *as a lover* in regard to Lesbia.

On this point Catullus may be distinguished from, for example, the love elegists of the Augustan generation. Propertius and Ovid own up to a roster of ethical inadequacies as lovers: these include infidelity, callous indifference and even cruelty.[117] In Catullus' poetry, conversely, these and all other faults, and all the moral turpitude underlying them, are on Lesbia's side. Her "offense" (*iniuria*, 72.7) and her "blameworthiness" (*culpa*, 75.1) have so cheapened Lesbia (72.6), and so deranged his own mind (75.1–2), Catullus claims, that he can never again respect her, and yet he will never leave off pining with love and burning with desire for her (75.3–4). The only consolation he can look forward to is the satisfied contemplation, in old age, of a blameless life; his only prayer to the gods, since even the gods cannot be expected to

---

[115] 66–7 above.

[116] Catullus as a poet of provincial mores living and writing in a sophisticated capital is a narrative at least as old as Havelock (1939). Wiseman (1985) 107–75 develops an especially compelling version of it.

[117] E.g. Prop. 1.3 (he returns late to Cynthia's bed after a revel) and, most notoriously, Ov. *Am.* 1.7 (he has struck Corinna in the face and torn her hair). Tibullus' abject stance is closer to that of Catullus.

make *her* want to recover a shred of decent shame, is to be cured of the passion that has become for him a torment, a monstrous affliction (Poem 76).[118] The speaker's amatory claims pass, in Poem 77, into a kind of self-mythologizing: no woman was ever so loved as Catullus loved Lesbia, no faithfulness in a bond of love was ever so great as his. Remarkable as that claim is, perhaps even more astounding, in the Roman cultural context, is the claim at 72.5 to have loved Lesbia as a father loves his sons and sons-in-law: here it is as if love of Lesbia had taken the place of *pietas* and even of *natura* in Catullus' subjectivity. An unsubstantiated but longstanding view of Roman paternity as a tyrannical and grimly loveless exercise of *patria potestas* has arguably obscured this assertion's full force.[119]

If we set aside for a moment the different gender of their addressees and read the Lesbia epigrams in light of the poetic epistles to men discussed earlier in connection with Poem 51, the petulantly self-righteous and hyperbolically self-aggrandizing claims of the two sets of poems sound, I think, remarkably similar. The sense of rhetorical outbidding is arguably even stronger in the Lesbia epigrams: they often give an impression of racing toward the single most invincibly outrageous declaration of a blighting, withering passion – a declaration performed with all the epigrammatic pith of their genre. Racing toward it, planting a flag in it and daring all comers to top it: other poets of Catullus' generation were almost surely making comparable, perhaps even explicitly competitive, claims in similar poems.[120] A male audience is implicitly but palpably present in the epigrams to Lesbia. Their speaker even seems often to turn away from her to address his claims of all-surpassing amatory excellence to them. On this reading, the aggressively outrageous self-abasement manifested in those claims is thus paradoxically the very feature that makes them most performative of a poetics of manhood.

---

[118] Booth (1997) has recently read Poem 76 as the account of its author's "classic case of reactive depression" (167).

[119] No evidence supports the modern popular view of the late republican *paterfamilias*. Roman *pietas* was reciprocal between family members and regarded as "natural," belonging to the *ius gentium* (Saller [1994] 103–32). I think it likely that a Roman reader would have regarded this statement as Catullus' strongest declaration of love for Lesbia in the poems.

[120] Interesting in this regard to note that Catullus appears to link poetic excellence to excellence in love (through attractiveness or fidelity) in his praise of two fellow poets: Caecilius (Poem 35) and Calvus (Poem 96).

CHAPTER 4

Towards a Mediterranean poetics of aggression

I'll tell you.
About my *poetics* –
Louis Zukofsky, *A-12*

CATULLUS AND THE PROBLEM OF AGGRESSION

Clinical psychology gives the name "aggression" to any action delivering "noxious stimuli to another organism" with intent to cause physical or psychic injury, including acts of speech and gesture productive of shame or humiliation.[1] On that definition, well over half the poems of the corpus (I count sixty-nine) feature Catullus performing or threatening aggression against an interlocutor or third party, or else decrying, suspecting or fearing aggression in the behavior of others.[2] No getting around it: the speaker of Catullus' poems is not a nice man, by any stretch of imagination or interpretation. Aggression poses an ethical problem in any context. Catullus' aggression, the question of how he came to be such a good hater, continues to pose a critical problem as well.

A Romantic answer to that question, already rehearsed here, located the source of his florid outbursts in the personal disillusionment of a heart broken and a life wrecked at the hands of a "worthless mistress."[3] Much of the fiercest Catullan vituperation

---

[1] Buss (1961) 1–6, cited in Gilmore (1987) 2.
[2] Aggression is the performance of an affective state, and judging the affect of a poem is inevitably a subjective matter. The sixty-nine poems I have in mind are: 5, 6, 7, 8, 10, 11, 12, 14, 15, 16, 17, 21, 22, 23, 24, 25, 26, 27, 28, 29, 33, 36, 37, 39, 40, 41, 42, 43, 47, 49, 52, 53, 54, 56, 57, 58, 59, 61, 67, 69, 71, 74, 78, 78b, 80, 81, 83, 84, 88, 89, 90, 91, 92, 93, 94, 95, 95b, 97, 98, 103, 105, 108, 110, 111, 112, 113, 114, 115 and 116. That count seems to me a conservative application of the stated definition. A broader application would add many others to the list, e.g. Poem 32 to Ipsitilla or even Poem 4, where Fitzgerald (1995) 104–10 has discerned, rightly I think, an aristocratic contempt in the speaker's portrayal of the little boat.
[3] Quinn (1972) 220.

can be, and was, woven prosopographically back into the Lesbia novel, chiefly by making the male victims of his poetic aggression into rivals for her love; what could not be conscripted into that service (or characterized, alternately, as "political invective") was taken as an indicator of the depths to which a young man so lately callow had sunk.[4] On the one hand, that interpretation is of course not entirely without basis in the poems themselves. Catullus' self-representation gives us Catullus' version of whatever story we construe from the poems, and we should not be surprised if those poems respond to a reading of their speaker as a sympathetic character, even on cultural terms other than those of late republican Rome. On the other hand, most (though not all) Catullans have by now put the ironizing distance of one or more critical/theoretical models between their own Catullus and the strong version of a Romantic one. The application of newer models of reading, however, has hardly made the insistent presence of verbal aggression on nearly every page of the shorter poems less of a question to be answered or less of a problem to be negotiated.

If Romantic readings of Catullus tended to excuse his aggression where they could not ignore it, postromantic ones have tended either to attempt to explain it or else, more recently, to decry it. The first of these modern strains, for the most part (vernacularized) Freudian or at least psychologizing in approach, has been predicated in each instance on some version of poetry in general, and Catullus' poetry in particular, as "self-revelation" rather than self-representation or self-fashioning, as more confessional (or at least "introspective") than performative.[5] Those models, it has already been suggested here, are closely affiliated with a neo-Romantic Modernist poetics of the kind typified, in Perloff's view, by the poetry of Wallace Stevens.[6] The recent critical work of Laura Quinney has traced a "poetics of disappointment" running as a continuous line through Anglophone poetry from Wordsworth to middle and late twentieth-century poets like John

---

[4] Arkins (1982) makes a particularly thoroughgoing attempt to read Catullan invective as stemming from rivalry for the love of Lesbia. As for "political invective," in the wake of Syme (1939) 149–61 it has often served critics as an all-purpose formula for ethical whitewashing of Roman verbal aggression, since "it was a point of honour in a liberal society to take these things gracefully" (152).

[5] Adler (1981).

[6] 24–5 above.

Ashbery.[7] What Quinney calls "disappointment" – a "distinct, fearsome psychological state" of "the self estranged from the hopes of the self" – is not hard to find in Catullus, if our literary formation has taught us to read poetry with the expectation of finding it. The canonically central poetry of Romantic and modern disappointment, it is true, offers few parallels to Catullus' scatological effusions. But with "our Catullus" admitted into the ranks of the moderns, it has been only natural to take even the harshest invective poems, wherever possible, as expressive and symptomatic of a "distinct, fearsome psychological state" of de-idealization and disenchantment at the level of individual subjectivity, rather than as social performances belonging to a radically foreign cultural context.

A second line of response to Catullan aggression, that of showing it up and decrying it on ideological grounds, is more recent than romanticizing or modernizing explanations, and has in large measure arisen in response to these, especially in light of heightened sensitivity in contemporary public discourse to the ways in which the use of language marginalizes and stigmatizes those whose identity stands outside a culturally defined center, or whose behavior or other characteristics are perceived to deviate from stated or implicit social norms. If we take the lowest level consensus of opinion among citizens of postindustrial Western societies as to what constitutes ethical behavior and human decency, the person or "persona" construed by a straightforward reading of Catullus' poems comes off by that standard as a morally reprehensible one.[8] The thing needed saying, and a debt of gratitude is owed to the critics who have said it.

That such a critical stance applies contemporary ethical standards ahistorically and anachronistically to an ancient author goes without saying (though perhaps it goes better, as Voltaire once quipped, if we do say it). But ahistoricism is a charge that can equally well be leveled against earlier Catullan criticism. Ahistoricism is arguably a condition of literary study itself: most critics have by now accepted, with varying degrees of enthusiasm or resignation, the proposition that a radical and completely successful

---

[7] Quinney (1999) ix.

[8] In fact, an earlier (19th and early 20th century) moralizing strain of criticism had condemned Catullus' "pornography." Granarolo (1967) 160–204 responds admirably to that charge.

historicizing, if it were possible, would necessarily reduce a text's interpretability to zero, and that interpretation of a text always proceeds by eliding historical difference to some extent. Still under this second rubric, an alternate and somewhat more complex version of an ethically engaged reading of Catullus' aggressive verbal abuse has been put forward by some of his best recent critics. Here it is still a matter of applying modern standards to an ancient text, but that text, instead of being denounced for the ethical stance it voices, is read as a "critique" or "deconstruction" of the ethical norms of its own cultural context.[9] Catullan aggression itself is still decried on this reading, but "our Catullus" is detached from that aggression, made to stand critically aloof from it and to verge toward the ethical stance of his modern readers.

In all these romantic and modern readings of Catullan aggression, whether Catullus is taken as culpable, pardonable, or critically detached, the nature and character of aggression itself, as an ill to be condemned in whatever form it takes, remains immune to question. To suggest that things might be regarded otherwise seems at best an impertinence and at worst an act of treason against modernity itself. We are not certain where human aggression comes from: perhaps it is inherited instinct (Darwin, by way of biologist Konrad Lorenz); or possibly a psychic drive (Freud), though one that, unlike the libidinal drive, cannot be sublimated and made into a civilizing force, but must instead be mitigated as best it can or else deflected into less dangerous channels such as public sporting events; or again, perhaps it is learned behavior imprinted on a *tabula rasa* of childhood innocence by corrupt and corrupting social institutions (sociologist C. Wright Mills, and ultimately Rousseau).[10] To these theories of aggression's origin are attached the names of thinkers who stand as so many milestones in our coming to modernity. They differ as to whether aggression belongs to "nature" or "culture," whether its roots lie in the individual human subject or in human communities.[11] They agree, however, that aggression serves no good or useful purpose, but is rather a symptom of maladaptive disfunction at the level of the

---

[9] Two of the most sophisticated examples of this gesture: Skinner (1989), for whom Poem 10 "deconstructs its own *urbanitas*" and Selden (1992) 484, for whom Poem 42 "offers a wry critique of *flagitatio* as a judicial institution."

[10] Gilmore (1987) 14–18 and references there.

[11] Corbeill (1996) 14–16.

individual, and a dangerous toxin at the level of the social group. Aggression, whatever form it takes, is a problem. Nor is an exception to be made for speech or gestural acts of "symbolic" aggression (such as poems): first, because of a nearly axiomatic assumption that nonphysical aggression is either a prelude to, or at least an indicator of a propensity toward, acts of physical violence; and second, because of a recognition that abusive acts of speech and gesture produce suffering no less real, and often have personal and social consequences no less grave, than the effects of a physical wound.

PROBLEMATIZING THE PROBLEM

Consensus on at least that last point would seem to include not only Western moderns but ancient Romans as well. Roman law took a dim view of *uis* (force, assault) and *iniuria* (wrongful injury) in every form, and it appears that the Roman republic's constitutive document had provided the harshest of sanctions against verbal abuse in the form of poetry:[12]

nostrae inquit contra duodecim tabulae cum perpaucas res capite sanxissent, in his hanc quoque sanciendam putauerunt, si quis occentauisset siue carmen condidisset quod infamiam faceret flagitiumue alteri. praeclare: iudiciis enim magistratuum disceptationibus legitimis propositam uitam, non poetarum ingeniis, habere debemus, nec probrum audire nisi ea lege ut respondere liceat et iudicio defendere. (Cic. *Rep.* 4.12, in Augustine, *Civ.*2.9)

[Scipio, in Cicero's dialogue on the republic] said: "Our twelve tables, on the other hand, while providing for the death penalty in very few matters, provided it in this one: 'if anyone have sung or composed a song against another so as to give defamation or public disgrace.' Excellently so: for we ought to have our lives laid bare not by the genius of poets, but by magistrates' judgments and legal disputations, nor should we be spoken to insultingly except on condition that we have the opportunity to respond and to defend ourselves at trial."

Apart from the severity of its contemplated penalty, this apparent guarantee of full protection and recourse against verbal aggression (at least of the kind that scans) provided by the Twelve Tables and explicated by Cicero in the persona of Scipio Africanus

---

[12] The Twelve Tables contained provisions against both *uis* and *iniuria*. On violence in republican Rome, Lintott (1968).

sounds remarkably similar to modern Western legislation against slander and libel. Citizens of modern egalitarian democracies are not in the habit of taking laws with a grain of salt, to say the least, and for over a century now, modern Catullans in discussing the social context of Roman invective have tended to take Roman "law on defamation" at face value.[13] That face, for all its seeming familiarity, is almost surely deceptive. A first question: precisely whom did the law protect, and from whom?

We know very little about the tabular law's scope and application, but Augustine gives us the context of Cicero's (Scipio's) remarks on it: a comparison between the unbridled *ad hominem* attacks of Attic Old Comedy and the constraints put on such utterances by the Romans of the early republic (*ueteres Romani*).[14] It is significant, I think, that Scipio's (Cicero's) examples of persons to be protected by law from such abuse are all patricians of the highest nobility, with the hypothetical offenders very much their social inferiors. While grudgingly accepting Old Comedy's lampooning of such "seditious" *populares* as Cleon and Cleophon (though adding that an imposition of censorial *infamia* would have done the job better than a poet's attack), Scipio draws the line at invective against *optimates*, or Greek equivalents thereof: "to do violence in verse" (*uiolari uersibus*) on stage to a man like Pericles, after he had governed the state with the greatest *auctoritas* for many years, would have been as improper, he opines, "as if our own Plautus or Naevius had chosen to insult (*maledicere*) Publius or Gnaeus Scipio, or as if Caecilius had chosen to do the same to Marcus Cato."

Of the tabular law it is difficult to say more than this: there is no evidence of anyone being put to death at Rome for invective poetry, and not a single extant instance of a judicial proceeding under it. By the late republic, however, defamation of every kind seems to have been subsumed into the more general law of *iniur-*

---

[13] Lafaye (1894) 11: "La loi romaine était sévère pour le genre de poésie qu'Archiloque avait créé." (For Lafaye, the license allowed to poets in the late republic was something new, the result of "a weakening of the aristocratic spirit," political chaos, the fierce passions aroused by the civil wars and the loosening of social ties.) Selden (1992) 483, discussing Poem 42: "To the Roman mind, insults of this type were not a trifling matter, but explicitly forbidden and policed by law. Under the XII Tables, slander was punishable by death, and intermittent prosecution impressed upon the populace the gravity of the offense."

[14] See *OCD* s.v. "*iniuria* and defamation" with references there.

iae.[15] In principle, then, recourse under that law should have been available to the parties injured by this not uncharacteristic piece of Catullan aggression:

> O furum optime balneariorum
> Vibenni pater et cinaede fili
> (nam dextra pater inquinatiore,
> culo filius est uoraciore),
> cur non exilium malasque in oras
> itis? quandoquidem patris rapinae
> notae sunt populo, et natis pilosas,
> fili, non potes asse uenditare.   (Poem 33)

> O finest of the thieves that haunt the baths,
> Vibennius Sr., and you too, little faggot Jr.
> (Sr.'s the one with the itchier fingers,
> Jr.'s the one with the hungrier hole),
> why not head for exile and some sick
> shore? I mean, after all, Sr.'s pilfering is
> public knowledge by now. And Jr., you can't get a
> dime for those hairy buttcakes.

The circulation of this poem ought to have constituted, at the very least, an actionable *iniuria*; a public performance before its addressees would conceivably also have come under more specific legislation. But if Vibennius *père et fils* (assuming they were actual persons) were inclined to seek redress against the author of Poem 33, there would have been considerable factors to discourage them, perhaps even to bar them, from doing so.

If the poem's accusations were grounded even partially in truth, or simply widely believed to be likely, then Roman legal process, that crossfire of vituperative wit, would have been at best a pointless exercise for the Vibennii and at worst a grave risk. The pros-

[15] Three recorded incidents are generally brought forward in connection with this tabular law: (1) a poetic feud between Naevius and Q. Caecilius Metellus (consul 209 BCE) that was said (centuries later, by Aulus Gellius 3.3.15, who calls it a *fabula*) to have ended with the poet thrown into chains by the *imperium* of the triumvirs (and so no judicial proceeding); (2) an unsuccessful suit brought by the poet Lucilius (second century) against a fellow poet who had lampooned him on stage; and (3) a suit filed by the poet Accius (first century) on similar charges, successfully this time. The source for these last two incidents (*Rhet. ad Her.* 2.19) implies that both cases were tried under the law of *iniuriae* (and so not the tabular law against abusive poetry, which appears by this time to have been subsumed into *iniuria*). Koster (1980) 97 and Selden (1992) 504 nn. 106–110 with references there, esp. Daube (1948).

pect of "losing face" was an important factor inhibiting every manner of civil litigation at Rome. Condemnation on particularly disgraceful charges (like the ones named in Catullus' poem) brought with it a mark (*nota*) of "praetorian" *infamia* or *ignominia*, and this carried certain lasting legal consequences for its bearer.[16] In the instance imagined here, however, it is frankly hard to believe that things would ever have reached that point. *Infamia*, not a legal technical term, was simply "disgrace." Its taint could be applied by the community as well as by a praetor or a censor. (And though Cicero's Scipio dislikes the thought, a memorably snappy poem probably in fact did the job better than the mark of a severe old censor.) Catullus' claim that the elder Vibennius' thievery at the baths was "well known to the people" (33.7) seems to imply that the community had long since placed such a damning mark on the latter's reputation. In any case, the prosopographical silence surrounding his family name suggests that the elder Vibennius was a person of relatively little consequence. As for the social standing of Catullus, he belonged to a family whose name appears on public building projects in the area of Verona.[17] He called Julius Caesar a *pathicus* ("anal receiver") in his poetry (57.2), and if we believe Suetonius, Caesar responded by attempting a reconciliation with the young poet by way of his father at Verona.[18]

It is questionable whether a Roman praetor would have heard a case brought by the Vibennii against Catullus, and if one had, "controlling laughter" would perhaps have brought the proceedings to a quick close, with dire social consequences for the plaintiffs, perhaps so dire as to necessitate the self-exile recommended in Catullus' poem.[19] Further, if the elder Vibennius was the lowly

---

[16] On *uituperatio* as the norm in Roman litigation (including ordinary civil cases), on *infamia* (not a legal technical term) and on "loss of face" as a factor inhibiting litigation at Rome, Kelly (1976) 93–111. See also Barton (1993) 184 n. 31.

[17] Wiseman (1985) 107–15. On the social and economic status of Roman poets, see White (1993).

[18] Suet. *Jul.* 73.

[19] Corbeill (1996) 106–27 on Cicero's use of derisive humor in litigation. Laughter does not, as a rule, bring court proceedings to a close in modern postindustrial communities or even (in principle) influence their outcomes. Herzfeld (1985) 26–7 cites an instance of laughter successfully overturning a case in a small Mediterranean community. An elderly and crippled man, while accompanying his son on a sheep raid, had beaten a police officer senseless with his stick. The officer brought charges. "When the case finally came up for adjudication, the judge asked the suspected sheep thief's father to stand up. The old man did so. Was *this* the Glendiot who had so badly mauled the healthy young police officer? Assured that indeed it was, he dismissed the case amidst derisive laughter."

personage I have speculated, and if his reputation already labored under taint of *infamia*, then there is room to question whether he could ever in the first instance have successfully brought Catullus to trial.[20] At the other end of the spectrum, a vastly superior plaintiff like Julius Caesar obviously *could* have compelled an annoying young municipal equestrian to answer charges for Poem 57 and similar verses. That is, if Caesar was willing to become a laughingstock: he could never have lived down the ridiculous figure he would have cut at such a trial. If it is true, as Mauss pointed out, that we owe the concept of "person" to Roman law, it remains that Roman law was a respecter of persons, and of personal honor and shame, to a degree that makes its operation quite alien to modern understanding.[21]

If Vibennius was really so unequal an opponent, then we may wonder why Catullus chose to attack him and his son so bitterly in Poem 33.[22] It is hard to make a case for the poem's abusive language as justified by a political motivation. To be sure, the text constitutes a social and political act of a sort: the invitation to opt for self-exile (33.5–6), with its silent threat of unlovely things to come if that invitation is declined, recalls some of the rhetoric of Cicero's first speech against Catiline. But Poem 33 resists classification as "political invective" of the kind that wins the modern reader's sympathy when Catullus takes on Caesar and Pompey, or when the young Zukofsky goes after Henry Ford.[23] Reasons of the heart offer no better justification than those of politics. Neither

---

[20] Kelly (1966) 29: "the irreducible fact remains that a powerful and intractable defendant who was not sensitive about his public reputation" (or who, while sensitive about it, had nothing to fear in its regard from his opponent) "could and doubtless very often did frustrate the just claim of a plaintiff by resisting summons or execution, and this situation must have continued to exist for so long as the State took no hand in physically assisting the wronged plaintiff." The Roman state began providing such assistance only about the time of Antoninus Pius.

[21] Mauss (1938).

[22] On "equal opponents," Barton (1993) 185.

[23] Zukofsky (1978) 25–6 in *A-6*, inveighing against Ford: "(Disposed of: the short change of labor.) As for labor,/'There are more people/Who won't try to do anything,'/Says Henry,/'Than there are who don't know what to do,/I am in the business of making automobiles/Because I believe I can do more good that way/Than any other.'" In later sections of *"A"* Zukofsky invokes Catullus' Caesarian invective against Mamurra, making the ancient poet a political ally by intertextuality, in *A-8*: "Lollai, lollai, litil child, Whi wepistou so?/For the estates Mentula had, that you will have?/Lollai, lollai, litil child, Child, lolai, lullow!/Now drinkes he up seas, and he eates up flocks," (50), and again: "Whether a Cincinnatus conducts/the labor process by tilling his little farm,/Or whether Tom Dick/Wears his vest in summer/And sells refrigerators to the Eskimos ..." (62).

elder nor younger Vibennius comes off as the kind of "descendant of great-souled Remus" (58.5) toward whom the tastes of Lesbia ran, as Catullus' poetry represents her, and in any case no one, so far as I know, has ventured the suggestion that either of the Vibennii was Catullus' amatory rival. We are of course at liberty to imagine the poem's speaker as one of the elder Vibennius' victims, and still smarting from the embarrassment of having to send a slave home from the baths to fetch a spare tunic. Perhaps; but elsewhere, when he has lost an expensive and treasured napkin (Poem 12) to theft (or perhaps better to say, to an aristocratic practical joke) or a set of writing tablets (Poem 42) to a borrower's contempt of a loan, the Catullan speaking subject is only too forthcoming with details on the nature both of his loss and of the redress sought or retribution threatened.

I have suggested that the Vibennii were as real as the persons behind most or all of the other names of male addressees in the corpus, and that they were not members of an elite family whose power the society had an interest in curbing, through mockery of the kind that assigned insulting hereditary *cognomina*.[24] I suggest as a further possibility that Catullus mentions no personal injury of any kind at their hands because he has received none, and that the Vibenii were neither personal rivals, nor personal friends, nor even personal enemies. That reading is speculative, of course, but nothing in the poem or elsewhere in the corpus argues against it. Nothing, that is, other than the dark picture it paints of "our Catullus." Whether Poem 33 is obscene is an interesting question. The speech act here represented is not devoid of what the judicial ruling in a famous American obscenity trial called "redeeming social value": its language affirms social norms of behavior and harshly punishes deviance from those norms through public disgrace. But at the level of the individual composing or reciting it, the poem appears chiefly to express and embody the sheer enjoyment of heaping communally shared derisive laughter upon victims who lack recourse or defense of any kind.[25] Its speaker, so

---

[24] Corbeill (1996) 57–98.

[25] On enjoyment (*jouissance*) as a political factor, Zizek (1991). Corbeill (1996) 8 aptly quotes Frye (1957) 224: "It is an established datum for literature that we like hearing people cursed and are bored with hearing them praised, and almost any denunciation, if vigorous enough, is followed by a reader with a kind of pleasure that soon breaks into a smile."

construed, offers a performance rather than a detached and wry critique of the aggressive act of public shaming that the poem represents. It is in this sense that Poem 33 can be said to offer one of the strongest and most unmitigated instances of a "poetics of aggression" that pervades the Catullan corpus.

The poem to the Vibennii is not a nice one, and critics have for the most part shown it their backs. Is it a bad one?[26] The tightly interlocking structure of the series of responsions between father and son make it difficult to read these eight giddy verses aloud twice without getting them by heart: sound and form burn their words onto the memory like the red-hot *lammina* ("metal plates") applied by the Roman torturer. A first verse addressing the father alone and a final one aimed only at the son stand as symmetrical poles highlighting the two-part structure of the composition. The poem's first half strings together two repetitions of the paired victims with perfect symmetry of epithets and body parts. The second half begins by inviting the addressees into exile in the form of a question – precisely the tack so effectively taken by Cicero in the first speech against Catiline.[27] Fitzgerald has noted that *natis pilosas* ("hairy buttcakes," 33.7), directly beneath the prior verse's *patris rapinae* ("father's thefts," 33.6) might be taken as a near pun (with different quantities of the first vowel) between *natis* ("buttocks") and an implied *nati* ("of the son").[28] There is a similar pun between *notae* ("the father's thefts are *known* to the people," 33.7) and the *nota* ("mark," again with differing quantity of the first vowel) of *infamia* branded on the bodies of father and son by the performance of the poem. The last two verses contain a treble alliteration of a consonantal pair that might suggest the speaker actually spitting in the direction of the addressees (*notae ... populo*; *natis pilosas*; *non potes*).

The poem's eight verses make a demonstrably well-wrought urn, then. Is there anything more, any better reason why Catullus (if the editing hand was his) included the piece in his collection? I think there is. The poem ends on a *para prosdokian* ("surprise") with teeth, one that probably would have raised uproarious laughter

[26] Quinn (1972) 218 on Catullus' "bad verse."
[27] Cic. *Cat.* 1.13–20 and passim.
[28] Fitzgerald (1995) 82–3, who says of this poem: "Son and father are both complementary and interchangeable; as a unit they are obscene because they produce a confusion of categories and a promiscuous profusion of relations that could also be described as poetic."

from a contemporary Roman audience and almost certainly compelled its aesthetic admiration. By closing on the observation that the son's pederastic charms have faded and so no longer constitute a profitable asset of the family enterprise, the speaker recharacterizes his utterance in a remarkable way. This parting shot functions as a kind of jump back from the stance of sternly moral public upbraiding (*flagitium*) to that of a blandly helpful remark; it might even be thought to preserve the speaker's "deniability" on the former count.[29] Up to the last verse the poem's message had read: "you, father, are known for a thief, and you, son, for a *cinaedus*; you are both disgraced; leave town." Now it admits a second reading: "since the people are on to your thieving, father – they'll be on their guard now – and since your garden is overgrown with weeds, son, you both have lost your marketable trades here, your two means of support by theft and commerce: perhaps it's time to consider relocating your operations." To put the thing into Roman terms: this Catullan coda, tacked on in the guise of a thoughtful piece of financial advice and career counseling to a youngster, has all the air of unstudied improvisation, of inevitable but quite unforeseeable brilliance, and of perfect contextual aptness, that Catullus' audience would have associated with an elegant performance worthy of the name *facetiae* ("wit").[30] And *facetiae* in place of *petulantia* ("brute violence"), as Cicero teaches us in a well known passage in the speech for Caelius, is the quality that promotes *maledictio* ("insulting language") from mere *conuicium* ("verbal abuse") to the aesthetic rank of *urbanitas*.[31]

Poem 33, I wish to suggest, is a taste of Catullan *urbanitas*. Its *urbanitas*, further, is precisely the quality that can be said to make this act of poetic aggression into the performance of a Herzfeldian "poetics of manhood": a self-allusive bid for recognition of the aesthetic excellence of its performer. The "stylistic transformation" of performative verbal wit foregrounds the poem's aesthetic value over its ethical content. Poem 33's referential meaning, its primary "message," after all, is the same thing that other members of Catullus' community can be imagined to have cried or mut-

---

[29] Corbeill (1996) 17: "Part of the accuser's skill depends upon his ability to expose the faults of a defendant without slipping into slander." Compare the remarks of Fitzgerald (1995) 72–5 on "staining without being stained"; also Richlin (1983) 26–31.

[30] Cic. *de Orat.* 2.217–90 (Caesar Strabo's discourse) on the theory and practice of wit offers numerous examples. Discussion in Corbeill (1996) 20–2 and passim.

[31] Cic. *Cael.* 6: *Maledictio autem nihil habet propositi praeter contumeliam; quae si petulantius iactatur, conuicium, si facetius, urbanitas nominatur.*

tered when such persons as the Vibennii passed by in the street. What distinguishes Catullus' utterance is not an ethical "being good" that makes him a social critic, but rather a performative "being good at," summed up in the word *urbanitas*, that gives him social mastery.[32]

A distressing critical result. Or at least a problematic one, and not merely for those critics who seek from poetry the Palgravian function of "leading us in higher and healthier ways than those of the world."[33] Can Poem 33, for all its bad taste, for all its ethical vileness, really be counted as a performance of Roman *urbanitas*? If Cicero's forensic speeches against Vatinius, notable for their gleeful mockery of the *strumae* ("bloody pustules") on the latter's face and neck, could be characterized by a later author as Cicero's *urbanitas* against Vatinius, then perhaps it is our understanding of the term within Catullan criticism that needs reevaluation.[34] The performative "being good at" called *urbanitas* by the Romans, it appears, not only had very little to do with "being good," by almost any modern reader's understanding of ethical norms, it had just as little to do with what the last few centuries have meant by "good taste."

Catullus' modern critical reception has held a very different view of what constituted *urbanitas*, and of how Catullus embodied it in social performance: "*urbanitas*, that aura of sophistication that elite Romans deemed essential for the fashionable man and that Catullus and his circle in turn elevated into a guiding aesthetic and moral principle." Under that construction of *urbanitas*, Poem 10 – in which Catullus claims ownership of a friend's parked sedan chair and bearers, only to be shown up when another friend's *scortillum* ("little whore," 10.3) calls his bluff by asking to borrow it – responds admirably to a reading according to which it "offers a parable of false *urbanitas* chastised and simultaneously manifests the ironic self-awareness that distinguishes the urbane gentleman at his civilized best."[35]

---

[32] Herzfeld (1985) 16; 60–2 above.
[33] Palgrave (1861); 21–2 above.
[34] Sen. *Dialogi* 2.16. 1–3. Mockery that Catullus seems to have known and remembered with enjoyment at 52.2. Corbeill (1996) 45–55.
[35] Skinner (1989) 8–9. At the time of its writing, this enunciation of Catullan *urbanitas* represented the critical *communis opinio*, supported by a respectable body of scholarship (see esp. Ramage [1973]). Other examples of a similar tone could easily be collected in the writing of twentieth-century Catullans. Skinner's version stands out chiefly by its clarity, elegance and critical tact.

This twentieth-century Catullan critical take on ancient Roman *urbanitas* is predicated, I think, on a number of sweeping social and cultural changes most of which had taken place in modern Western industrialized nations during the previous century. At least in Britain and the United States, the nineteenth century witnessed, along with the continuing rise of a middle class, the crystallization of a ideology of gentility based not on nobility of birth but on such considerations as ethical conduct and manners.[36] The class distinctions marked by those externals of behavior were themselves increasingly occluded, allowing for a new construction of the "gentleman" (and the "lady") based on a collapsing of moral, aesthetic, and even religious criteria of valuation and approbation into social and economic ones. The same century, not coincidentally, witnessed an unprecedented rise in the criminalization of (largely male) aggression.[37] By the beginning of the twentieth century, on both sides of the Atlantic, physical violence had become in theory (and, in many places, to a considerable degree in practice) an almost exclusive legal monopoly of the state, through the criminalization of a wide range of aggressive and violent behaviors that the judicial institutions of earlier centuries had treated as personal matters between the parties involved, or at least punished with relative leniency. High Romantic "gentlemen," unlike Renaissance and Baroque ones, did not fight each other in taverns and alleys with fists or knives.[38] A continuation of that same "civilizing process" (what Marx called capitalism's "science of renunciation") came to its flower in the modern "gentleman," of professional rather than leisure class, a man who not only neither brawls nor duels, but carefully eschews every coarseness of speech and gesture.[39]

Catullan criticism, in the wake of such powerful narrative models as Quinn's "*urbani* and their mistresses," has in effect been

---

[36] The process was of course already underway before the nineteenth century and continued into the twentieth. On English and American "gentlemen," Castronovo (1987) and (1991). On the medieval genealogy of modern manners, Arditi (1998). Bourdieu (1979), though focused on contemporary French society, has provided a vocabulary and theoretical framework now widely applied in the sociology of class and "distinction."

[37] On Victorian "criminalization of men," Wiener (1998).

[38] On early European (specifically French) manhood as a "culture of the sword," and its nineteenth century modification, Nye (1998). On similar developments in modern Germany and Italy, Frevert (1998) and Hughes (1998).

[39] "Civilizing process": Elias (1994). "Science of renunciation": Marx (1963) and discussion in Adams (1995) 107–47.

forced to deal with the problem of how a modern "urbane gentle-man" could have written such pieces as Poem 10 or – an even longer stretch – Poem 42, in which Catullus calls his hendecasyl-lables to swarm and publicly shame (*persequamur eam et reflagitemus,* 42.6) the "stinking slut" (*moecha putida,* 42.11, 12, 19, 20) who re-fuses to return his tablets. A solution to that problem, the only workable one under the given assumptions, was sought in an intri-cate elaboration of something that Quinn, again, had already suggested: the notion of Catullus as a poet of "social comment."[40] On that view, "the poet" didn't mean these poems, saw through their ugly aggression and stood aloof from it. And the detach-ment of the ethical stance of Catullus the poet from that of "Catullus" the persona could be carried out in the name of a criti-cally sophisticated modernist rejection of naïve Romantic "bio-graphical criticism." Poem 33, however, and others like it in the corpus reproblematize the ethical problem of Catullan aggression. They offer no foothold for a critical saving of the appearances by positing "ironic self-awareness" (a strand in the fabric of the "meditative introspection" of modernist poetics) at the center of the Catullan speaking subject.

The modern and modernist confidence in the ethically enno-bling power of self-awareness may have been overly optimistic from the outset. As Slavoj Zizek has put it, the formula for ideol-ogy is not "they know not what they do," but rather "they know what they do, and they do it anyway."[41] In his funeral orations pronounced over the corpses of seventeenth-century French nobles and royals, Bossuet gave thundering voice to a Christian discourse on earthly vanity that, from a postchristian modernist viewpoint, might just conceivably be construed as a self-aware cri-tique or even a "deconstruction" of the artificiality and unreason of the distinction of a nobility of birth. But no one is likely to claim the staunchly royalist bishop of Meaux, or any other prelate of the *ancien régime,* as an unsung precursor of revolution and the Rights of Man. Likewise, if I am a nineteenth-century English "urbane gentleman" poet, my allowing that Gunga Din is a better man than I am, for all its civilized and ironic self-awareness, is not a term in a syllogism whose conclusion will relieve my shoulders of the white man's burden that I continue to take up every day with

---

[40] Quinn (1972) 204–82. [41] Zizek (1991).

an imperially world-weary sigh. Awareness of the contradictions inherent in ideology produces cognitive dissonance – but only to the extent that the ideology under scrutiny is not *my* ideology.

That Catullus' own resentments, frustrations and anxieties *vis-à-vis* the Roman Symbolic order will have engendered in his conscience, by algebraic substitution or categorical imperative, an ethical concern for women, slaves, or overtaxed Bithynian provincials, is neither a certainty nor even a likelihood. If by "social critique" we mean a stance outside the ideology of the society in which he lived, I question whether we may hope to find social critique at all in Catullus' poetry.[42] In any case, my reading of the poems discerns in them no voice groping toward an ethical stance I wish to embrace or recognize as kindred. And yet I continue to read these poems with pleasure, to teach them with all the persuasiveness I can muster, and to celebrate them through literary criticism (always a celebratory act, even in its most denunciatory and debunking versions). This is by now a recognizable and familiar dilemma, one that feminist classical scholarship grappled with over the last few decades of the twentieth century. Among the conclusions of that debate was a nearly universal, and I think clearly correct, rejection of the ingenious but ultimately too comfortable ethical solution of discerning a feminism *avant la lettre* in, for example, Euripides, and so conscripting him as an ally (or at least a double agent) for the critic's own cause.[43]

If the problem of a genuinely noble and beautiful literary text of impossible valuation as ethically normative is not solved by that complex solution, the same is truer still of the two straightforward solutions to the same problem.[44] Simple and outright ethical denunciation of an ancient Greco-Roman text sits ill, even a little bizarrely, on the lips of one of its purveyors in the context of a literary market from whose center "the classics" have long since been displaced. The other simple solution, the "commonsense" one of closing off the possibility of ethical comment on ancient literature by raising the wall of cultural relativism, ultimately cre-

---

[42] The old New Historicist refrain, perhaps, but a proposition still very far from the banality of axiom within Catullan studies.

[43] Michelini (1987) 3–51, also Rabinowitz (1993) 14: "It would be a mistake, even a waste of time, to try to decide whether Euripides was a misogynist or a feminist."

[44] The phrase "impossible value" is from a study of Nahum Tate's *Lear* by Strier (1995) 203–32.

ates more problems than it solves. If it were desirable in any instance, this stance is particularly problematic in the case of a text in whose critical reception, at every point, assertion of cultural authority and overthrow of that same authority have been commingled, and in the case of an author whose relation to canonicity has manifested a Klein bottle's paradoxical confusion between inside and outside.[45]

If it is (1) impossible to excuse Catullan aggression and (2) equally impossible to denounce a character whom centuries of reception history have found invincibly sympathetic, and if the stratagem of making Catullus into our man in Rome, our secret periscopic eye viewing his world from our own ethical viewpoint, is found out, then how are we to proceed toward an account of the "poetics of aggression" embodied in a text whose genuine poetic status we refuse to reject? I have suggested one avenue of response to impossible critical binarisms by triangulating them, and doing so in Catullus' case specifically through the introduction of a third term from other moments in literary history and from Mediterranean cultural anthropology. I return now to the latter of the two, in the form of recent work on the role of aggression in Mediterranean communities. I put forward this comparative material and the conclusions drawn from it as one possible way of heartening the aesthetic appetite for cultural difference without putting the faculty of ethical judgment into an overfed stupor. Contemporary Mediterranean evidence has the further advantage of offering a cultural context that is not only comparable but also cognate with Catullus' own, a world inhabited by many of the same structures and constructs, even calling them by names that Catullus would have recognized.

VERONESE CATULLUS AS AN ANDALUSIAN DOG

In the social interaction of a small *pueblo* in Andalusian Spain, cultural anthropologist David Gilmore came to discern, just beneath a smooth and unbroken surface of affability, the ever present threat and fear of aggression. Every public interchange he witnessed manifested the highest degree of gentility in manners.

---

[45] Three narratives of three very different aspects of Catullus' (long) modern reception: Gaisser (1993), Wiseman (1985) 211–45, Fitzgerald (1995) 212–35.

Every social gathering of men gave voice, with "lyric loquacity," to pronouncements of neighborly civic solidarity and mutually loyal friendship based on masculine honor. "Only later," says Gilmore, "did I realize such declarations are prophylactic formulae to ward off suspicion, betrayal, and anxiety about others' motives."[46] The modern, academically trained "urban intellectual," Gilmore suggests, experiences the shadow presence of aggression in the small Mediterranean community – through silently implied, vigilantly feared threats of betrayal by friends and resulting public disgrace – as a profound cognitive dissonance. Knowledge of travelers' tales about Andalusian "Judas kisses," and a specialist's familiarity with the considerable body of previous anthropological literature on the ethos of "agonism" in Mediterranean culture, proved insufficient to buffer the shock of lived experience. The straightforward confidence in face values that Gilmore brought to his fieldwork was quickly unsettled.

Gilmore recounts a private conversation with a particularly amiable and gregarious young male informant that took place in the month of his arrival. At the end of an afternoon spent in a neighborhood bar where conversation over glasses of sherry had centered around "the obligations and rewards of masculine friendship – loyalty, honor, and all that," the young man excused himself and, with a concealed gesture, invited Gilmore to follow. Once out of the bar and in an alleyway far from observers, the young man began to ask advice on a financial matter involving a local merchant. Producing at length from his pocket a crumpled dunning letter he had received after falling behind in payments on the time purchase of a television set, he asked the visiting professor from America by what way a poor man, but an honorable one, and entirely without experience in the newfangled ways of consumer finance, might be able to obtain a delay in his payment schedule "without compromising his honor and reputation." Gilmore continues:

Uneasily, I inquired if the matter could not best be resolved by mobilizing Alfonso's network of friends. After all, we had just spent hours listening to expressions of undying support and loyalty. "Of course I will intervene if you want," I stammered, "but surely your pals in the bar –" With a wave of his hand, Alfonso cut me short. "My friend, you must be

---

[46] Gilmore (1987) 5.

joking," he retorted, shooting me a reproachful look. "They're the last people I would confide in. It would be all over town in ten seconds. And *Dios mio* [my God], the lies they would tell to torment me with!" He concluded this denunciation of the same men he had just warmly embraced: "Damn them, the worst enemies of all are your friends."[47]

Alfonso's "cynical statement," following so quickly on the heels of loud protestations of mutual loyalty, produced in Gilmore a brief "sense of unreality." The sentiment expressed by Alfonso toward his friends is foreign in more ways than one. In the cultural context of a postindustrial Western urban community, asking friends for a petty loan does not ordinarily provide material for defamation, nor is it immediately obvious how the report of having done so could be elaborated with lies in such a way as to torment the unfortunate debtor. Readers of Catullus, however, will know a striking pair of examples of the kind of abusive speech Alfonso appears to have had in mind. In two invectives addressed to Furius, Poems 23 and 26, Catullus publicizes his victim's shameful insolvency with verve and precision (whether truthfully or not we shall never know). In both poems, the punch line, the climax of the speaker's aggressive enjoyment, comes in the revelation of the exact sum of money involved: in Poem 23, a petty loan of one hundred sesterces; in Poem 26, a mortgage on Furius' villa in the amount of two hundred fifteen thousand. In Poem 23, discussed earlier, not only is Furius' penury metaphorized as an obscenely excessive bodily dryness, his father and stepmother are implicated as well: the whole family is contaminated by the taint of a foully healthy dryness and hardness, not without vague hints of an incestuous *ménage à trois*.[48] If Alfonso could envisage something resembling Catullus' gleefully defaming exposure of the financial (and familial) situation of one of his so-called *comites* ("companions," 11.1), the young man's mistrust of his friends at the bar was anything but misplaced.

Some weeks after that incident, dinner at the neighboring house of a widow and her unmarried daughter operated a similar effect of cognitive dissonance on Gilmore and his wife. At the end of a long and pleasant conversation whose topics had included the sense of obligation, mutual loyalty and interdependence among neighbors, Gilmore's wife received a surprising answer to an innocent

---

[47] Gilmore (1987) 6.   [48] On Poem 23, see 73–4 above.

question about their hosts' social life. No invited guests had ever before been received into the widow's house, for dinner or any other social reason. "People do not *entertain* here, as you call it," the widow explained, adding that Gilmore and his wife "must be mad" to think otherwise. The daughter gave the reason: if a neighbor gains access to the secret sanctuary of your house, she conducts a minute surveillance of the place "like a ferret." Anything out of place, any foible or eccentricity in the house or its inhabitants, would be public knowledge by the next morning, and neighbors are worst of all in this regard. (Visiting foreigners, on the other hand, were safe enough for curiosity to outweigh mistrust.)

These fears and suspicions were no more unfounded than Alfonso's. Continued observation brought home to Gilmore the truth, in its own cultural context, of the proverb: *la lengua no tiene dientes, y mas que ellos muerde* ("the tongue has no teeth, yet bites deeper").[49] He recounts, for example, the story of Conchita, a young woman whose upcoming marriage was overshadowed by the (apparently true) report that she had been seen in an alley during a festival necking, or "skinning the turkey" (*pelando la pava*), with her young fiancé. (Both the scene and the quaint culinary metaphor are strangely reminiscent of Catullus' depiction, at 58.5, of Lesbia "shucking" the men of Rome in alleyways and streetcorners.) As rumors escalated, men began to stare at Conchita with insulting bluntness when she passed in the street, sometimes whistling or howling; old women covered their mouths and spoke to each other in stage whispers. Rumor, true to its descriptions in the *Aeneid* (4.173–95) and Don Basilio's aria on *la calunnia* ("calumny") in *The Barber of Seville*, had quickly snowballed by the accretion of elaborate falsehoods: it was over town that Conchita was pregnant, that the marriage had been forced by her father and its date moved up on the calendar. The witness of Conchita's moment of festive indiscretion, and the ultimate source of the ensuing gossip, it turned out, had been the girl's best friend Maria, spurred on by envy of Conchita's beauty and carefree happiness. Conchita and her family launched a retaliatory campaign of gossip against Maria and hers. Conchita's wedding, in the event, took place as originally planned, and her story, from the viewpoint of the *pueblo*'s ethical norms, can be said to have had a desirable and

---

[49] Gilmore (1987) 53.

even a happy conclusion: she no longer wore sleeveless dresses, no longer entered bars where (like the *puella* in Poem 37) she was the only woman among men, whether to deliver a message to her new husband or for any other reason. She no longer manifested her quick wit and easy laughter in public. Conchita had become, in short, and with no irony about it, "modest and upright" (*pudica et proba*, 42.24): an exemplary model of the feminine probity that the power of gossip had extorted from her through the punishment of exposure and the threat of worse things to follow.

Not every aggressive exercise of the communal power of gossip and verbal abuse produces a mutually tolerable (albeit grim) resolution for all parties. At the time of Gilmore's visit, townspeople still told the story of Juanillo de la Quiniela ("Lottery Johnny").[50] Some years before, a lucky number at the soccer lottery had made poor Juanillo suddenly a rich man. He had bought a fancy new car, redecorated his home, and even gone so far as to have the bars on his doors and windows (a feature of every Andalusian house) replaced with a new set. Custom-designed by an artist from Seville, the new iron grates bore the crest of the beloved soccer team that had enriched Juanillo: a "pretentious" detail of the sort to draw hostile attention, to give envy its focus and mockery its fuel. After a few months of performing the generosity implicitly demanded of him in his new circumstances, Juanillo realized that his winnings would soon be depleted if he continued to buy drinks and give gifts at the expected rate. He began to charge interest on loans, grew irritable and quarrelsome, and eventually stopped frequenting the neighborhood bar altogether. Soon he had acquired the reputation of living like a *señorito* (a contemptuous term for the rich), of being *cursi* ("pretentious") and, perhaps worst of all, of being *cerrado* ("closed," "secretive") rather than *abierto* ("open"). Juanillo's wife, for her part, was now known as an obnoxious haggler in the marketplace. Along with Juanillo, she and their children became objects of ridicule and of increasingly hostile pranks. An invective song, lovingly composed in advance, was directed at Juanillo at the next carnival. During that same festival, a group of masked revelers cornered him and, with no act of physical aggression other than refusing to let him pass, hurled verbal abuse at him for hours, calling him a whoreson and worse names than that:

[50] Gilmore (1987) 47–9.

a precise enactment of *flagitatio*, the public shaming by swarming that Catullus wittily invokes in Poem 42 and that Catullans since Usener have described, quaintly, as a manifestation of "Italische Volksjustiz."[51] By the close of the year, Juanillo and his family had opted for precisely what Catullus recommended to the Vibennii in Poem 33: self-imposed exile. Lottery Johnny had relocated to Barcelona, and his house, empty and falling into ruin – no one had been willing to purchase it – stood in the middle of town at the time of Gilmore's stay, the invidious soccer crests on its iron grating still provoking passersby to gloating merriment over the fortunes of their ruined owner.

This is perhaps the moment to state what is obvious enough: there are fundamental cultural and social differences between late twentieth-century Andalusian Spain and late republican Rome. Further, Catullus' elite status within his society was very far from the social class of most of Gilmore's informants, and the macho prudery performed so vividly in Catullus' sexual invective is far from being the only strand in his poetics of manhood. There is a Catullan manhood of delicacy as well, one that the next chapter's discussion will characterize as a stance of cosmopolitan and erudite elegance thrust performatively forward to the point of provocative effeminacy. Though I shall argue that this aspect of Catullan manhood too is informed by a recognizably Mediterranean competitive ethos of "agonism," its distinctly Hellenistic and metropolitan glamor finds no direct counterpart in the small rural communities where cultural anthropologists of the Mediterranean carry out their fieldwork.

Those caveats having been stated, however, it remains that Catullus' representations of the power (and the powerfully delicious appeal) of private gossip and public verbal aggression resemble, to a remarkable degree and with a nearly encyclopedic completeness, the modulations and even the lexicon of verbal abuse in small Mediterranean communities of the kind studied by Gilmore. (But then, encyclopedic completeness is easily achieved where the circle of concerns is claustrophobically small.) The "Priapic" Poem 17, for example, with no other editing than the necessary geographic and cultic alterations, would be perfectly

---

[51] Usener (1901). On the Andalusian public shaming ritual known as *vito*, Pitt-Rivers (1961) 171 and Gilmore (1987) 49.

suitable for performance at an Andalusian carnival.[52] Its speaker targets a certain countryman (presumably at Verona) as a prime candidate to be thrown off an old bridge into the muddy river beneath it. The poem's allegations include sexual neglect of a beautiful young wife, impotence, and cuckoldry born either of compliance or of ignorance. The closing lines suggest that a dunking might do the victim some good, making him shake off the stupid and shameful laziness of his member and his mind alike, leaving both behind in the mud:

> O Colonia, quae cupis ponte ludere longo
> et salire paratum habes, sed uereris inepta
> crura ponticuli axulis stantis in rediuiuis,
> ne supinus eat cauaque in palude recumbat:
> sic tibi bonus ex tua pons libidine fiat,
> in quo uel Salisubsali sacra suscipiantur,
> munus hoc mihi maximi da, Colonia, risus.
> quendam municipem meum de tuo uolo ponte
> ire praecipitem in lutum per caputque pedesque,
> uerum totius ut lacus putidaeque paludis
> liuidissima maximeque est profunda uorago.
> insulsissimus est homo, nec sapit pueri instar
> bimuli tremula patris dormientis in ulna.
> cui cum sit uiridissimo nupta flore puella
> et puella tenellulo delicatior haedo,
> adseruanda nigerrimis diligentior uuis,
> ludere hanc sinit ut lubet, nec pili facit uni,
> nec se subleuat ex sua parte, sed uelut alnus
> in fossa Liguri iacet suppernata securi,
> tantundem omnia sentiens quam si nulla sit usquam;
> talis iste meus stupor nil uidet, nihil audit,
> ipse qui sit, utrum sit an non sit, id quoque nescit.
> nunc eum uolo de tuo ponte mittere pronum,
> si pote stolidum repente excitare ueternum,
> et supinum animum in graui derelinquere caeno,
> ferream ut soleam tenaci in uoragine mula.   (Poem 17)

> Colonia! You're eager for some festal fun on your long
>   bridge,
> you've got everything ready for dancing, but you're afraid –
>   she's still

---

[52] Among recent studies of Poem 17 see esp. Cenerini (1989), Fedeli (1991) and Kloss (1998).

standing, the old bridge, but on wobbly legs, with recycled
    timbers –
she's about to go belly up and lie down in the bottom of the
    swamp.
Here's wishing you a fine bridge, the bridge of your dreams,
a bridge where even the leaping priests of Salisubsalus
could carry out their rites. But Colonia, you've got to give
    me a laugh
as a gift in return, a big one. I want to see a certain
    countryman of mine go
headlong off your bridge, into the mud, head to toe,
(and I mean that part of the whole lake and stinking swamp
where the quagmire's deepest and the mud muddiest).
He's an idiot, this one, without the sense of a two-year old
boy asleep in the dandling cradle of his father's arms.
He's got a wife, though, a girl at the peak of her flower,
(and I mean a girl more skittish than a youngling kid,
a girl for guarding with care like a harvest of the very
    blackest grapes),
but he lets her play as she will, he doesn't give a flip.
And for his own part, he doesn't give himself a lift. He just
    lies there,
like an alder in a ditch when a Ligurian hatchet's hacked its
    hams.
He's as aware of what's going on as if the woman didn't exist
    at all.
This friend of mine, the walking stupor, sees no evil, hears
    no evil,
isn't sure of his own name – isn't even sure whether he's
    dead or alive.
Now, *he*'s the one I want to throw head first off your bridge.
It's worth a try. Maybe it'll stir up his stupid torpor.
Maybe he'll leave his old mind behind in the heavy slime
like a mule losing an iron shoe in sticky clay.

The message is of course unmistakable, and it is a message appropriate to the poem's Priapic metre. Yet the propriety, the fastidi-
ous indirection, of Catullus' diction here surprises the reader of
the whole collection, and may perhaps point to an actual public
performance of this piece at a festival in "Colonia."[53] In any case,

---

[53] Wiseman (1987) 333–4 notes that contemporary inscriptions from the region include the
names of Valerii on public building projects and speculates that Catullus' family may
have received a request for funds toward the new bridge. If so, Poem 17 takes on a
sharper point, as does its aggression, thanks to its speaker's considerable position of
power and influence.

we may easily compare Poem 17 to an invective song written for actual performance at Trebujena's 1964 carnival. The Andalusian poem takes a similar approach to the same theme as Catullus', though in somewhat more explicit terms and on a more modest scale poetically:

El tío de las escobas	The fellow with the brooms
está loco por un niño	is mad for a son,
pero gasta un zoquetito	but his prick is tiny and
arrugao como un pestiño.	shriveled like a honey doughnut.
Eso lo sabe tó Trebujena	All Trebujena knows this fact:
que de sarasa tiene una vena;	he has a queer streak;
a su señora, a la pobre, la trae frita	his poor wife is fed up with him
porque dice que no llega al sitío	because, she says, he can't get there
¿con qué? con su cosita.	– with what? – with his little thing.[54]

The victim of this fiercely aggressive defamation, though not mentioned by name or even nickname, was fully identifiable to the audience from the first line of the poem as a certain vineyard worker who, as a sideline, also made brooms from palm leaves. The identity of Catullus' victim, though unrecoverable to us, would presumably have been similarly identifiable to a Veronese audience (though not to a Roman reader of the collection). Further, the carnival song clarifies what was almost certainly the implicit departure point and ultimate trigger of the Catullan poem's attack. It is a point not likely to leap to the mind of the post-industrial urban reader, but Gilmore's fieldwork made him acutely aware of it. If the first year of a marriage does not produce a child, people in the Andalusian *pueblo*, and in many other Mediterranean communities, take notice, and they begin to talk. A young married couple confided to Gilmore with an air of resignation that although they wanted a small family and were in no particular hurry to start one, they had not begun to use artificial birth control until their marriage had produced a first child.[55] They knew what manner of attention a childless marriage, and particularly a childless young husband, could be expected to attract.

[54] Mintz (1997) 153–4.   [55] Gilmore (1987) 69.

Poem 17 would have had little force, and probably would never
have been written, if its young victim had been granted the wish
that Catullus expresses for Torquatus, the new bridegroom in
Poem 61: the speedy arrival of a son whose unmistakable resemblance to his father leaves no room for wicked tongues to do their
work (61.204ff).

The opposite situation, that of a bride no longer a virgin and
perhaps already pregnant, while a common enough occurrence in
rural Andalusia, is also a focus of anxiety for the parties involved
and of hostile attention from the community.[56] Here again Catullus offers a point of comparison in another poem set in his own
native town. Poem 67 is a dialogue with the talking front door of a
house in Verona. The poem opens with an interlocutor, apparently male, greeting the door with wheedling politeness and begging it to speak. The door at length complies, and its revelations
proceed in the order of an escalating campaign of gossip against
the household dwelling behind it, starting with the newlywed
mistress:

> primum igitur, uirgo quod fertur tradita nobis,
>   falsum est. non illam uir prior attigerit,
> languidior tenera cui pendens sicula beta
>   numquam se mediam sustulit ad tunicam;
> sed pater illius gnati uiolasse cubile
>   dicitur et miseram conscelerasse domum,
> siue quod impia mens caeco flagrabat amore,
>   seu quod iners sterili semine natus erat,
> ut quaerendum unde unde foret neruosius illud,
>   quod posset zonam soluere uirgineam.   (67.19–28)

Well, then. First of all, as for her having been brought to us
a virgin: that's a lie. And it wouldn't be her *husband* touched
    her first –
not him, with his little dagger that hangs limper than a beet
    root
and never yet has lifted itself up to the middle of his tunic.
No: they say it's his father. Violated his son's bedchamber,
    he did,
and brought the stain of sin on an unlucky household,
either because his criminal mind was on fire with secret lust,

---

[56] Mintz (1997) 156–60.

or else because his son was born worthless, with barren seed,
so they had to go looking somewhere, anywhere, for
    something
harder, something that could undo a virgin's belt.

After a maliciously amused response from the interlocutor cast
sarcastically in the language of moral approbation, the door goes
on to catalogue earlier indiscretions committed by the bride in her
hometown of Brixia (modern Brescia), before her arrival at Verona. Anticipating the question how a door attached to a house at
Verona could have news of events at Brixia, she assures the interlocutor that her source is the young woman herself, who has been
overheard whispering to her handmaids about her crimes. The
door's speech, and the poem as well, climax and close by slyly fin-
gering a male victim whose identity, like that of the victim of the
Andalusian carnival song, looks to have been unambiguously clear
in context.[57] Of course, no one is *named*, and if the man in question were to proceed against Catullus, or even merely to protest,
he would thereby be owning up to the poem's accusation of adulterous dalliance with the materfamilias behind the door:[58]

> praeterea addebat quendam, quem dicere nolo
>   nomine, ne tollat rubra supercilia.
> longus homo est, magnas cui lites intulit olim
>   falsum mendaci uentre puerperium.   (67.45–8)

> [The bride] also added a certain party, someone I don't
>   want
> to mention by name; he'd raise those red eyebrows of his.
> A tall man, he is, and involved some time ago in a big
> lawsuit about a faked delivery from a lying womb.

---

[57] Richlin (1992) 153 notes that many Catullan invectives offer similarly "concrete but non-
specific details" about their victims and suspects the obscurity may be deliberate. Our
prosopographical ignorance makes it impossible to pronounce either way in most instances, but the Andalusian material here cited offers examples of similar invectives
whose victim's identity was made unambiguously and brutally clear in the context of
performance.

[58] Mintz (1997) 151 records an Andalusian carnival poet's reasoning along these lines: "I
won't mention his name to avoid further charges. Because, if he catches me in a slip,
he'll turn me in again, and I'll be in a bigger jam. I'll do it so that he'll say: 'That one
was meant for me.' Yet he won't be able to turn me in because I won't use any names.
No one will be able to bring up any charges."

Many critics have tasted a distinctly small-town flavor in the petti-
ness of this poem's gossip.[59] Probably rightly so, though Cicero's
speech for Caelius makes it clear that rumors of incest, at least,
could still set the most sophisticated Roman tongues wagging with
as much gusto as the provincial ones represented in Catullus'
poem.[60] That consideration points toward a question that seems to
have gone unanswered and even unasked here: precisely *whose*
tongue is wagging in Poem 67? Who is speaking this poem, and
what is the nature of the scenario it represents? Commentators
remind us that Roman elegiac poets also have conversations with
doors, and indeed they do, but for a very different reason.[61] The
Veronese door is certainly not being asked to swing open, and
Poem 67 has nothing to do with the song of the frustrated lover
outside a locked door known as *paraclausithyron*.[62] What does it
mean, dramatically, to approach a door, to greet it with ingrati-
ating commiseration, to beg it tenderly to speak, to listen to it
attentively and eagerly, and then to recount its conversation, a
conversation in which the door claims to have heard the lady of
the house within whispering her sins to her slaves? There is of
course a very real and potentially dire social sense in which a
house's front door can be said to have an ear and a tongue (67.44)
and to serve its masters well or badly (67.3–6), incurring their angry blame (67.9–14) in the latter case. The door of a house is its
sensitive and vulnerable membrane. It functions as both conduit
and seal (though not a hermetic one) between the guarded world
within and the dangerous one without. Catullus, I think, has given
us in Poem 67 a thinly troped poetic representation of a scene of
eavesdropping.[63]

---

[59] Fitzgerald (1995) 203–7 on Poem 67 as an expression of "Transpadane" pride and anxiety.

[60] In the same speech in which he seems to warn against unbridled defamation (*Cael.* 6, see
n. 31) and complains that no one can escape gossip (*fama*), "especially in so badmouthing
a town" (*praesertim in tam maledica ciuitate, Cael.* 38) as Rome, Cicero makes his famous
comic "slip," referring to P. Clodius Pulcher, Clodia Metelli's brother, as her husband.
He corrects himself: "I always make this mistake" (*semper hic erro, Cael.* 32).

[61] Quinn (1970) 369 and Thomson (1997) 466 compare Prop. 1.16. Kroll (1968) places the
dialogue with the door in the context of Hellenistic epigram.

[62] Prop. 1.16 has the door speaking, but the story it tells is still that of a paraclausithyron; a
lover is complaining outside, but no information about happenings within the house is
revealed. The door does however complain (Prop. 1.16.9–11) that she has been unable to
protect her mistress from defamation.

[63] Pedrick (1993) arrives by a different route (not in the context of Poem 67) at a strikingly
similar picture of the invective Catullus as an eavesdropper who abuses his "internal audience" (what I have called the "addressee") while flattering the wider audience.

The poem's relation to gender ideology becomes, on this reading, satisfyingly complex in a way that appears to be culturally accurate as well. At the surface of Poem 67 is a dialogue between a male interlocutor and a female door. While no pronoun or modifier disambiguates, the interlocutor's speech is fairly clearly gendered male – Cicero could easily have said, in a forensic speech, *egregium narras mira pietate parentem* ("an excellent father, that, whose tale you tell, a man of wondrously strong family feeling," 67.29), with just the same moralizing sarcasm – and on some level he seems to be a version of the Catullan speaking subject. As for the door, its feminine gender is made insistently clear (*iucunda ... iucunda*, 67.1) before its nature as a door is ever revealed, so that the first time reader initially assumes that the interlocutor's addressee is a literal woman. Just beneath that surface dialogue, however, is a narrative spoken entirely in the male voice and recounting publicly the secrets of a household, secrets whose veracity he authenticates for his audience by impersonating the door from which (at which) he has heard them. The interlocutor's poetic conceit is thus, in effect, that "I heard it from the door," or "the door told me herself." Note too that in the last four lines of the poem (67.45–8, cited above), the two voices seem almost to merge dialogically – surely it is both the door and the interlocutor giving the gleefully teasing physical description of the poem's final victim – and from there it is only a step to reading the entire poem as a dialogue spoken in a single voice.[64]

Commentators, trusting in what Gilmore called "the luminous surface of things," have tended to read the talking door as the simple personification of a gossipy maidservant and consequently to interpret Poem 67 by transcribing the blandly tolerant misogyny ("women are gossips") of its surface.[65] The poem's ventriloquized door serves, I suggest, as a ruse to cover an uncomfortable but inevitable fact about invective poetry: while the performance of poetic verbal aggression belongs to the blazing sunlight of the public forum and is as such both the exclusive province of men and a performance, in the most literal sense, of a poetics of manhood, it remains that the aggressive act of shaming regularly

---

[64] On dialogism, Bakhtin (1981). On its application to Catullus, Miller (1993b) and (1994) 44–51 and passim.
[65] Kroll (1968) 212–13 on Poem 67's door as a gossipy housekeeper.

involves publicizing *private* details about the victim. In consequence, the material, the message, of male-gendered invective
utterance (unless completely without basis in fact or likelihood, in
which case it is far less effective) can have been obtained only
through the male speaker's prior involvement in the shady, clan-
destine and "unmanly" activities of peeping, snooping and gossip-
ing. In the case of Poem 67, we as critics have been only too eager
to further the ruse, to help the Catullan speaking subject put the
best face on things.

Andalusians also say that women are the ones who gossip. They
say it and presumably on some level even believe it, but – like the
Ethiopian Christian shepherd who "believes" that wolves are
practicing Christians and therefore abstain from eating flesh meat
on Fridays – they do not enjoy the luxury of applying that ideological proposition with naïve earnestness to the context of guarding against the real danger of aggression (and the Ethiopian
shepherd does not fail to guard his flocks on Friday).[66] Men, no
less than women, are devoted practitioners of the fine art of
"murder by language" (Barthes' definition of gossip), and in the
small Mediterranean community they are in fact the more to be
feared: men can stroll or loiter unaccompanied in the day without
attracting attention, and they can prowl at night with relatively
little fear of scandal.[67] And of course, they are the ones who
compose and perform the invective carnival songs that are remembered and quoted throughout the year. Gilmore tells of a
voluntary association that, until the authorities shut it down, had a
thriving activity in his Andalusian *pueblo*, a community where
being a "joiner" (*lioso*) was otherwise regarded as despicable and
dangerous. The club's membership was restricted to men, and the
sole business of its meetings consisted in going about the *pueblo*
after sunset to peep through windows and listen at doors.[68]

Nonviolent aggression, as Gilmore argues, can indeed function
as a positive force for social cohesion in small communities, rather
than being always a symptom or cause of disfunction.[69] That
social cohesion is bought at considerable cost to each member of
the community, and few "urban intellectuals" would consider the
trade-off a favorable one. The individual, motivated by the fear of

---

[66] Sperber (1975), cited in Veyne (1988b) xi.   [67] Barthes (1977) 169.
[68] Gilmore (1987) 37–9.   [69] Gilmore (1987) 10–28.

verbal aggression to guard family matters and other private business with the tightest possible secrecy, is simultaneously constrained by that same threat to manifest a public behavior that gives every appearance of living fully in the open, with nothing to hide, and no distinctive idiosyncratic excesses of any kind. Cicero is perhaps the only individual from whom we have enough material to evaluate that formulation as a description of the elite Roman man's subjective experience. Even there the evaluation is itself inevitably subjective, but in light of the self-allusivity so clearly and loudly embodied in Cicero's public performances (and characterized by so many modern readers as an unbearable arrogance), and in light of the suspicion and duplicity toward friends and associates so frankly avowed in his private letters (by which even Cicero's devoted admirers have been scandalized all modernity long, starting with Petrarch), it seems at least plausible that comparative material from "agonistic" Mediterranean communities of the kind discussed in this section can move us toward a richer cultural contextualization of the most aggressively hypermasculine aspects of Catullus' own poetics of Roman manhood.[70]

WICKED TONGUES AND EVIL EYES

Maud Gleason has described Greco-Roman elite male social interaction as the individual's dangerous passage through a "forest of eyes."[71] A revelatory and instructive formulation, but perhaps the full picture is something still more dire. Work like Gilmore's suggests that Mediterranean eyes (and ears) do more than merely lie in wait as passive observers: they prowl and devour. In Andalusian Spanish, to give someone a "hard look" (*mirada fuerte*) is "to eat him with the eyes" (*comérselo con los ojos*), and it is understood that "wicked tongues" (*malas lenguas*) will soon pour out into the light of day what eyes have eaten and ears have drunk in the shadows.[72] The hard stare of aggressive eyes is both a symptom and an embodiment of *envidia*, a word that in Catullus' Latin (*inuidia*), as in Andalusian Spanish, is connected ideologically with the fear of what wicked tongues will say. Latin *inuidia*, of course,

---

[70] "agonistic society": Pitt-Rivers (1977) 92; Gilmore (1987) 96.
[71] Gleason (1995) 55.
[72] Gilmore (1987) 34, 161.

means both "envy" and "the evil eye."[73] It means both, arguably, because the two are precisely the same thing. The ideology of the evil eye, a "spiritual construct" of the greatest antiquity and nearly pan-Mediterranean pervasiveness, gives a magical force, metaphorically and metonymically, to what is at the same time a social inevitability: if I overstep communal norms in a way that draws attention, or if someone merely looks askance at my excessive happiness and good fortune, I can expect to suffer from it.[74]

That is perhaps a valid principle in most or all human communities, but one whose discursive construction varies widely among cultures. What separates Catullus' world from ours on this point, perhaps, is not only the fact that we find it quite inconceivable even to joke about the brutally violent retributions threatened or performatively accomplished in Mediterranean messages of nonviolent verbal aggression: for example, orally raping (Poem 21) a *stuprator* (sexual miscreant), tying his feet to doorposts and sodomizing him with radishes and mullet (Poem 15), or merely terrorizing him by wiring his door shut in the middle of the night and then singing invective songs into a rifle barrel inserted through a hole in the door.[75] It is not only that; it is also that the so-called "puritanical" Anglophone and northern European moralizing discourses of the nineteenth and twentieth centuries have tended to mystify something that victims and perpetrators of verbal aggression in the premodern Mediterranean often express openly and with perfect lucidity: namely, that the individual aggressor is motivated not so much by love of righteousness as by envy, jealousy or hatred toward the victim, and perhaps even more fundamentally by an overwhelmingly strong libidinal investment in the pure enjoyment of aggression itself.[76]

Catullus, I think, performs the *jouissance* and the potential terror

---

[73] On Roman envy and "fascination": Barton (1993) 85–175.
[74] On the evil eye in the Mediterranean: Maloney (1976), Herzfeld (1981), Di Stasi (1981), Gilmore (1987) 154–170, Dundes (1992) 93–133.
[75] Pitt-Rivers (1961) 171–2, cited in Gilmore (1987) 49.
[76] Gilmore (1987) 68: "The motive [for gossip] is envy or simply spite. The Andalusians are the first to admit this." Mintz (1997) 150 records a carnival poet's statement of his motivation in composing defamatory verses: "I say things that people would rather keep under wraps. They don't want gossip ... gossip. Say a brother and sister are fooling around. Well, they don't want anyone to know. Boy! That's the sort of thing I like about carnival." Compare Catullus' similar tone, at once apologetic and defiant, at 54.6–7: "you'll be angry again at my iambs, though they don't deserve it, O one and only general."

of hard looks and hard words with that same lucidity, and nowhere in the corpus more explicitly and elegantly than in a sequential triplet of poems that are almost never discussed together, since the bookends of the set are central Lesbia poems and its middle member contains primary obscenity and not a hint of Lesbia's presence. When they are read in their received order, however, these three pieces take on the look of a remarkably coherent and satisfying mime in miniature on the aggressive power of evil eyes and wicked tongues:

> Viuamus, mea Lesbia, atque amemus,
> rumoresque senum seueriorum
> omnes unius aestimemus assis.
> soles occidere et redire possunt:
> nobis cum semel occidit breuis lux,
> nox est perpetua una dormienda.
> da mi basia mille, deinde centum,
> dein mille altera, dein secunda centum,
> deinde usque altera mille, deinde centum.
> dein, cum milia multa fecerimus,
> conturbabimus illa, ne sciamus,
> aut ne quis malus inuidere possit,
> cum tantum sciat esse basiorum.   (Poem 5)

> My Lesbia, let us live, and living love,
> and give all outcries from severe old men
> full due consideration: one red cent.
> The sun that sets tonight can rise again;
> but we, when once our too brief light is set,
> must sleep a single night that never ends.
> Give me a thousand kisses, next a hundred,
> another thousand, plus another hundred,
> then yet another thousand, next a hundred.
> And when we've racked up thousands after thousands,
> we'll lose count, we'll make sure that we're not sure,
> and that some fiend can't cast an envious eye
> with knowledge of how many are our kisses.

> Flaui, delicias tuas Catullo,
> ni sint illepidae atque inelegantes,
> uelles dicere nec tacere posses.
> uerum nescio quid febriculosi

scorti diligis: hoc pudet fateri.
nam te non uiduas iacere noctes
nequiquam tacitum cubile clamat
sertis ac Syrio fragrans oliuo,
puluinusque peraeque et hic et illic
attritus, tremulique quassa lecti
argutatio inambulatioque.
nam nil ista ualet, nihil, tacere.[77]
cur? non tam latera ecfututa pandas,
ni tu quid facias ineptiarum.
quare, quidquid habes boni malique,
dic nobis. uolo te ac tuos amores
ad caelum lepido uocare uersu.   (Poem 6)

It's about your girlfriend, Flavius. From where
Catullus sits, either she's not exactly what you'd call class
or you'd be telling me about her, couldn't shut up.
No. It's some working-girl health risk that's won your
affection and esteem: that's what you're ashamed to admit.
And no, you're not spending nights all alone these days.
Your quiet bedroom doesn't convince: it *screams*,
all reeking of garlands and olive oil from Syria.
So does your bedroll with its twin depressions.
So does your cracked and creaky bedstead: it's walked
out into the middle of the room to denounce you.
No use, trust me, keeping quiet in the face of all that.
Why indeed? Your thighs wouldn't be fucked down
to the bones if you weren't in some business on the nasty
        side.
So look. Whatever you've got going, good or bad,
come on and tell me. I want to send you and your darling
up to the sky on a surge of lovely poetry.

Quaeris, quot mihi basiationes
tuae, Lesbia, sint satis superque.
quam magnus numerus Libyssae harenae
lasarpiciferis iacet Cyrenis
oraclum Iouis inter aestuosi
et Batti ueteris sacrum sepulcrum;
aut quam sidera multa, cum tacet nox,

<hr>

[77] Lachmann's emendation. Mynors prints and obelizes the transmitted text of the verse's opening: *nam inista preualet.*

furtiuos hominum uident amores:
tam te basia multa basiare
uesano satis et super Catullo est,
quae nec pernumerare curiosi
possint nec mala fascinare lingua.   (Poem 7)

You ask me, Lesbia, how many kissings of you
would be enough and more for your Catullus.
So great a number as grains of Libyan sand
that lie in Cyrene, the land where silphium grows,
between the oracle of Jove of the Burning Heat
and ancient Battus' ancient hallowed tomb;
or as many as the stars that, when night is quiet,
look down upon the furtive loves of mortals:
that's how many kisses to kiss you with
your crazed Catullus would count enough and more,
a count that prying minds could never complete
or lay their curse on with a wicked tongue.

The speaker of both Poems 5 and 7 is a young man in love and in open defiance of societal norms, including norms of masculine behavior. The last point is one worth stressing, since it is only in light of recent work on Roman sexuality that it is possible to see it clearly. Similar effusions of amorousness in a modern context are unlikely to register as behavior inappropriate for a man. Quite the contrary: it is always possible to read modern male expressions of unbridled *amour-passion* as performances of the machismo of a Romeo (if truthful) or a Don Juan (if not), and the very intensity of the desire expressed may be taken as a measure of the speaker's manhood. The Roman man, conversely, if he was true to the letter of his ideology of masculinity, did not languish in desire. He *took* sexual pleasure, to his fill but no more, and without relinquishing control either to the object of his appetite or to "desire" itself.[78] The speaker of Poems 5 and 7, by his abject dependence on the beloved, by his turn away from phallic pleasure to oral, and perhaps most of all by the uncontrolled unrestraint (*impotentia*) of his gluttony for kisses, impersonates and performs a provocative

---

[78] On sexual excess and Roman "heterosexual" effeminacy: Richlin (1992) 139, 222 and passim; Cantarella (1992) 120–54; Edwards (1993) 81–4; Parker (1997); Williams (1999) 138–59 and passim.

effeminacy that has been effectively invisible to much of Catullus' modern reception.[79]

Poem 5 begins by inviting Lesbia to join Catullus in a society of two, in defiant deviance from the norms of the community expressed in the "outcries of overly stern old men." The third line's verse-final *para prosdokian* – the unexpected appearance of an *as*, the smallest unit of Roman currency – retrospectively gives a sylleptic, or punning, sense to the verb of the last member of the floridly rhetorical ascending tricolon that opens the poem. *Aestimare* is "to value," "to assign worth." A Roman man's *aestimatio* (more commonly *existimatio*) was his "good name," his "face," what Andalusian men of earlier generations (less so now), described, without irony, as the thing a man must at all costs not lose, and all is not lost if that one thing is not lost.[80] But *aestimare* and its cognate forms, precisely like English "value" and "worth," admit, alongside their ethical sense, a purely economic one. It is this latter sense that Catullus' performative wit brings flashing out at the end of the third verse, cracking the tail of its whip in the "face" of the *senes seueriores* ("overly stern old men") and openly debunking their loudly proclaimed ethical norms.[81]

The Roman ethical quality of *seueritas* might be rendered as "censoriousness." *Seuerus* seems in fact to have been a common epithet of the Roman censor, the official who policed the morals of senatorial men, punishing misconduct either by placing a mark of *infamia* ("disgrace") by their names or else by removing them from the senatorial roster altogether.[82] Latin *census* and its cognate forms manifest a semantic nexus interestingly similar to that of *aestimatio*. As Dumézil showed, *cens-* is the Latin reflex of an Indo-European root signifying the approbation of (chiefly poetic) praise, and so represents a survival of prehistoric ideology of praise and blame.[83] That aspect of the root survived in the *censura* (the office and function of the censor), and in the verb (*censeo*) with

---

[79] Quinn (1970) 145: "Can anyone doubt, after reading Poems 5 and 7, that Catullus is a man?" Discussed at Fitzgerald (1995) 251 n. 10.
[80] On Andalusian honor, Pitt-Rivers (1966). On its recent modification, Gilmore (1987) 128.
[81] On *aestimatio* and *existimatio* as economic terms coopted into the ethical sphere, Habinek (1998) 45–59.
[82] *Censorum seueritas*: Cic. *Rep.* 4.6.15, Val. Max. 2.9, Gell. 4.20.1. On censors and senators, Suolahti (1963).
[83] Dumezil (1943) and (1969) 103–24.

which a Roman senator officially put forward a motion. At the same time, *census*, like *aestimatio*, admits a financial sense, and does so in a way that lays bare one of the ideological connections between the two meanings. A Roman man's *census* was the value of his property, and since membership in the senatorial and equestrial orders required minimum levels of wealth, his financial worth (*census*) could come under the censor's severe scrutiny no less than his publicly perceived moral worthiness (*aestimatio*).[84]

The Latin name, then, both for the process of kiss-counting that Poem 5's Catullus performs with loud outrageousness and for the final tally of kisses he claims, just as outrageously, to be at pains to confound (many readers have seen here the image of an abacus being shaken to spoil the count) is the same word: what the poem's speaker is performing, and making a great fuss of concealing, is the *census* of his kisses.[85] Nothing in that formulation, I think, is apt to jar the modern ear. It might even sound a bit hackneyed. The kiss poems look and feel remarkably like European sonnets, and kisses-as-coins and love-as-wealth are, in that subgenre, standard and very ordinary fare indeed. In the poem's own cultural context, however, the thought of a *census* of kisses, and one so great as to defy exact count, would almost certainly have been an image so striking as to rivet the attention upon the speaker who had framed it. A Roman reader could easily have found something vaguely obscene in the image of counting all those thousands. Showy excess of (literal rather than figurative) wealth was associated with effeminacy and with the laxness of morals said to have followed upon the end of the wars with Carthage and the concomitant disappearance of a salutary *metus hostilis* ("fear of an enemy").[86] Further, there was even a famous story involving a kiss and a censor. Cato the censor, paragon of *seueritas* and all the other old Roman virtues, was said to have struck from the senatorial roster a certain Manilius, on the grounds that the man had offended public decency by kissing his own wife in public.[87] Whether the story was true or believed to be so in Catullus' time is not the point. The

---

[84] Shatzman (1975), Nicolet (1976).
[85] Many readers have seen in Poem 5 a reference to the image of calculating on an abacus. Levy (1941).
[86] Sallust *Cat.* 9–10 is the locus classicus.
[87] Plut. *Cato Maior* 17.7, discussed in Segal (1968) 98 and Williams (1999) 17–18, 266 n. 14.

decadent Catullus of Poem 5 is going against a cultural grain quite alien to our own.[88]

Poem 5's Catullus, as Fitzgerald has pointed out, is a tease.[89] This is one of the poems that, as the speaker of Poem 16 boasts, "can stir up an itch" (*quod pruriat incitare possunt*, 16.9). What is being dangled before the reader, just out of the reach of knowledge, is the *census* of Catullus' kisses, kisses that have all the unreality of unfulfilled desire, and all its powerful sway over the imagination. Precisely by the insolent absurdity of its poetic logic, the poem takes readers in, compelling us to assign the valuation (*aestimatio*) of burning interest to this incalculable *census* that is both an enviably vast magnitude and a countable but tantalizingly inaccessible quantity. If we read the poem with hypermasculine and hostile Roman eyes, disgusted and roused to punitive aggression (like Sulla before the young Caesar, or like the Catullus of Poem 17) at the sight of a man reduced to infantile orality, the state of a "two-year-old boy asleep in his father's dandling arms" (17.13), then the poem flicks two apotropaic spurs in our faces: one at the beginning, with the news that our "outcries" (*rumores*, 5.2) have been appraised and found to possess the value of a single penny (*unius . . . assis*, 5.3) for the whole lot; and another at the end, with the brusque demystification of our moralizing as pure viciousness (*malus*, 5.12) and envy (*inuidere*, 5.12) of a young lover's happiness and good luck in love.[90]

On the other hand, if our eyes are friendly, if we read the poem sympathetically, giving in to the aesthetic *aestimatio* of Catullus' mad passion of kisses and sharing Catullus' glee at the scandal of the *seueriores*, we are no less suspected and feared by the poem's speaker. If we read the poem as if we were (that most dangerous kind of enemy) Catullus' friend, or as if we were Lesbia, or even if we identify with Catullus himself, our eyes must still be kept far

---

[88] Valerius Maximus (early first century CE) records another story of a punished kiss, perhaps dating from the late republic (see Pauly-Wissowa s.n. Maenius 13), and told in moralizing language strangely reminiscent of Catullus' mockery in Poem 5: Publius Maenius is said to have punished (how severely we are not told) a beloved freedman when the latter had given Maenius' daughter an innocent kiss. Maenius "kept a severe guard over modesty" (*seuerum pudicitiae custodem egit*) and so "counted it worth much" (*magni aestimauit*) "to teach his daughter by so grim an example that she should keep not only her virginity untouched for a husband, but her kisses intact as well" (Val. Max. 6.4).

[89] Fitzgerald (1995) 54–5.

[90] On Sulla's urge to kill the young Caesar for his effeminately girded tunic, Dio 43.43.1–4, discussed in Edwards (1993) 90.

from the knowledge of the precise number of kisses that the poem teasingly incites us to try and calculate. Two can keep a secret, this poem seems to say, but only if neither of them knows it. What *we* (Catullus and Lesbia) must not know (*ne sciamus*, 5.11) is precisely what none of *them* must know (*ne sciat*, 5.13): the exact numerical quantity of our kisses. For what is known is seen, what is seen can be given a hard look, and what is given a hard look sickens and withers under the aggressive power of *inuidia*: the evil eye, synonymous and conterminous with envy, just as *tantum ... basiorum* (5.13) is both the fact of the kisses being enviably numerous and also their exact number, a sum whose knowledge would give an enemy magic power (and excellent material for invective).

On the other side of Poem 6 comes a second kiss poem. Poem 7 is thematically a recapitulation of Poem 5 (a "reprise," as Fitzgerald calls it) though with some important differences.[91] While Poem 5 began by drawing an apotropaic circle around Catullus and Lesbia, separating "us" from "them," Poem 7 opens with Catullus repeating or ventriloquizing a question from Lesbia: "How many kisses are" not just enough, but "enough and more" (*satis superque*, 7.2)? Readers have, as always, taken the tone variously, but many have seen in this opening question a first hint of exasperation on (the represented) Lesbia's part, and of suspicion on the part of the speaking Catullus: a suggestion that the apotropaic cartouche that set Poem 5's *Liebespaar* off from the rest of humanity has already begun to reconfigure itself as a line of demarcation between the pair's two members, a madly desirous Catullus and an unreciprocating Lesbia.[92] On this reading, Poem 7 can be seen to stand in a linear narrative relation to the immediately following Poem 8, whose speaker claims to have experienced some manner of definitive rejection from the *puella* and urges himself to respond in kind. The structure of Poem 7 seems to corroborate that reading. If Poem 5 implicitly identified the envious "fiend" (*malus*, 5.12) in its last verse but one with the *senes seueriores* (5.2) of its second verse, a comparable symmetry in Poem 7 seems to range Lesbia at verse two, with her unwelcome question, among the dangerous *curiosi* (7.11) of the poem's penultimate verse.[93]

Poem 5 closed by warding off *inuidia*: envy and the evil eye.

---

[91] Fitzgerald (1995) 54.
[92] E.g. Rankin (1972).
[93] On the identification of Poem 5's *quis malus* with the *senes seueriores*, Fredricksmeyer (1970).

Poem 7, in a similar ending, locates the feared threat in the curse or bewitchment (*fascinus*) of wicked tongues (7.12). *Fascinus* was the Latin name given both to magic spells and also to the phallic charm worn around the neck to avert them.[94] Significantly, Catullus may have regarded the Latin word as a calque or equivalent of Greek βασκανία, a word that, like *inuidia*, carries the social meaning of "envy" alongside the magical one.[95] What are these poems' apotropaic gestures protecting? An expression of passionate love, certainly, and one that a Roman reader could have chosen to find grotesquely effeminate; but there are other tender presences in both poems as well. Catullus' poetics of Roman manhood in these two poems, provocatively and agonistically delicate, seems to be informed by what we might call a Callimachean poetics of art and an Epicurean poetics of life.[96]

Poems 5 and 7 have long stood at or near the center of Catullus' reception, for scholars, critics and poets alike. The poem they flank is somewhere at the opposite end of the spectrum of valuation, excluded not only from critical discussion of the kiss poems but from the memory of many readers (and excluded, notoriously, from at least one scholarly edition of the poems).[97] The interlardment of Poem 6 between the kiss poems is arguably the single most striking and aesthetically jarring instance of juxtaposition in the entire collection – that is, if we read against Catullus' modern reception and insist on taking these three poems together in their received order.[98] I have already swerved from that aim by discussing the two kiss poems first, but a sequential "first reading" of the triplet would have been not only uneconomical but artificial: the kiss poems are simply too well known for the exercise to have its effect. And again, the translation of Poem 6 here offered, like many other versions, has obscured the external formal similarity

---

[94] *OLD* s.v. *fascinum*.
[95] Callimachus in the *Aetia* prologue (1. Fr. 1.17 Pfeiffer) had referred to the "Telchines" as Βασκανίης ὀλοὸν γένος ("envy's dire spawn"). Cairns (1973) suggests that Poem 5 may allude specifically to this passage.
[96] Poem 5's speaker is, I think, at least a "vernacular" Epicurean, with a mortal soul. On Catullus' possible Epicurean connections or leanings, see Giuffrida (1948) *pro* and Granarolo (1967) 205–24 *contra*.
[97] Fitzgerald (1995) 54 observes that the themes of hiding and revealing link Poem 6 to Poems 5 and 7. The edition of Fordyce (1961) omits Poem 6.
[98] See most recently Thomson (1997) 221: "Intercalated between two of the most ardent poems arising out of C.'s own passion for Lesbia, this occasional piece removes us temporarily from all deeper and more personal feeling."

of all three poems. In Catullus' Latin, all three poems share the Phalaecian (hendecasyllabic) metre of the opening dedication and the sparrow poems (Poems 1 through 3), and Poem 6 begins and ends with verses whose preciousness of diction seems to link it with that parade of elegant performances. *Flaui, delicias tuas Catullo* ("Flavius, your *deliciae* to Catullus ...," 6.1) recalls the opening of the first sparrow poem – *passer, deliciae meae puellae* ("sparrow, *deliciae* of my girl," 2.1) – not only by the presence of *deliciae* (*délices*, the "joys" and "toys" of sixteenth-century English poets), but also by setting forth an intriguing threesome of players, with a direct address to one of them, in the poem's first verse. At the end of Poem 6 comes the promise to put Flavius' loves to verse (or, what is more likely, the self-allusive claim to have now done so, by the performance of the present poem) – *ad caelum lepido uocare uersu* ("to call [you and your loves] to the sky in verse that is *lepidus*," 6.17) – and the epithet would seem to assign to Catullus' performance the same mark of aesthetic approbation he claimed for his *libellus* at the opening verse of its dedication: *cui dono lepidum nouum libellum?* ("To whom do I give this little book that is *lepidus*?" 1.1). But alongside this aesthetic meaning ("charming"), *lepidus*, as the *Rhetorica ad Herennium* attests, had in Catullus' time the plainer meaning of "comical": a joke, even a cruelly aggressive one, could be *lepidus* simply by being funny, by raising a laugh.[99]

A further point of similarity between Poem 6 and the kiss poems is the one I take as crucial. Like Poems 5 and 7, Poem 6 strongly demarcates between inside and outside, between a public and private space, the two being configured as a tender center framed by a hard exterior. If anything, the demarcation is in Poem 6 drawn with brighter lines and marked with a more perfect symmetry. At the precise center of this piece in seventeen verses comes a description of Flavius' bedchamber, opening and closing (if the first word of a garbled text at line 12 is right) on verses beginning with the same causal conjunction (*nam*, "for," 6.6, 6.12). This detailed excursus on Flavius' love nest, poised at the poem's dead center, is a cadenza of Hellenistic elegances evoking specific images found also in the epigrammatists of the Palatine Anthology, but with an important difference.[100] In those epigrams, the symptoms of love

[99] *Rhet. Her.* 4.32.
[100] Kroll (1968) ad loc. adduces epigrams of Meleager (*AP* 5.175), Callimachus (*AP* 12.71) and Rufinus (*AP* 5.87). Morgan (1977) 340 n. 4 adds Asclepiades (*AP* 12.135).

were on the lover's person: sleeplessness, disheveled hair still
bearing the imprint of a garland, panting breath, a faltering gait.
In Poem 6 Catullus has instead transferred those symptoms, or
evidences, of love and lovemaking to the bedchamber itself and its
furnishings.[101] Though the conceit is unquestionably elegant and
the poem unmistakably learned, this personification, rather like
that of the door in Poem 67, is both strange and strangely insistent. Still, we have so far seen nothing in Poem 6 to compel us to
the conclusion that the Catullus who wrote the kisses and the
sparrows – the Catullus we love as the world loves a lover – has
attached anything other than a positive valuation to Flavius and
his dalliance.

What critical discussion this poem has received is focused in
large measure on precisely this question: is the Catullan speaker's
disposition toward Flavius ultimately a nice or a nasty one? Read
the poem from the outside in, and from both directions the
speaker seems careful to leave that question open as long as possible. At the poem's extremities stand two symmetrical five-line seg-
ments, located not in Flavius' bedchamber but in full public view
and earshot (as is, of course, the whole poem). After a potentially
flattering first verse comes a first hint of trouble in the second:
Flavius' companion must be "charmless" and "inelegant," (6.2),
the speaker suggests, and the proof that she is so lies in Flavius'
silence, described in a line whose hyperbolic rhetorical outbidding
is intensified by the grammatical palindrome (modal, infinitive,
conjunction, infinitive, modal) of its structure: *uelles dicere nec tacere
posses* (6.2). "Did I say you would *want* to tell me? *Immo uero* (*nec*
does the duty of a Ciceronian 'nay rather'), silence would be *impossible*." On the face of things, the aggression seems mild enough
at this point, vaguely comparable to the speaker's blunt sizing up
of a friend's "little whore" (*scortillum*, 10.3) in another poem, and in
any case the envisaged object of any possible abuse would so far
appear to be not Flavius but his unknown and completely invisible
beloved. Similarly, at the end of the poem, just before the ostensibly flattering announcement of an intent to make Flavius and his
loves into lovely poetry, there is a final attempt to conjure Flavius
out of his silence: *dic nobis* ("tell me," 6.16). What Flavius is invited
to tell is "whatever you have, good or bad," *quare, quidquid habes*

---

[101] Morgan (1977) 340.

boni malique (6.15). The phrase, while not exactly flattering, is even more innocuous than the second verse's uncharitable surmise. Horace, as commentators have noted, uses part of the same phrase in a remarkably similar context.[102] What the Horatian speaker says to *his* young friend, however, is instructively different from Poem 6:

> quae te cumque domat Venus,
> non erubescendis adurit
> ignibus ingenuoque semper
> amore peccas. <u>quidquid habes</u>, age,
> depone tutis auribus   (Hor. *Carm.* 1.27.14–18)

> Whatever Venus is taming you,
> she never burns you with fires that give you
> cause to blush; the love by which you sin
> is always high-born. <u>Whatever you have</u>, come,
> entrust it to safe ears.

Horace may well have had Catullus' poem here in mind. Indeed, the best argument for direct reference, apart from the shared phrase, is the fact that Horace's speaker seems at pains specifically to unwrite Poem 6.[103] Under his garlanded grey hair, with a *bienséance* that is autumnal, Augustan and Anacreontic, he reassures his young friend that (1) he has no cause to blush, since (2) his love of the moment is, as ever, a person of good birth, and in any case (3) the Horatian speaker's ears can be trusted with a secret. It was precisely those three points that Catullus' speaker in Poem 6 had sharpened into prongs at the end of a verbal pitchfork for skewering Flavius. Flavius, according to Poem 6, is silent because (1) he is ashamed to confess the truth (*hoc pudet fateri*, 6.5), and (2) the truth is that Flavius' new love is not only charmless and inelegant (*illepidae atque inelegantes*, 6.2) but worse: the object of Flavius' tender affection must be some fever-stricken whore (*nescio quid febriculosi scorti/diligis*, 6.4–5). Further, Catullus' stated reason for prodding

---

[102] Horace's ode instantiates the same commonplace situation as the Hellenistic epigrams cited above (n. 101): a young man is obviously in love, but the identity of his beloved remains mysterious. On the topos, see Leo (1912) 145, Jacoby (1914) 398–405 and Wheeler (1934) 227.

[103] An instance of what Newman (1990), viewing Latin literature through the strong lens of Russian formalism, calls the "Augustan deformation" of Roman "recapitulation of genres."

and poking Flavius is that (3) he intends to write (and, in the event, has already written) a clever poem publicly sending Flavius and his love up to the sky (6.17).

Evaluating just how aggressive Poem 6 is hangs (and critics have seen this) on the precise interpretation of the phrase *nescio quid febriculosi scorti*.[104] If the "fever" from which the *scortum* suffers can be taken as a metaphor for sexual heat, as in the popular speech of the middle twentieth century, then it is just possible to construe the poem's abuse as "roughly congratulating" and an instance of "male bonding": an utterance, in other words, that one English-speaking, city-dwelling, twentieth-century straight boy could have directed at another in a comparable circumstance.[105] There is in fact only one prior Latin attestation of the adjective *febriculosus*, and it occurs in a comic (but roundly damning) inventory of the attributes of the lowest class of prostitutes.[106] The "fever" that Flavius' *scortum* has to offer him is decidedly not that of constant sexual excitation. The word almost certainly describes someone suffering from malaria.[107] Though the speaker has never seen Flavius' new love and does not know his or her name, he claims to deduce the lover's vile degradation – to Flavius' shame – from a series of clues: (1) Flavius' silence, (2) his bedchamber which, though silent, screams out (*clamat*, 6.7) damning evidence, and (3) Flavius' "fucked-out thighs," emaciated in the way that only shameful sex can emaciate. Compare another poem where Catullus constructs a similar evidentiary argument from silence, but this time to sting his victim with a far more shameful charge:

> Quid dicam, Gelli, quare rosea ista labella
>   hiberna fiant candidiora niue,
> mane domo cum exis et cum te octaua quiete
>   e molli longo suscitat hora die?
> nescio quid certe est: an uere fama susurrat
>   grandia te medii tenta uorare uiri?
> sic certe est: clamant Victoris rupta miselli
>   ilia, et emulso labra notata sero.   (Poem 80)

---

[104] And they have generally downplayed the phrase's aggressivity: esp. Friedrich (1908) ad loc., Quinn (1972) 226. But see Morgan (1977) 339.

[105] Johnson (1982) 108–10, to whose reading of Poem 6 I owe much.

[106] Morgan (1977) 340, Thomson (1997) ad loc.

[107] So Kroll (1968) and Lenchantin (1945) ad loc.

To what should I attribute the fact, Gellius, that those
  rosy-pink
lips of yours come out whiter than winter snow
when you emerge from your house of a morning
and when the eighth hour, on a long summer day, rouses you
  from a sweet little siesta?
It's got to be *something.* Can it be that it's true what rumor
  whispers:
that you're munching the big hard-on between a man's legs?
That's what it's got to be. And what screams it out is Victor's
  busted nuts,
poor sod, and your lips, marked with the mark of the semen
  you milk.

Poem 80 positions Gellius on the other side of a sexual gridline
from Poem 6's Flavius, both for a modern reader, since the sexual
partners are unambiguously of the same biological sex, and also
for an ancient Roman one, since Gellius is here made a *cinaedus*:
penetrated rather than penetrating, and that in the more shameful
and degrading of the two possible orifices.[108] The poem's technique of shaming by induction is nonetheless remarkably similar
to that of Poem 6. *Nescio quid* (80.5, 6.4) again serves as the place-
marker of unseen but suspected sexual misconduct. Silent evidence is again made to "shout" (*clamant*, 80.7; *clamat* 6.7) through
the operation of the speaker's hostile eyes and tongue. Whatever the precise anatomical location and nature of the symptom
described as Victor's *rupta ... ilia* (80.7–8), it appears to represent,
like Flavius' *latera ecfututa* (6.13), something that the poem's speaker
(and imagined audience) can *see* and take as evidence of excessive
sexual activity. The odd-sounding name of Gellius' bedfellow is
unknown to us. Might Victor have been a gladiator? If so, then
not only would the poem's speaker be pointing to a man whose
body everyone would have an opportunity to scrutinize, he would
also make Gellius share with Flavius the shame of having taken a
lover from the very lowest end of the social spectrum.

Poem 6 may be distinguished instructively from Poem 80 on two
further related points. First, in Poem 6, the Catullan speaker has
gained access to Flavius' house, and so can use the state of his

---

[108] Williams (1999) 175–88 argues that the term *cinaedus* referred not only to men who were
anally penetrated but more generally to male "gender deviants."

bedchamber, along with his *latera ecfututa*, as irrefutably damning evidence. In Poem 80, conversely, the interior of Gellius' house remains sealed off from the public eye, and what takes the place of Flavius' bedchamber, as corroboration of publicly visible physical symptoms, is the presence of *fama* (80.5): personified gossip. In Poem 80, then, the speaker does not adduce any evidence that is not already public knowledge; he simply applies his eye and tongue to silent (but fully visible) evidence in a way that converts the whisper of gossip to the shout of public shaming. Second, Flavius, unlike Gellius, and unlike most victims of Catullan invective, is being prodded into speech, at least ostensibly – though it is admittedly hard to imagine what Flavius could have offered by way of reply, except of course by composing an invective poem of his own against Catullus. But Gellius, so far from being invited to speak, is silenced by Poem 80. Or rather, he is *read* as already having been silenced by submitting orally to Victor (irrumation silences, and Poem 74 has already accused Gellius of silencing his own uncle in precisely this manner). Gellius is silenced, but the community, through gossip (*fama*), has already spoken, already ruled on his case, and already constituted the mark of whiteness on his formerly rosy (and so already effeminate: the materiality of the *cinaedus*) lips as a disenfranchising *nota* ("mark") of *infamia* upon his *aestimatio*.[109]

The charge against Flavius is, again, far less shaming than that against Gellius. And in the case of Gellius, Catullus proceeds in the manner of an openly avowed enemy (it is on that open avowal, Poem 116, that the collection closes), having access to no material for verbal aggression other than what public eyes and ears can know. Against Flavius, conversely, Catullus has been able to maneuver from a far more dangerous and insidious position: that of friendship. The middle section of Poem 6 proclaims to the world that Catullus has entered Flavius' house, presumably by invitation, and has even been admitted to (or was able to sneak a glimpse of) the master bedchamber, an area of the Roman house not ordinarily open to guests.[110] Precisely as Gilmore's widowed neighbor feared, Catullus has gained access to Flavius' house under guise of

---

[109] Richlin (1993).
[110] On public and private spaces within the Roman house, Wallace-Hadrill (1994) 10–11, 17–37 and passim. On "public" and "private" in late republican Rome, Treggiari (1998).

friendly or neighborly sentiment only to scour every inch of its interior with a hard look, "like a ferret," and he has departed with a pair of eyes glutted on damning sights, bloated with them like a leech full of blood, and eager to pour hidden knowledge out into the public "sky" upon the "charming verse" (6.17) of a wicked tongue. Poem 6 is all the more effective as an act of aggression for beginning and ending on a tone that can be construed as a friend's sincere good wishes.[111] Indeed, if Flavius is a member of Catullus' circle of friends, part of the Catullan *jouissance* of the poem (its choicest part) may be read to reside in the delicious knowledge that Flavius must now submit to the poem's abuse under the social obligation to "take a joke."

Poem 6 is inhabited, then, by the same themes and concerns as Poems 5 and 7: two versions of a lover's secret carefully concealed from the malice of eyes and tongues flank a lover's secret gleefully betrayed through the omnipresent and powerful aggression of eyes and tongues. What Poem 6's Catullus personates and carries out is precisely what the Catullus of Poems 5 and 7 simultaneously wards off and invites: a stern, severely moralizing public exposure fueled by personal envy, prurient curiosity and pure malice. The twin guilty secrets – nowhere revealed, but held up, dangled, just beyond the reach of our eyes and ears in flurries of languid Hellenistic elegances – are in both instances a single and specific piece of knowledge, a number and a name: in Poems 5 and 7, the shameful multitude of kisses that Catullus desires from Lesbia; in Poem 6, the shameful identity of Flavius' new love. Both secrets are subject to discovery, or at least to the suspicion that leads to discovery, through the twin routes of sight and speech. The aggression of a malevolent gaze (*inuidia*) and maliciously framed poetic speech (*fascinatio*) that Catullus wards off in Poems 5 and 7 – all the while defying it, tempting its envy and teasing its curiosity with virtuoso bravura – is exactly the aggression he performs in Poem 6. Poem 6's performance is distinguished from the ones framing it by a Herzfeldian "stylistic transformation" of a stunning sort, a self-allusive bid for what the chess masters call "brilliancy points": without having gained access to the kind of

---

[111] Indo-European blame poets, it seems, liked to couch invective in language that could be construed on first hearing as praise, and whose invective sting, once felt, was thus all the sharper. Ward (1973) 136.

damning certainty about Flavius' love that the Catullus of the kiss poems is careful to protect in his own case, the Catullus of Poem 6 has pilloried Flavius, nailed him to the wall poetically, and has done so as successfully and conclusively as if his eyes, his ears and his aggression had penetrated far deeper than into Flavius' empty and silent bedroom.

CHAPTER 5

Code models of Catullan manhood

We fill pre-existing forms and when we fill them we change
them and are changed by them.

Frank Bidart, "Borges and I"

THE TEXTUALITY OF CATULLAN MANHOOD

If Poems 5 through 7 respond to a reading that takes them as a
triplet, with the Catullan speaking subject moving from the stance
of a fearfully defiant lover (in Poem 5) to that of an aggressive
moralizer (in Poem 6) and back again (in Poem 7), what poetic
meaning, and indeed what social and ethical meaning, are we to
attach to this flashing oscillation? Despite the last chapter's argument against reading a Catullus critically detached from his own
poetically performed aggression, surely there is some kind of role
playing (*prosopopoeia*) in this three-act mime, and hence surely it is
possible, here and elsewhere in Catullus' poetry, to draw some
kind of distinction between role and actor, between mask and
man. *Some* kind of distinction there is, but I think it need not
take the form of the neat demarcation, derived from modernist
"persona criticism," between Catullus the poet and "Catullus" the
persona, a binary division that a generation of Catullan criticism
taught its students to make and maintain carefully, on pain of falling back into what it saw as the hopeless naïveté of Romantic
"biographical criticism."[1] It is a question, again, of who is speaking, and of the nature of the speaker's engagement with the words
being spoken, especially where those words are ethically unpalat-
able to the reader by the aggression they perform. Here again a
postmodern critical stance may offer a richer and deeper reading

[1] Sarkissian's (1983) interpretation of Poem 68 is perhaps the most thoroughgoing application of this critical binarism, showing its possibilities as well as its limitations.

of ancient Catullus than was provided by modernism's saving of the appearances through positing a "literary persona."[2]

"Persona" is an authentically ancient critical term, and a subject on which one could likely have had an interesting discussion with the poet from Verona. Catullus and his more learned ancient readers surely knew the Hellenistic Greek technical term *prosopopoeia*, which appears in Philodemus' treatise on poetics.[3] Cicero amply attests a contemporary self-consciousness about the act of speaking rhetorically under an assumed or "introduced" persona. His dressing down of Clodia under the *introducta persona* of Appius Claudius Caecus, in the speech for Caelius, is only the most memorable of numerous examples.[4] Outside the speeches, two late philosophical dialogues, on old age and friendship, begin with prologues in which Cicero tells his dedicatee Atticus (and the reader) explicitly that in what follows he will discourse under the assumed persona of Cato or Laelius.[5] Perhaps even more intriguing is Cicero's explanation, in *De Oratore*, of how he prepares for an upcoming court case, after the interview with his client, by privately acting out the entire trial, assuming in turn the three roles, or personae, of the plaintiff's counsel, the defendant's counsel (here Cicero impersonates Cicero), and the praetor hearing the case.[6]

These instances of Ciceronian rhetorical *prosopopoeia*, however, differ crucially from the operation of a modernist "literary persona" on two related counts. First, the words uttered through Cicero's personae, in the philosophical dialogues no less than in the speeches, cannot be said to belong, by virtue of their status as literary artifacts, to that "world apart" that was the province of poetry and of literature in general under the modernist critical models discussed in previous chapters. Second, the Ciceronian speaker cannot be said to stand in a relation of "aesthetic distance" or critical detachment toward his speech performances

[2] On the "literary persona," Elliott (1982).
[3] Philodemus *Po.* 5.12; the first extant Latin attestation comes much later, and just where we might have expected it, in Quintilian's treatise on the training of an orator (*Inst.* 1.8.3 and passim).
[4] *Cael.* 34
[5] *Sen.* 1.2, without mention of the term *persona*; *Am.* 1.4–5, with discussion of both dialogues and their *personae*.
[6] *de Orat.* 2.102. Trendelenburg (1910), Elliott (1982) 25–7 and Gill (1988) discuss various aspects of *persona* in Cicero and elsewhere in Latin writings.

under assumed personae. His utterances are in every case purposive, urgently so. Cicero does not impersonate both sides of a case, for example, in order to show up, through "social critique," the "moral bankruptcy" of the society or the legal system of his day, but rather to prepare himself to win his case. Nor, obviously enough, does this lack of detachment make his relation to his performance one of (Romantic) "sincerity," of inspired emotion getting the better of intellect and self-interest. It is true that an oratorical speaker's words may stand in direct opposition to that speaker's interests, as when Cicero impersonated his legal opponent (or when Catullus seems to betray his own guiltiest secrets to the reader). They may be, alternately, a matter of relative indifference to those interests, as when a Roman youth practiced the rudiments of argumentation through *controuersiae* on historical subjects.[7] In all these instances, however, the *performance* of the speaker's words, quite independently of what the words say, constitutes a bid for social and hence political mastery on the part of the speaker, and it is precisely through performance that that mastery is attained. I have argued in previous chapters for the prevalence of a similar bid for social mastery in Catullus' poetic performances of his manhood.

In the hands of the literary critics who formulated it, most notably R. P. Blackmur, the modernist concept of the literary persona offered a profound and sophisticated tool for thinking about the process of literary creation.[8] But in its subsequent application to individual texts both ancient and modern (Juvenal and Catullus were chief targets within Latin literature), it often tended to serve a different purpose, as a way of rehabilitating, of naturalizing canonical authors (and especially the questionably canonical ones, like Juvenal and Catullus) by reassuring the modern reader that whatever dreadful things great writers might have *said* in their Great Books, what they really *meant* – and this could be seen once the necessary adjustments for detached irony were made – never failed to embody the cultural and ethical values of the modernist new humanism. While for Blackmur the persona had been both "I" and "not I" – a formulation reminiscent of Rimbaud's *Je est un*

---

[7] See examples at *Inv.* 1.17.
[8] Blackmur, in *The Language of Silence*: "a *persona* is the invoked being of the muse: a siren audible through a lifetime's wax in the ears; a translation of what we did not know that we knew ourselves: what we partly are." Cited by Elliott (1982) 1.

autre – this simplified and didactic version of persona criticism drew the brightest of lines between "poet" and "persona." Gilbert Highet's condemnation of persona criticism as a distorting fiction achieved through the introduction of a "ventriloquist's dummy" contains, I think, a considerable grain of truth.[9] The fictional construct posited by this working version of persona criticism is to be found, however, not in the persona but rather in the "poet": a stable, serenely omniscient "I" whose ethical viewpoint and presuppositions, in the last analysis, are those of (who else's could they be?) the critic reading the poem.[10]

Not only twentieth-century critics, but a considerable number of twentieth-century writers, furthered this "seductive and even oddly comforting" binary opposition of "I" and "author," with its implicit presupposition of an "I" that remains always protected, essential and identical to itself in "life" (i.e., non-literary utterance), but is always deranged, falsified, exaggerated (i.e., aestheticized), solely and uniquely in the act of "making literature."[11] In a prose poem named after (and in some measure parodying) Borges' short story "Borges and I," Frank Bidart has raised a strong voice in critique of that remarkable certitude:[12]

The desolating landscape in Borges' "Borges and I" – in which the voice of "I" tells us that its other self, Borges, is the self who makes literature, who in the process of making literature falsifies and exaggerates, while the self that is speaking to us now must go on living so that Borges may continue to fashion literature – is seductive and even oddly comforting, but, I think, false.

The voice of this "I" asserts a disparity between its essential self and its worldly second self, the self who seeks embodiment through making things, through work, who in making takes on something false, inessential, inauthentic.

... When Borges' "I" confesses that Borges falsifies and exaggerates it seems to do so to cast aside falsity and exaggeration, to attain an entire candor unobtainable by Borges.

---

[9] Highet (1974), invoking Cherniss (1962) and polemicizing against Anderson (1964).

[10] I am grateful to Paul Allen Miller for showing me a manuscript in progress in which he expresses similar reservations, and comes to similar conclusions, about the application of persona criticism to Roman love elegy.

[11] See Halpern (1995) for essays on "the authorial I" by distinguished twentieth-century authors, including Borges and Bidart.

[12] Bidart (1997) 8–9 places this poem, interestingly, just after a version of Catullus' Poem 85, under the title "Catullus: Excrucior."

The "I" therefore allows us to enter an inaccessible magic space, a hitherto inarticulate space of intimacy and honesty earlier denied us, where voice, for the first time, has replaced silence.

– Sweet fiction, in which bravado and despair beckon from a cold panache, in which the protected essential self suffers flashes of its existence to be immortalized by a writing self that is incapable of performing its actions without mixing our essence with what is false.

Bidart has put his finger squarely on what is at stake in this "twin selves" theory of literary creation, the notion that whoever writes "has a self that has remained the same and that knows what it would be if its writing self did not exist," and no less squarely on its nostalgic appeal and the brave despair of its affect. The orders created by his own poetry books, Bidart suggests, are not parallel universes produced by a phantom author-self but mirrors of his own universe, albeit "cracked and dirty" ones. "Everything in art is a formal question," Bidart says, and what he seems to put forward in place of a "Frank and I" binarism is the statement that gives this chapter its epigraph: "We fill pre-existing forms and when we fill them we change them and are changed."[13]

Bidart's formulation, and his description of his poetry as forming an "order," are more than a little reminiscent of T. S. Eliot's essay on "Tradition and the Individual Talent" (and the present study has taken enough shots at Modernism; its author is long overdue to quote one of its giants with due respect):

[W]hat happens when a new work of art is created is something that happens simultaneously to all the work of art which preceded it. The existing monuments form an ideal order among themselves, which is modified by the introduction of the new (the really new) work of art among them. The existing order is complete before the new work arrives; for order to persist after the supervention of novelty, the *whole* existing order must be, if ever so slightly, altered; and so the relations, proportions, values of each work of art toward the whole are readjusted; and this is conformity between the old and the new. Whoever has approved this idea of order ... will not find it preposterous that the past should be altered by the present as much as the present is directed by the past.[14]

[13] This apothegm appears three times in Bidart (1997): at the beginning (9) and near the end (11) of "Borges and I," and near the end (56) of a long poem inspired by Ovid's Myrrha episode in the *Metamorphoses*.

[14] Eliot (1950) 5. See Martindale (1993) 23–9 on Eliotic and Gadamerian models of tradition.

Bidart's words resonate with Eliot's – as do Eliot's with Bidart's, so that Eliot's text is altered for the reader who comes or returns to it by this route – and both texts resonate with the late twentieth-century (postmodern, but the periodizing terms have grown difficult to sustain) critical stance that views all forms of signification, without distinction between literary and non-literary, as taking place within an intertextual universe of discourse.[15] Eliot's model of "tradition," like Bidart's "pre-existing forms," seems startlingly close to – indeed seems to explicate, in language less openly technical – the notion of an intertext that informs a new text, gives that text its signifying force, renders it decipherable, and is itself in turn made new by the inscription of that new text upon itself.

The text that Catullus inscribed upon his intertext-tradition, and that we read inscribed upon ours, is both a series of poems and a performance through those poems of self and manhood, a performance whose poetics I have attempted here to trace. The Catullan self that we construe by reading the poems, the Catullan persona (in Cicero's sense of the term), has its own textuality, is itself a text. My reading of that text has pointed to specific moments of intertextuality at the level of "character," as when the speaker of Poem 37 momentarily fills the boots, and the pre-existing form, of the stock comic Braggart Soldier.[16] Other readers have highlighted the presence of other "character intertexts," such as the comic lover in Poem 8.[17] These intertextual gestures appear to be drawn not so much toward a specific textual model (Poem 37, for example, does not seem to *allude* to Plautus' *Miles Gloriosus*) as toward what might be called recognizable speech genres. But alongside the momentary appearances in Catullus of stock characters and individual "literary" characters like Odysseus (in Poem 101), there are moments in the Catullan persona-text where it is possible to discern character intertexts whose features, and whose names, are those of poetic personae belonging to specific poets in Catullus' tradition. These presences are of course in *some* measure textually imbedded in the words of Catullus' poems and thus

---

[15] One of the early enunciations of this Kristevan model whose currency remains wide is Barthes (1973).

[16] On the notion of "character intertext" as a potentially fruitful approach awaiting exploration, see the suggestive remarks of Laird (1997). On Poem 37, see 80–7 above.

[17] See ch. 3, n. 40 and text.

describable, at least in places, by a philological "rhetoric of allusivity," but they cannot be so entirely, and need not be.[18] In the attempt to discern those presences we inevitably underread at moments, because of the fragmentation of our evidence, and overread at others, through the nostalgia and enthusiasm that impel toward restoration of the fragmentary. To hope that the two tendencies will offset each other would be optimistic; to view them as dangers to be avoided (and avoidable), and to try and steer a conservative middle course between them, would precondition the results as insufficiently interesting to merit the effort of attempt.

This final chapter will examine the presence, in the text of Catullus' performed manhood, of two specific poets from very different historical moments in Catullus' poetic tradition. Both have been discussed, at various points in the history of Catullus' scholarly reception, as Catullan literary models. While I shall inevitably be renewing some of those discussions in their turn, my chief interest will be in their presences as persona-intertexts in Catullus' persona-text, or I as prefer to call them, borrowing a term of Conte's, "code models" of Catullan manhood.[19] These code models form part of the speech and gestural lexicon of Catullan self-fashioning, as markers for individually recognizable modes of Catullus' poetic performance of manhood: an Archilochian mode, characterized by aggressively hypermasculine invective of the kind discussed in the previous chapter; and a Callimachean mode, standing – or appearing to – at the antipodes of the Archilochian, fragrant with the sophistication of erudition and with the manhood of a "feminine" delicacy, but ultimately no less agonistically performative of its own excellence.

ARCHAIC BLAME AND THE SHAME OF BEING ARCHILOCHUS

No other ancient Greek poet, not even Sappho, presents a starker contrast than Archilochus between the luster of the ancient reputation and the present decomposition into fragments of the received corpus. The seventh-century poet from Paros was throughout antiquity regularly assigned a place at the top of the poetic roster of the Greek language, alongside Homer himself (sometimes with the

---

[18] On "rhetoric of allusivity": Hinds (1998) 5–10 and passim.   [19] Conte (1986) 31.

addition of Hesiod).[20] The invention of *iambos* seems to have been credited to Archilochus (though it was by no means the only generic form in which he composed), giving him the status as founder of a genre to answer Homer's paternity of *epos*.[21] A later epigram composed in Greek by that most conspicuous Hellenophile among the Romans, the emperor Hadrian, framed the conceit that Archilochus' genius had been deflected from epic into "raging iambs" (λυσσῶντας ἰάμβους) by the Muse in answer to a prayer of Homer, who presumably had divined that if his epigone were to follow in his footsteps, the primacy of the *Iliad* and *Odyssey* was at risk.[22]

That educated Romans of Catullus' generation took Archilochus' preeminence for granted is suggested by a passing remark of Cicero near the opening of the *Tusculan Disputations*, in one of those moments of Roman anxiety vis-à-vis the superior prestige of Greek literature so common in Cicero and other Latin writers (and so conspicuously absent from Catullus). The three pinnacles of archaic Greek poetry are here taken as given, beyond dispute:

> Greece used to outstrip us in learning and in every genre of literature. It was easy to outdo us in this area: we were not competing. For while among the Greeks, the class of the poets was composed of learned persons from the earliest antiquity (Homer and Hesiod lived before Rome was founded, and Archilochus while Romulus was king), we have been comparatively late in taking up the poetic art. (*Tusc. Disp.* 1.3)

Archilochus' ancient critical reception seems to have produced a body of work commensurate in volume with the centrality of his position in the canon. Three librarians from the Museum at Alexandria, for example, appear to have written on Archilochus. Catullus will have known something (probably a great deal) of this critical literature, as did Cicero, who records in passing a witticism of Aristophanes of Byzantium, one of Archilochus' Alexandrian exegetes, to the effect that the best of that poet's *iamboi* were those that went on the longest.[23]

---

[20] Tarditi (1968) 233 catalogues the ancient testimonia naming Homer and Archilochus together.

[21] A claim attested no earlier than Clement of Alexandria *Strom.* 1.21.117, but surely reflecting earlier tradition.

[22] *AP* 7.674.

[23] The three librarians who appear to have written on Archilochus are Apollonius of Rhodes (Ath. 10.451d), Aristophanes of Byzantium (Cic. *Att.* 16.11.2, also Ath. 3.85e) and Aristarchus (*Et. Gud.* 305.8).

Aristophanes' remark has a defensive ring, and apologia presupposes attack or at least critique. Critical censure of Archilochus – or rather, what could have appeared as such to Hellenistic readers – is attested as early as Pindar, focused on just that ethical character of his iambic poetry hinted at in Hadrian's epigram: the unbridled, albeit stunningly artful, invective expression of violently aggressive rage.[24] In one of Pindar's odes to Hieron, tyrant of Syracuse, the epinician speaker seems to assert that "being Archilochus," or being an Archilochian blame poet, is bad business, in every sense – as indeed it is, for a praise poet.[25] And later, in Hellenistic Egypt, while the head librarians at Alexandria were pleading Archilochus' case, their colleague Callimachus seems to have taken the other side of the debate, insisting on the ethical vileness of Archilochian iambic invective, calling its poet-speaker "wine-drunk" in one fragment and likening his poisonous mouth to that of a dog or wasp in another.[26] If the epithet "wine-drunk" refers, as seems likely, not only to literal intoxication but also to the hypermasculine, aggressive railing associated with a drunken bout, then Callimachus' remark can be situated within the tradition of a poetic conceit that was to become common coin among Hellenistic epigrammatists before Catullus, imperial ones after him, and Augustan poets in Latin as well: the division of male poets into wine-guzzling he-men (like Homer and Archilochus) and water-sipping nellies (like the refined Callimachus himself).[27]

Catullus draws this same line between wine and water in a short poem near the midpoint of the polymetrics as we have them:

---

[24] Heraclitus had already condemned Archilochus, but as a poet *tout court* rather than as a blame poet: his blanket rejection covered Homer as well (D. L. 9.1; Heraclit. fr. 42 Guthrie). For a sketch of Archilochus' critical reception, both ancient and modern, see Bossi (1990) 31–53. See also Rankin (1977) 1–9 on the ancient reception. We probably do not possess any characteristic samples of Archilochus at his most fiercely aggressive (even with the addition of the Cologne epode, which won him Merkelbach's [1974] 113 characterization as "ein schwerer Psychopath"), and if he was as foul-mouthed at his worst as the ancient critics seem to suggest, the gap in our tradition is probably not accidental.

[25] Pindar, *Pythian* 2.52–6: "I must flee the constant bite of wicked speech, for, though being distant from it myself, I have seen Archilochus the blamer (ψογερόν) often reduced to a state of loss (τὰ πολλ' ἐν ἀμηχανίᾳ) through fattening himself on heavy-worded enmities (βαρυλόγοις ἔχθεσιν πιαινόμενον)." Pindar's characterization most likely reflects an antithesis between praise and blame belonging to the tradition of the genres rather than a personally held authorial opinion. See Nagy (1976) 195–6.

[26] Call. frs. 544, 380 Pfeiffer.

[27] Wimmel (1960) 225, Degani (1977) 110ff., Crowther (1979), Knox (1985), Bossi (1990) 33–4, Cameron (1995) 364–7.

Minister uetuli puer Falerni
inger mi calices amariores
ut lex Postumiae iubet magistrae
ebrioso acino ebriosioris.
at uos quo lubet hinc abite, lymphae,
uini pernicies, et ad seueros
migrate. hic merus est Thyonianus.   (Poem 27)

Cup-bearer boy of finely aged Falernian,
bring me in some bitterer cups to drink.
Postumia's in charge now, and here's her law:
"drunker than the drunken grape itself."
And as for you, water: Away! Make tracks,
you spoiler of wine, go visit the strait-laced.
The god of wine is here, and here we take him straight.

If Catullus had written it in Greek couplets instead of Latin Phalaecians, this poem would be fully at home in the pages of the
Palatine Anthology by its structure, its theme and its diction. A
Greek epigram written in Augustan Rome by Antipater of Thessalonica comes perhaps the closest to Catullus' version of the topos,
and Antipater's version nicely renders explicit what is almost
certainly the poetic and programmatic meaning of the Catullan
imagery:

Φεύγεθ', ὅσοι λόκκας ἢ λοφνίδας ἢ καμασῆνας
    ᾄδετε, ποιητῶν φῦλον ἀκανθολόγων,
οἵ τ' ἐπέων κόσμον λελυγισμένον ἀσκήσαντες
    κρήνης ἐξ ἱερῆς πίνετε λιτὸν ὕδωρ.
σήμερον Ἀρχιλόχοιο καὶ ἄρσενος ἦμαρ Ὁμήρου
    σπένδομεν· ὁ κρητὴρ οὐ δέχεθ' ὑδροπότας.
                                    (*AP* 11.20)

Away, you tribe of poets that sing of "mantillas,"
"tapers," "tunnies" – every word a prickle! –
and, fretting every verse's tortured structure,
sip simple water from a sacred spring.
Today we drink to Archilochus, to Homer: men.
No place around the wine-bowl for drinkers of water.

The same nexus of symbols appears in numerous Hellenistic epigrams well predating Catullus.[28] Given all the evidence, in fact, it

---

[28] Gutzwiller (1998) 157–82 cites examples and discusses Poem 27 in their context..

seems likely that this poetic standoff between wine and water harks back to a third-century Alexandrian critical debate (if not a full-blown *Querelle*). Archilochus, by the fierce aggression of his verse and perhaps also thanks to his colorful ancient biography, looks to have been chief and eponymous hero among the poets of rough and ready wine-drinking inspiration (and hence, presumably, all the critical apologetics in his favor). On the other side of the debate, we seem to discern Callimachus occupying the front lines (or at least conscripted into them later), both as a critical voice and as a poetic exemplar of the water-drinking mode of delicate refinement.[29]

The first-time reader of the received corpus is not made to wait an instant for the fulfilment of Poem 27's promise of bitterer cups filled with the unmitigated wine of manly aggression.[30] The next two poems make good the promise, by personating a recognizably Archilochian mode.[31] The tightly linked pair formed by Poems 28 and 29 strikes a new note, not so much by its violent sexual aggression alone (we have already seen Poem 16 and the others to Furius and Aurelius) as by its politicizing and indeed universalizing of that sexual aggression. Sexual violence is here imbedded in the poet's personal history and in the Roman political order itself (from which Catullus is anything but critically aloof). The aristocratic political system of patron-client alliance is here characterized as a promiscuous economic exploitation (operating in both vertical directions), and that exploitation is in turn figured, at every turn, as brutally aggressive sexual penetration:

> Pisonis comites, cohors inanis,
> aptis sarcinulis et expeditis,
> Verani optime tuque mi Fabulle,
> quid rerum geritis? satisne cum isto
> uappa frigoraque et famem tulistis?
> ecquidnam in tabulis patet lucelli

---

[29] Antipater's "simple water from a holy spring" (*AP* 11.20.4) seems to recall Callimachus' "stream that creeps, pure and undefiled, from a holy spring, the choicest of waters" from the end of the hymn to Apollo (ἥτις καθαρή τε καὶ ἀχράαντος ἀνέρπει | πίδακος ἐξ ἱερῆς ὀλίγη λιβὰς ἄκρον ἄωτον, *H.* 2.111–2). Cameron (1995) 366, Gutzwiller (1998) 168.

[30] Latin *amarus*, like Greek πικρός (and English "bitter"), described both a taste upon the tongue and an ethical quality. It is perhaps worth remarking that a Hellenistic epigram attributed to Meleager, and so probably known to Catullus, uses the epithet πικρός of Archilochus (*AP* 7.352.3).

[31] Wiseman (1969) 7–8; Skinner (1981) 27–8

expensum, ut mihi qui meum secutus
praetorem refero datum lucello?
o Memmi, bene me ac diu supinum
tota ista trabe lentus irrumasti.
sed, quantum uideo, pari fuistis
casu: nam nihilo minore uerpa
farti estis. pete nobiles amicos!
at uobis mala multa di deaeque
dent, opprobria Romuli Remique.   (Poem 28)

Piso's retinue, empty-handed cohort,
traveling light, just a handy little rucksack,
excellent Veranius and you my dear Fabullus,
how are you making out? Had enough freezing
cold and hunger along with that flat-wine loser?
Do your checkbooks show substantial revenues ...
spent? Just like me: I went and served with my
praetor, and I count to my credit what I gave.
Memmius, you really threw me down on my back
and rammed me slowly, good and hard, in the mouth
with that big, heavy two-by-four of yours.
But it looks like you two had the same good luck
as me: you both got stuffed with no less dick.
"Get yourself some noble friends." Yeah, right.
But may the gods and goddesses damn you all
handsomely, you blots on the names of Romulus and Remus.

Quis hoc potest uidere, quis potest pati,
nisi impudicus et uorax et aleo,
Mamurram habere quod Comata Gallia
habebat ante et ultima Britannia?
cinaede Romule, haec uidebis et feres?
et ille nunc superbus et superfluens
perambulauit omnium cubilia,
ut albulus columbus aut Adoneus?
cinaede Romule, haec uidebis et feres?
es impudicus et uorax et aleo.
eone nomine, imperator unice,
fuisti in ultima occidentis insula,
ut ista uestra diffututa mentula
ducenties comesset aut trecenties?
quid est alid sinistra liberalitas?
parum expatrauit an parum helluatus est?

paterna prima lancinata sunt bona,
secunda praeda Pontica, inde tertia
Hibera, quam scit amnis aurifer Tagus:
nunc Gallicae timetur et Britannicae.
quid hunc, malum, fouetis? aut quid hic potest
nisi uncta deuorare patrimonia?
eone nomine, urbis o potissimi
socer generque, perdidistis omnia?   (Poem 29)[32]

Who can watch? Who can bear the sight
(someone who lives for sex and food and dice,
that's who) of Mamurra owning everything
that long-haired Gaul and far Britannia used to?
Faggot Romulus, will you just watch and take it?
There he is now, swollen up and spilling over,
coming to do the tour of every man's bedroom
like the little white dove, like the god Adonis,
and faggot Romulus, will you just watch and take it?
That someone who lives for sex and food and dice
is you. Was it really for him, O one and only
general, you went to the isle at the world's west end,
so that your friend, this Dick that's all dicked out,
could munch his millions two and three at a time?
You have to admit it's a strange kind of generosity.
Hasn't he pigged out, hasn't he daddied out enough?
Daddy's fortune was the first he busted through,
the second one the spoils of Pontus, and third
was Spain's, where the Tagus flows with yellow gold.
Now we're afraid for Gaulish fortunes, British ones:
they're next. Why the hell do you cherish this man?
What talents does he have – apart from a deep throat
for swallowing down big, juicy patrimonies?
You mightiest men of Rome, by marriage son and father,
was it really for *him* you wasted the world?

All the players in this pair of poems are adult Roman males, and
none of them escapes the stinging skewer of emasculation in some
form. Certainly not Catullus himself: Poem 10's Catullus had

---

[32] The text printed here is not Mynors' but Thomson's, reflecting two important emendations on which the sense of the poem turns: Schwabe's *ante* at line 4 (*uncti* was a conjecture as well, for V's nonsensical *cum te*, and *ante* seems inevitable in light of Pliny's remark
at *Hist. Nat.* 36.48) and Badian's (1977) brilliant restoration of line 20 (*Gallicae* and
Britannicae for *Galliae* and *Britanniae*). I have altered Thomson's text only to make its
orthography consistent with other Latin texts cited here.

called his praetor Memmius an *irrumator* ("oral penetrator"), and
Poem 28 makes clear how keenly and materially the Catullan
speaker feels that emasculation.[33] Certainly not Catullus' friends:
Veranius and Fabullus have suffered under Piso the penis (*uerpa*,
28.12) the same treatment that Memmius accorded to Catullus.
Not Pompey, the most likely candidate for identification with
"faggot Romulus" (28.5, 9).[34] Not the men of Rome, who are
about to be cuckolded universally by Mamurra's Adonaic proces-
sion through their bedrooms – and who are implicated in Poem
29's opening *quis*, since they, like Pompey, look on and just take
it.[35] Not Caesar: he is of course implicated here as well, and Poem
29 forms part of the Catullan smear campaign that Caesar is supposed to have tried to abate by conciliation through the poet's
father.[36] Not even the Great Penetrators themselves: by the logic
of the ideology of Roman manhood, that very excess of appetite
with which Piso, Memmius and Mamurra are pumping the system
is itself a symptom of ethical weakness, *impotentia*.[37] Piso (and so
too Memmius by analogy) is not only a *uerpa* (28.12) but also a
uappa (28.5): the "wine" of his manhood is stale, flat, vapid. And
Mamurra, Caesar's detachable penis, is by that same logic "dicked
out" (*diffututa*, 29.13) and rendered orally receptive (*helluatus*, 28.16;

---

[33] The Catullan speaker's readiness to characterize being wronged by a social and political
superior as sexual penetration seems to reflect the hypermasculine aggression of such
violently policed hierarchical communities as men's prisons and barracks. Walters (1997)
41–2 has suggested that military service – being "under orders" and under threat of cor-
poral punishment – posed a particular problem to the elite Roman man's stance of
manhood. *Irrumator*, as Richlin (1981) has argued, never loses its literal force – or at least
if it does momentarily, that literal force (as Catullus shows us here) is always subject to
immediate reactivation. As Lenchantin (1945) suggested ad loc., the word probably
belonged to the *sermo castrensis* ("military slang") of Catullus' time.

[34] On *unice imperator* as possibly echoing an imperial acclamation given to Caesar, and on
the identification of *cinaedus Romulus* as Pompey, see Cameron (1976), also Lenchantin
(1945) ad loc. Young (1969) and Scott (1971) take *Romulus* to stand for "the Roman
people." I consider that the men of Rome are ultimately implicated in the poem's invective, but *Romulus* seems to have been a common ironic insult for hurling at a politico:
see Quinn (1970) ad loc.

[35] On Adonis and the dove in this poem, see Allen (1984).

[36] Poem 29 was the most memorable of Catullus' Caesarian poems for subsequent readers,
as Quintilian (*Inst.* 9.4.141) and Pliny (*Hist. Nat.* 36.48) seem to attest, and it is here that
the identification of the sobriquet Mentula with Mamurra is made explicit. Suet. *Jul.* 73
claims that Catullus had permanently stained Caesar's reputation: its refrain would have
been suitable for quoting in Caesar's face or behind his back (the words *socer generque*
would recall the entire poem and so suffice to raise a laugh).

[37] See ch. 4 n. 79.

deuorare 28.22), precisely by his ravenous ingestion of fortunes on a global scale.

What, then, is specifically Archilochian about the mode of manhood personated in this pair of poems? Archilochus may well have been a great political lampooner – the fragments feature some animadversions on the wealth of tyrants and a memorable bit of grumbling about one Leophilus – but we lack the evidence to judge the extent of Archilochus' presence as an "exemplary model" in Poems 28 and 29.[38] Certainly the bite and sting of the two poems could have led an ancient reader to the judgment that Catullus had dipped his stylus in Archilochian bile and so delivered on the promise of unmitigated wine hinted in Poem 27. But a further and more specific aspect of Archilochian code modeling is discernible here, in a trait that modern readers notice in Catullus and that ancient ones were unlikely to miss. Catullus' "iambic" rage in these poems, as inventoried above, heaps emasculating shame not only upon his enemies, but also upon himself and, perhaps even more significantly, upon his friends as well. These were precisely the charges leveled against Archilochus by the fifth-century Athenian tyrant Critias, his sternest moralizing critic whose opinions are preserved to us. Here the grounds for condemnation, from a sort of man that Archilochus and Catullus can both be imagined lampooning with gusto, are themselves put forward in a mode of macho prudery and so rather different from those to be framed later by the partisans of water:

Critias reproaches Archilochus for speaking extremely ill of himself. For (so he says) if Archilochus himself had not given out so evil a report of himself among the Greeks, we would never have known any of the following: that he was the son of one Enipo, a slave-girl; that he left Paros because of destitute poverty and moved to Thasos; that he fell into disfavor with the inhabitants of this latter place; and that he spoke as abusively of his friends as he did of his enemies.[39] What is more (so Critias), we would never have known, had we not learned it from the man himself, that he was a philanderer (μοιχός), a lecher (λάγνος), a sex criminal

---

[38] On Leophilus: Archil. 115 West.

[39] We do have a bit of evidence for Archilochus' ancient reception in this regard. Aristides (*Or.* 46, 2.380.21) lists Archilochus' friend Pericles among the targets of the poet's invective, alongside Lycambes and Charilaos. Athenaeus (7f) preserves a brief sample of that "friendly" invective, accusing Pericles of gluttonously hurrying to symposia "like the (impoverished) Myconians" (Archil. 124 West).

(ὑβριστής), and further, what is most shameful, that he threw down his shield. Archilochus, then, was not a favorable witness in his own behalf, given the report of himself and the reputation he left behind. These reproaches are not my own, but rather those of Critias. (Archil. 295 West = Critias 88 B 44 Diels-Kranz = Aelian, *Var. Hist.* 10.13)[40]

Catullus elsewhere delights in coating himself (and his native Verona) with a liberal application of sleaze, and he elsewhere takes his friends to task and attacks his enemies, but Poems 28 and 29 arguably present the corpus' most concentrated and relentless condemnation of self, friends and enemies to scandalous shame, in a voice that could be characterized as hoarse with rage if only its diction were not so artful. But then, artfulness of diction does not of itself mitigate Archilochian bile: no critic seems ever to have dared call into question Archilochus' mastery of his own poetic forms.

Form, specifically metrical form, may be a further aspect of Archilochian intertextuality in the second poem of this pair. Poem 29 is one of three poems in the corpus composed in iambs. Of the other two, Poem 52, in four verses, shares with Poem 29 both its political subject matter (though its satire is meek in comparison) and the refrain-like repetition of an entire verse.[41] Poem 4 on the little boat, conversely, is very much a water-drinking poem, Hellenistic in style and tone and owing much to the Hellenistic topos exemplified in Callimachus' epigram on a conch shell.[42] Poem 4 does however share a formal trait with Poem 29 that makes them both remarkable as metrical *tours de force* in the Hellenistic style. With a single exception, both poems are composed entirely in perfect iambic feet, rather than in iambic metra allowing, as was the tradition of the form, for substitution of a long syllable in the first, fifth and ninth positions.[43] The single reversion to a more relaxed prosody, a spondee at the beginning of the twentieth verse of Poem 29 (*nunc Gallicae timetur et Britannicae*) has often been

---

[40] It is a twist worthy of a short story of Borges that the critique of the fifth-century BCE Athenian Critias against seventh-century Archilochus is preserved for us only in a work written long after Catullus' death, by the second- and third-century CE Hellenizing Italian writer Claudius Aelianus. Aelian's insistent distancing of himself from Critias' opinion probably reflects his knowledge of the critical polemics on Archilochus that occupied the intervening centuries.

[41] On Poem 52, see 100–1 above.

[42] Call. *Epigr.* 5 Pfeiffer.

[43] Noted already by Lafaye (1894) 13.

attributed to textual corruption. Corruption in the text of Catullus we shall always have with us, but if this (emended) verse is sound as it stands, then its opening spondee serves arrestingly to mark a climactic moment in the poem by the same kind of bursting of formal boundaries that Wiseman has pointed out in Poem 116.[44]

Poem 29 is thus by far the most Archilochian of Catullus' three iambic poems, the one where Catullus could be said to be "following Archilochus" by being (thematically) iambic, in the way that a writer of hexameter poetry could be said to be "following Homer" by being epic or "following Hesiod" by being didactic. Catullus speaks of his own *iambi* three times in the corpus.[45] All three instances, strangely, occur in poems whose meter is not iambic but Phalaecian. What is meant by "iambs" is however made clear in each case: invective poetry of the dangerously aggressive kind. Catullus most likely thought Archilochus to have invented the metrical form and so the genre of *iambos*. When Catullus speaks of iambs he does so to invoke "iambic" Archilochus as a code model for his own performance of masculine aggression.[46] Let us review the three instances.

Poem 54 details the physical abnormalities of three persons probably connected with Caesar or Pompey or both. The text is corrupt and difficult to interpret. After an apparent gap, the poem ends with the two lines: "you will once again be angry at my *iambi*, though they don't deserve it, O one and only general" (*irascere iterum meis iambis | immerentibus, unice imperator*, 54.6–7).[47] The "general" is clearly Julius Caesar, addressed with the same words (reversed, to fit the iambic metre) at 29.11, and it seems most likely that Poem 54 refers specifically to that earlier poem. If so, then *iambi* can be construed here (and here alone in the corpus) as referring to a poem actually written in an iambic metre.

Working backwards through the poems, the second appearance of *iambi* comes at Poem 40:

---

[44] See 56–7 above.

[45] A fragment contains a fourth occurrence, cited at 189 below.

[46] See Newman (1990) 43–74 on the ἰαμβικὴ ἰδέα in Catullus, also Puelma Piwonka (1949) 331–3. On ἴαμβος as a thematic designation before it was ever the name of a metrical form, see Dover (1964) 185–90, West (1974) 22, Nagy (1976) and (1979) 243–52.

[47] Others mark the end of Poem 54 at the previous verse, counting these lines as a separate poem or fragment (so, most recently, Thomson [1997]).

Quaenam te mala mens, miselle Rauide,
agit praecipitem in meos iambos?
quis deus tibi non bene aduocatus
uecordem parat excitare rixam?
an ut peruenias in ora uulgi?
quid uis? qualubet esse notus optas?
eris, quandoquidem meos amores
cum longa uoluisti amare poena.   (Poem 40)

Miserable little Ravidus, what mental instability
is pushing you head first into my iambics?
What god, offended by improper prayer,
is stirring you to a fight that's pure derangement?
What do you want? Celebrity at any price?
That's what you'll get, since you've decided to love
a love that's mine, at a price you won't stop paying soon.

Establishing the presence of Archilochus as code model here requires no elaborate argument, since this is one of the very few places in Catullus' text where we can point to Archilochus' real presence as an exemplary model, active in the text of the poem as well as the text of the persona.[48] The extant Archilochian intertext is from an epode addressed to Lycambes, the jilting father-in-law-to-be:

πάτερ Λυκάμβα, ποῖον ἐφράσω τόδε;
  τίς σὰς παρήειρε φρένας
ᾗς τὸ πρὶν ἠρήρησθα; νῦν δὲ δὴ πολὺς
  ἀστοῖσι φαίνεαι γέλως.   (Archil. 172 W)

Old papa Lycambes, just what were you thinking here?
Who unhitched the hinges of your brains?
They used to fit together. But now you're a big
joke to everybody in the city.

It was Scaliger who first remarked that Poem 40 is "altogether similar" (*omnino simile*) to the Archilochus fragment. Scaliger possessed only the fragment's first two lines.[49] There already the

---

[48] The other notable instance is Poem 56 (*o rem ridiculam.*) and Archil. fr. 168 West. See Newman (1990) 195–6.

[49] Hendrickson (1925) 156. Most commentators agree that the similarity is too striking to be other than a genuine allusion. Fordyce (1961) ad loc. is unconvinced, but it seems fair to say that Fordyce's is a critical stance particularly inhospitable to what is most Archilochian, wine-drinking, and "iambic" in Catullus.

points of kinship are striking, at levels of speaking stance, theme, diction, and even "melopoeia." Both poems accuse their victim of derangement by taking that condition as an established fact and wondering aloud, rhetorically, what could have caused it (Catullus' *quis deus* seems to explicate Archilochus' τίς: the divine agent of an "inspired" madness). Both poems open by addressing the victim directly (Λυκάμβα, *Rauide*) with a contemptuous term of mock pity (*miselle*) or respect (πάτερ). And both poems intensify that contempt by the epithet's inclusion in a pounding alliterative series (πάτερ, ποῖον, ἐφράσω, παρήειρε, φρένας; *mala, mens, miselle, meos, iambos*). Add the second pair of Archilochian lines and the similarity is more striking still. Both poems point to the victim's wrecked reputation in his community (ἀστοῖσι, *ora uulgi*), and in so doing, both appear to invoke (Catullus again more explicitly) the ancient Indo-European blame poet's power to adjust an individual's reputation and community standing. Both poems are thus performative, in the strictest Austinian sense: both poems designate or "dub" their victims as laughably mad by the speech act that is the poem itself.[50] Lycambes is a "laughingstock" (γέλως) to the townspeople because Archilochus finds him so, and Ravidus' unsavory celebrity has been guaranteed and memorialized by the poetic performance that is Poem 40. Precisely because of the Catullan poem's performativity, it seems fair to take the *iambi* into which Ravidus has been pushed head first as the verses of Poem 40 itself, Phalaecian in metre but "iambic" by the Archilochian sting they personate.

A further piece of evidence (once again from a Greek author postdating Catullus) strengthens the argument that by *iambi* in Poem 40 Catullus means "Archilochian invective." Lucian's *Pseudologistes* begins with an explicit invocation of the Archilochian mode so closely resembling the situation of Poem 40 that scholars have been tempted to apply this passage by triangulation to a restoration of the Archilochus fragment:[51]

τὸ δὲ τοῦ Ἀρχιλόχου ἐκεῖνο ἤδη σοι λέγω, ὅτι τέττιγα τοῦ πτεροῦ συνείληφας. καὶ σὺ δή, ἔφη, ὦ κακόδαιμον ἄνθρωπε, τί βουλόμενος ποιητὴν λάλον παροξύνεις ἐπὶ σεαυτὸν αἰτίας ζητοῦντα καὶ ὑποθέσεις τοῖς ἰάμβοις; (Lucian, *Pseudol.* 1)

---

[50] Austin (1962).   [51] See esp. Hendrickson (1925).

That famous saying of Archilochus is just what I'm saying to you now: you've "grabbed hold of a cicada by the wing." "You poor madman," he said, "what do you hope to accomplish by stirring up, against *you*, a poet who loves to talk and is on the lookout for grievances and subjects for his iambs?"

It is impossible to say whether Lucian's quip about the invective poet's iambic chip on the shoulder reflects lost material from the epode to "papa Lycambes" (or some other poem of Archilochus), or lost material from the intervening centuries of Archilochus' reception, chiefly in Hellenistic poetry and criticism. In either case, however, the tradition reflected here by Lucian is likely to have been known to Catullus and so points again toward the "pre-existing form" of an "iambic," specifically Archilochian, mode of hypermasculine aggression familiar enough that Catullus could invoke it with a subtle gesture.

The remaining occurrence of *iambi* belongs to a Catullan poem already discussed here in detail.[52] In Poem 36, Lesbia's vow as reported by the Catullan speaker had been to burn the "worst poet's choicest writings" (36.6–7) if Catullus would be reconciled to her and leave off "brandishing" or "hurling" his "fierce iambs." Lesbia is here portrayed as "talking back," responding to Catullus' "iambic" blame poetry by a performance of her own verbal wit, a performance that Poem 36 attempts to turn back upon Lesbia and so reestablish Catullus' mastery. The poetic representation of a woman responding to a poet's verbal attack upon her reputation was not a Catullan innovation. Catullus and his contemporary readers will have known such epigrams as this one, attributed tentatively to Meleager and spoken in the personae of Lycambes' daughters, who were said to have been driven to suicide along with their father by Archilochus' invective shaming.[53] Their words rise with measured dignity from the grave:

---

[52] See 75–80 above.

[53] The preceding epigram in the Anthology, of Dioscorides (*AP* 7.351), similarly personates Lycambes' daughters on the same theme. It is impossible to say how "biographical" or "fictional" Archilochus' poems, and the stories attached to them, are. Lycambes is probably a "meaningful name" (West [1974] 23–30), as is perhaps Neobule ("she who changes her mind"). But as Irwin (1998) points out, a meaningful name can be coined and attached to a real person. Irwin suggests that Archilochus criticism may have drawn too stark a dichotomy between biography and fiction. In any case, I think the comparative material from the previous chapter is enough to suggest the social verisimilitude of the Archilochus narrative in the context of a small Mediterranean community.

Δεξιτέρην Ἀίδαο θεοῦ χέρα καὶ τὰ κελαινὰ
ὄμνυμεν ἀρρήτου δέμνια Περσεφόνης,
πάρθενοι ὡς ἔτυμον καὶ ὑπὸ χθονί· πολλὰ δ᾽ ὁ πικρὸς
αἰσχρὰ καθ᾽ ἡμετέρης ἔβλυσε παρθενίης
Ἀρχίλοχος· ἐπέων δὲ καλὴν φάτιν οὐκ ἐπὶ καλὰ
ἔργα, γυναικεῖον δ᾽ ἔτραπεν ἐς πόλεμον.
Πιερίδες, τί κόρησιν ἐφ᾽ ὑβριστῆρας ἰάμβους
ἐτράπετ᾽, οὐχ ὁσίῳ φωτὶ χαριζόμεναι;   (*AP* 7.352)

By the right hand of Hades, by the black bed
of Persephone, we do solemnly swear: we are
virgins, most truly, even beneath the earth.
Archilochus in his bitterness spewed bluster
of abuse upon our maidenheads. He turned lovely
verse to unlovely matter: to war on women.
Muses, why did you turn ravaging iambs
upon maidens? Why grant an unholy man your favor?

Lycambes' daughters show Archilochus' "poetics of manhood" in its grimmest light. "Ravaging" is not a strong translation for the act of *hubris* wrought by his poetry, through the performative, aesthetic excellence of poetic charm granted by the Muses to their soldier-squire.[54] The poetic aggression of his iambic shafts, it is not excessive to say, has raped and murdered the daughters of Lycambes.[55]

While Poem 36 cannot be said to "allude" to this epigram, the two poems resonate intertextually, by the common theme of a woman defending herself against poetic abuse, and by two prominently shared tropes: one on the paradoxical distinction between ethical "goodness/badness" and performative "being good/bad at" (ἐπέων δὲ καλὴν φάτιν οὐκ ἐπὶ καλὰ | ἔργα; *electissima pessimi poetae | scripta ... pessima puella*, 36.6–7, 9), and another on invective

---

[54] The speakers of this poem seem in the final couplet to recall the famous boast of Archilochus' sphragis: "I am the squire (θεράπων) of Lord Ares, and I possess by knowledge the Muses' lovely gift" (1 West). See discussion of this epigram, and of *AP* 7.351 as well, in Irwin (1998) 180–1.

[55] The epithet ὑβριστής seems to reflect an ancient critical commonplace about the expression of sexual desire in Archilochus. Compare Critias' remark that Archilochus had characterized himself as ὑβριστής (175–6 above), and also the ethical condemnation of Maximus of Tyr: "To Archilochus' desire I say no thanks: it's violent" (Ἀρχιλόχου ἔρωτα, ὑβριστὴς γάρ, χαίρειν ἐῶ, Archil. 295 West = Max. Tyr. 18.9, p. 230, 10 Hobein).

iambs as weapons of physical violence (ὑβριστῆρας ἰάμβους; *truces uibrare iambos*, 36.5). Just as the Hellenistic epigram presupposes knowledge of Archilochus' poetry as part of its reader's "competence" – and probably incorporates more of that poetry by specific reference than we can see – so Poem 36 invites its reader to cast about in the collection for a specific piece of Catullan abuse toward Lesbia as the narrative motor of its dramatic situation. A few candidates present themselves – Poem 58, for instance, and perhaps *si optima fias* ("if you should become good as good can be," 75.3) in the epigrams could be thought to recall this poem's *pessima puella* – but none is more memorable, and none more harshly damning, than the only instance preceding Poem 36 in the corpus: Poem 11 to Furius and Aurelius. Here again it is possible to argue that this "final farewell" (to whose finality a Catullan reader does well to give the same credence she puts in his lover's oaths), this unforgettable instance of Catullus at his most Catullan, owes rather more of its rhetorical and "lyrical" power to archaic Greek modes of invective than is commonly recognized.

The attribution of the following epodic fragment is disputed between Archilochus and Hipponax:

> κύμ[ατι] πλα[ζόμ]ενος·
> κἀν Σαλμυδ[ησσ]ῷ γυμνὸν εὐφρονε [
>   Θρήϊκες ἀκρό[κ]ομοι
> λάβοιεν – ἔνθα πόλλ’ ἀναπλήσαι κακὰ
>   δούλιον ἄρτον ἔδων –
> ῥίγει πεπηγότ’ αὐτόν· ἐκ δὲ τοῦ χνόου
>   φυκία πόλλ’ ἐπέχοι,
> κροτέοι δ’ ὀδόντας, ὡς [κ]ύων ἐπὶ στόμα
>   κείμενος ἀκρασίῃ
> ἄκρον παρὰ ῥηγμῖνα κυμα .... δου·
>   ταῦτ’ ἐθέλοιμ’ ἂν ἰδεῖν,
> ὅς μ’ ἠδίκησε, λ[ὰ]ξ δ’ ἐπ’ ὁρκίοις ἔβη,
>   τὸ πρὶν ἑταῖρος [ἐ]ών.
>   (P. Argent. 3, fr. 1.1–16 = Hippon. 115 W)[56]

... driven off course by a wave;
and then at Salmydessos I hope
Thracians with mohawks get him when he's
naked, not a friendly face in sight,

---

[56] West attributes the epode to Hipponax. Diehl (1922) had assigned it to Archilochus.

and there he'll have a bellyful of pain,
eating the bread of slavery
and frozen stiff with cold.
Clumps of seaweed from the saltwater
should cling to him, his teeth should
chatter as he lies face down
like an incontinent dog
at the edge of the crashing sea,
[vomiting] a wave. And I should be there
to see it, to see the man who did me wrong,
the man who trampled on his promise,
the man who was my friend before.

The passage from rage to lament owes much of its effect, and much of its psychological verisimilitude, to its stunning abruptness. Both those affects, of course, modulate the speaker's self-righteous indignation, with the nostalgic grief at abandonment put forward as the implicit justification for the invective redress. The Catullan speaker ends Poem 11 by modulating through precisely the same keys:

pauca nuntiate meae puellae
    non bona dicta.

cum suis uiuat ualeatque moechis,
quos simul complexa tenet trecentos,
nullum amans uere, sed identidem omnium
    ilia rumpens;

nec meum respectet, ut ante, amorem,
qui illius culpa cecidit uelut prati
ultimi flos, praetereunte postquam
    tactus aratro est.   (11.15–24)

Take a message to my girl. It isn't long.
It isn't pretty.
Tell her she should fare well with her fuckers,
taking them on three hundred at a time,
giving good love to no one and busted groins to everyone,
every time.
Tell her she shouldn't look for love from me,
the way it was before. My love is fallen
the way a flower falls on the edge of a field: the plow
touches, and plows on.

The Dioscorides epigram already mentioned has Lycambes' daughters deftly refuting Archilochus' charges in a manner to suggest that his poems on them had similarly toggled between invective attacks on their modesty and expressions of grief at rejection and loss:

ἀλλὰ καθ᾽ ἡμετέρης γενεῆς ῥιγηλὸν ὄνειδος
φήμην τε στυγερὴν ἔφλυσεν Ἀρχίλοχος.
Ἀρχίλοχον, μὰ θεοὺς καὶ δαίμονες, οὔτ᾽ ἐν ἀγυιαῖς
εἴδομεν οὔθ᾽ Ἥρης ἐν μεγάλῳ τεμένει.
εἰ δ᾽ ἦμεν μάχλοι καὶ ἀτάσθαλοι, οὐκ ἂν ἐκεῖνος
ἤθελεν ἐξ ἡμέων γνήσια τέκνα τεκεῖν.   (*AP* 7.351.5–10)

... but Archilochus babbled terrific slander
and ill report against our family name.
By all the gods and spirits, we never saw Archilochus
in the streets, or in Hera's great temple precinct.
If we really *were* "wantons" and "scoundrels," we daresay
the man would never have wanted us to bear
his legitimate children.

If the middle couplet here cited (lines 7–8) reflects something in Archilochus' poetry – and it is hard to see its point if it does not – then a specific Archilochian intertext may underlie the Catullan speaker's claim at Poem 58 that Lesbia is doing nasty things with Romans in "streetcorners and alleyways" (58.4).

Catullus' poetic reception of Archilochus, his personation of an Archilochian mode of manhood, is woven of three separate threads, all of them largely mysterious to us: (1) the text of Archilochus' poetry, as Catullus read it and construed an Archilochian persona from it; (2) Catullus' knowledge of the Hellenistic (and earlier Roman) critical and literary reception of Archilochus available in his time; and, no less importantly, (3) the extent to which Catullus's performance of selfhood would have been "Archilochian" even if he had never heard the name of Archilochus: many of the ancient Mediterranean social and cultural constructs embodied in archaic Greek invective would have seemed natural and transparent to Veronese Catullus. These three strains make for the possibility of a rich "mapping" of Archilochian significance onto Catullus' poetry, and onto his poetic persona. It is precisely its richness that makes it difficult to explicate with precision.

A final speculation. It is remarkable that the daughters of Lycambes, at *AP* 7.352.8, take the Muses to task for granting favor to "an unholy man" (οὐκ ὁσίῳ φωτὶ). Doubly remarkable, since we now know from the Mnesiepes inscription that Archilochus had an important cultic role at Paros during his life (some have speculated that he was a priest of Demeter; he was in any case palpably ὅσιος), and we know further, from the same source, that in death he was honored alongside the gods, presumably as a hero (and so only marginally a φώς).[57] Might this epigram reflect a line of Hellenistic critique from the Callimachean water-drinkers to the effect that Archilochus' wicked tongue sat ill inside so sanctified a head?[58] If so, then Poem 16, again to Furius and Aurelius, may present a further instance of Catullus "being Archilochus," this time in a distinctly different mode. As Daniel Selden's brilliant reading of that poem has shown, the Priapic threat on which it begins and ends (*pedicabo ego uos et irrumabo*, "I'll fuck your hole, I'll fuck your little face," 16.1, 14) performatively exposes its two victims, and the reader of the collection as well, to the penetrative ferocity of the aggressive acts it names.[59] This poem most amply merits the epithet given by the (personated) daughters of Lycambes to Archilochian invective: Poem 16's hendecasyllabic Phalaecians are "ravaging" and indeed "raping" iambs (ὑβρισ-τῆρες ἴαμβοι). And yet it is at the center of this poem that Catullus lays claim, astonishingly, to a personal purity of life that seems all out of keeping with the lubricious "salt" of this and other poems, and with his gleefully sleazy accounts of himself:

> nam castum esse decet pium poetam
> ipsum, uersiculos nihil necesse est.   (16.5–6)

> See, the holy poet must keep his life pure.
> His *life.* His occasional verses labor under no such
> obligation.

[57] Burnett (1983) 17: "it is strikingly clear that antiquity did not regard Archilochus as a rebel or an iconoclast." For the Mnesiepes inscription and Sosthenes, see Tarditi (1968) 4–11 and Treu (1959) 152–4. On Archilochus as priest of Demeter, see Miller (1994) 25–6 and references there.

[58] The criticism would presumably have been meaningless to Archilochus and his contemporaries, but the priestly "holiness" of "the poet" seems to have been programmatic for Callimachus (e.g. *H.* 2.1–11), as it was to be for his Augustan imitators (Hor. *Carm.* 3.1, Prop. 3.1).

[59] Selden (1992).

In writing those lines, Catullus may have had before his eyes, and expected his reader to see as well, the most conspicuous example known to antiquity of a holy poet who wrote dirty poems.

HELLENISTIC DELICACY AND THE IMPORTANCE OF BEING CALLIMACHUS

If the presence of an Archilochian intertext in Catullus' poem-text and persona-text seems beyond controversy and has been admitted, in one formulation or another, by nearly every Catullan critic, the attempt to trace that presence's contours is inevitably in considerable measure a "readerly" enterprise. Catullus offers no poetic reference to Archilochus so explicit as to exclude all doubt. The presence of Callimachus, by contrast, is realized in Catullus' text richly and even, it seems, systematically. Two of the three mentions of Callimachus by (patronymic) name, roughly symmetrically arranged in our corpus, have already been discussed. A riddling one stands near the beginning of the polymetrics, in the second of the kiss poems.[60] A transparent one stands in the middle of the long poems, in the covering letter to the most explicit instance of Catullus' "being Callimachus," in his translation of an episode from the *Aetia*, a crucial intertext (and a crucially important translation as well) in the subsequent development of Latin poetry.[61] The third and final mention comes in the last poem of the corpus. It is here that the speaker most clearly and self-allusively invokes Callimachus as the code model of a very particular mode of male friendship, and it is here that he cuts the neatest binarism between the mode of "being Callimachus" on one side, and an iambic or Archilochian mode of invective aggression on the other.

Poem 116, the closing epigram of our corpus, is also the last in a series of seven invectives addressed to Gellius.[62] By its programmatic theme – the poem promises abuse of Gellius to come – it has often been read as making bookends with Poem 1's dedication to Cornelius Nepos, and reasonably so.[63] Further, by the opera-

---

[60] Discussion at 151–2 above.

[61] On Poem 66 and Latin love elegy, Puelma (1982).

[62] The other six are Poems 74, 80, and 88 through 91. Their addressee, if Wiseman (1974) 119–29 is right, was no inconsiderable personage: L. Gellius Publicola, grandson of a consul and consul himself in 36 BCE.

[63] Macleod (1973). Also see Dettmer (1997) 222–6 with references there.

tion of a readerly desire to make these poems tell a story (Janan's point, and Miller's as well, about the "Lesbia cycle"), Poem 116 has regularly been placed at the Gellius cycle's narrative beginning, since it merely threatens abuse, while the six previous epigrams have already given performances of an abuse so outrageous that it is hard to see what poetic threats Catullus has left to make.[64] Under a rhetorical reading, however, rather than a narrative one, these poems in their received order can be seen to trace a psychologically satisfying arc, in a recognizably Archilochian mode: aggression gives way to a grieving indignation put forward, climactically and analeptically, as that aggression's justifying motive.[65] After the charges of fellating Victor (in Poem 80, already discussed) and of incest with all the women in his family, comes Poem 91, in which Catullus seems to give the narrative background motivating this most relentless round of invective salvos in the entire corpus. Here the speaker reveals that he too, like Gellius' uncle and father, has been betrayed and cuckolded.[66]

Poem 91 makes three self-allusively outrageous revelatory claims about Gellius' motivation. First, Gellius' choice of female erotic objects from among his own kin is psychologized as the result of something in his *ethos*, a very particular sort of "perversion": Gellius gets his *gaudium* (91.9) precisely from the criminality (*culpa ... aliquid sceleris*, 91.10) of his incestuous acts. Second, Catullus claims to have thought his own love safe from Gellius because she was no relation to him (*quod matrem nec germanam esse uidebam*, 91.5), and so no paternal prohibition could be transgressed by Gellius in having her.[67] The third claim, taken together with the second, gives this epigram its flash of comic performative brilliance: Gellius, Catullus implies, has beaten a path to *gaudium* with Catullus' beloved by likening the act of seducing her to one of incest. This Gellius has accomplished through construing the relation between himself and Catullus as a bond of friendship so close and holy, so like a bond of kinship, that betraying it can afford Gellius a bit of the

---

[64] So most recently Thomson (1997) ad loc.

[65] See 182–3 above.

[66] On Poem 80, see 157–8 above. In Poem 90 the object of Catullus' love remains unindicated, but the language of the poem makes Lesbia by far the most likely choice.

[67] Incest, in its Greco-Roman construction, seems to have been in this sense more "homosocial," in that its horror lay far more in its cuckolding of the father (and mixing generations) than in the modern version, which places the chief point of taboo aversion in the kinship of the two persons physically involved.

old obscene thrill (his supply of unseduced kinswomen having perhaps been exhausted): "and though I was joined to you in considerable intimacy (*usu*), I hadn't thought that would be sufficient
cause for you. You counted it sufficient: that's how much you get
off on crime of every kind" (91.7–10).

The emotional focus of Poem 91's speaker is thus centered not
upon anguish at loss of the unnamed beloved, but rather upon the
friendship between the two adult males and that friendship's betrayal. Lesbia, if she is the beloved in question, is thus once again
relegated to a status of importance secondary to the "homosocial"
one. In the next and final poem to Gellius, the beloved's existence
is forgotten entirely, and the speaker's message announces and
justifies his shift from friendship to enmity in a way comparable
to Herzfeld's Glendiots, and even more closely comparable to an
iambic maxim of Archilochus: "I know how to be a friend to a
friend. I also know how to be an enemy to an enemy: by harming
him with my mouth, like an ant."[68] By a performative play on two
senses of the verb *mittere* – to "send" poems (as letters) but also
to "hurl" them (like weapons) – enmity and friendship between
men are characterized as two modes of epistolary commerce. The
one whose imminent delivery Catullus promises Gellius, as due
punishment, is invective, iambic and Archilochian. The one whose
loss Gellius is implicitly invited to mourn as his lost opportunity
to enjoy a charmed and charming friendship with (a suddenly
clean-handed) Catullus, appears, remarkably, to consist in "being
Callimachus":

> Saepe tibi studioso animo uenante requirens
>   carmina uti possem mittere Battiadae,
> qui te lenirem nobis, neu conarere
>   tela infesta meum mittere in usque caput,
> hunc uideo mihi nunc frustra sumptum esse laborem,
>   Gelli, nec nostras hic ualuisse preces.
> contra nos tela ista tua euitabimus acta,
>   at fixus nostris tu dabis supplicium.   (Poem 116)[69]

---

[68] Herzfeld (1985) 16, see 60–2 above. Archilochus: ἐπίσταμαί τοι τὸν φιλέοντα μὲν
φιλέειν, | τόν δ' ἐχθρὸν ἐχθαίρειν τε καὶ κακοστομέειν | μύρμηξ (fr. 23.14–6 West).

[69] A difficult received text here. I follow Thomson (1997) except in the first verse, where I
read V with Mynors (Thomson accepts Guarinus' *studiose*, disambiguating the verse's
syntax with minimal alteration of meaning).

> So many times I've cast about, my heart's gone
> hunting for how I could send the scholar that you are
> some songs of Battus' son to make you be kind
> to me, and make you stop trying to send
> hostile shafts whizzing toward my head.
> This task I've set myself is hopeless. I see that now.
> I see my prayers have meant nothing here.
> Every shaft you aim at me, I'll dodge.
> But mine will hit. You'll give me satisfaction.

The entire poem tropes on the physicality of poetry's effect, for good or ill, upon its addressee. Catullus' search for poetic inspiration is likened to the hunt (116.1), his stated aim in sending "songs of Battus' son" is to "soften" Gellius (116.3), and the rest of the poem has the two poets battling like gladiators or Homeric champions, with Catullus the certain victor. The final verse may be compared thematically with an iambic trimeter of Archilochus, a one-verse fragment probably referring to Lycambes (ἐμεῦ δ᾽ ἐκεῖνος οὐ καταπροΐξεται, "he won't get off unpunished by me," 200 West), and with a Phalaecian fragment of Catullus (*at non effugies meos iambos*, "but you won't escape my iambs," fr. 3).[70] This same verse's ambiguous scansion, as either a dactylic pentameter or a "comic" iambic trimeter, may thus point not so much to Catullus' future mime-writing career (Wiseman's suggestion) as to his ability, now fully demonstrated, to write both poetry of tender delicacy and iron-tipped "iambs," and to write both kinds of poetry in a multiplicity of poetic forms.[71]

That Poem 116 programmatically announces Catullus' ability to perform in two very different poetic modes, presented as "deliberately contrasted alternatives," has seemed evident to many readers of the poem.[72] Further, to call the hypermasculine and aggressive mode threatened in Poem 116 and performed in the earlier Gellius poems "Archilochian" (in the sense of code model, at the very least) and "iambic" (in the sense that Catullus himself gives the word) hardly seems overbold. But in what sense and to what extent can Callimachus really be claimed to function for Catullus as code model of the opposite mode? Given his well-known defense

---

[70] Newman (1990) 45–6 argues for an Archilochian model for Poem 116.
[71] Wiseman (1985) 188–9, 56–7 above.
[72] Macleod (1973) 305.

of himself, in the *Aetia* prologue, against the malicious gaze (βασκανία) of the rivals and critics he calls "Telchines," given his representation, in the hymn to Apollo, of the god giving envy (φθόνος) a good swift kick, and given that he composed not only a collection of *Iamboi* but also a poem named after a coprophagous bird (*Ibis*) and filled, it seems, with elaborate curses, Callimachus might seem an odd choice for the eponym of an "anti-iambic" delicacy pressed to the point of effeminacy. One might respond by pointing out that this is precisely what Catullus seems to evoke by each mention of Callimachus' name in the corpus, and that the images surrounding those mentions, by their operation in other Catullan poems, appear to have a similar force. But the suggested objection deserves a fuller answer.

Our text of the apologia against the Telchines in the *Aetia* prologue is incomplete, but well enough preserved to give the flavor of Callimachus' speaking stance.[73] The Telchines are first characterized as "ignorant and no friends of the Muse" and later addressed as a "race knowing how to waste away in its heart" (the text is damaged here).[74] After the well-known statement of his aesthetic program come the hardest extant words Callimachus has for the Telchines:

> ... ἐνὶ τοῖς γὰρ ἀείδομεν οἳ λιγὺν ἦχον
> τέττιγος, θ]όρυβον δ᾽ οὐκ ἐφίλησαν ὄνων.
> θηρὶ μὲν οὐατόεντι πανείκελον ὀγκήσαιτο
> ἄλλος, ἐγὼ δ᾽ εἴην οὐλαχύς, ὁ πτερόεις,
> ἆ πάντως, ἵνα γῆρας ἵνα δρόσον ἦν μὲν ἀείδω
> προίκιο]ν ἐκ δίης ἠέρος εἶδαρ ἔδων,
> αὖθι τὸ δ᾽ ἐκδύοιμι, τό μοι βάρος ὅσσον ἔπεστι
> τριγλώχιν ὀλοῷ νῆσος ἐπ᾽ Ἐγκελάδῳ.
> ... Μοῦσαι γὰρ ὅσους ἴδον ὄθματι παῖδας
> μὴ λοξῷ, πολιοὺς οὐκ ἀπέθεντο φίλους.
>   (Call., *Aetia* 1, fr. 1.29–38 Pfeiffer)

> ... for I sing to those who love the cicada's
> tenor chirp, not the braying of asses.[75]

---

[73] On the question of whether Callimachus gave the *Aetia* a "second prologue" in a later edition, see Cameron (1995) 104–32 and references there.
[74] νήιδες οἳ Μούσης οὐκ ἐγένοντο φίλοι ... τήκειν ἧπαρ ἐπιστάμενον (Call. *Aet.* 1 fr. 1.2, 8 Pfeiffer).
[75] τέττιξ (see *LSJ* s.v.) is a common designation for a poet.

Others may intone like the long-eared beast.
Me, I should like to be "the slight," "the winged,"
yes, and learn to feed my song on food
of dewdrops, freely given of air divine,
and cast off tattered age: age weighs on me
like the three-cornered isle on Enceladus the monster.
... when once the Muses have looked upon a child
not unkindly, they do not reject him, now grey, as a friend.

The speaker's abuse of his anonymous critics is no harsher than what educators in every century before the twentieth doled out to their students. Considerably less harsh, in fact, since Callimachus never calls the Telchines asses outright, preferring instead to pass quickly to a self-characterization as a "dainty" cicada-poet sipping dewdrops out of the divine air and enjoying the Muses' lasting friendship.

Envy's unpleasant conversation with Apollo at the end of *Hymn 2* casts the Callimachean speaker in a similar light. The poet's purity and sanctity is again symbolized by water, and his outright rejection of blame poetry is here rendered fully explicit:

ὁ Φθόνος Ἀπόλλωνος ἐπ' οὔατα λάθριος εἶπεν·
'οὐκ ἄγαμαι τὸν ἀοιδὸν ὃς οὐδ' ὅσα πόντος ἀείδει.'
τὸν Φθόνον ὡπόλλων ποδί τ' ἤλασεν ὧδέ τ' ἔειπεν·
"Ἀσσυρίου ποταμοῖο μέγας ῥόος, ἀλλὰ τὰ πολλά
λύματα γῆς καὶ πολλὸν ἐφ' ὕδατι συρφετὸν ἕλκει.
Δηοῖ δ' οὐκ ἀπὸ παντὸς ὕδωρ φορέουσι μέλισσαι,
ἀλλ' ἥτις καθαρή τε καὶ ἀχράαντος ἀνέρπει
πίδακος ἐξ ἱερῆς ὀλίγη λιβὰς ἄκρον ἄωτον.'
χαῖρε, ἄναξ· ὁ δὲ Μῶμος, ἵν' ὁ Φθόνος, ἔνθα νέοιτο.
(Call., *H.* 2.105–13)

Envy whispered in Apollo's ear:
"When a poet's poems are less than oceanic
in scope, I remain less than impressed."
Apollo answered Envy with a kick and a lesson:
"Mighty the flood of Euphrates: what it drags
on its water is vastness of mud, vastness of trash.
It isn't just any water the Bee-priestesses carry to Deo.
No. It must be pure and undefiled, must inch
its slender stream from a holy fountain.
It must be, in a word, of the highest water."
Hail, gracious lord! and Blame begone: go live with Envy.

Probably the feature of this famous passage best remembered by most readers is Apollo's kick, partly because of its vividness and partly because recent classical scholarship, reacting to earlier unsympathetic portrayals of Callimachus as a milksop, has tended to emphasize the vigor of Callimachus' critical agonism.[76] The aesthetic program is indeed stated with vigor, but the victim of Apollo's physical and verbal aggression is not one of the poet's enemies (even under a pseudonym) but rather personified Envy.[77] By the time we arrive at the closing rejection of "Blame," the focus of the speaker has shifted, as in the *Aetia* prologue, to an implicit characterization of his own poetic performance as refined and delicate, stated this time in terms that Antipater of Thessalonica seems to have had specifically in mind in his epigram against the water-drinking poets.[78]

As for Callimachus' iambic and "invective" poetry, nothing that we know of the fragmentary *Iamboi* or the lost *Ibis* suggests that either poetic production ever gave voice to verbal aggression in anything like an Archilochian mode. The collection of *Iamboi* was introduced by its poet speaking not *in propria persona* but rather in the voice, and the "limping iambic" (choliambic, or scazon) metre, of Hipponax. The iambic poet second in the canon (after Archilochus) announces his return from the dead "bringing *iambos* that sings no battle against [his chief victim] Boupalos" (φέρων ἴαμβον οὐ μάχην ἀείδοντα | τὴν Βουπάλειον, *Iamb.* 1.3–4 Pfeiffer). An extant summary (*Diegesis*) of the collection tells us that Hipponax's opening speech continued with an injunction to the Alexandrian *philologoi* to put down their *odium philologicum* and treat each other kindly: a suggestion very much in keeping with Callimachus' stance in the passages already quoted, and comparable to nothing extant in Archilochus or Catullus, even at their most self-righteous and self-justifying.[79] It does appear from the *Diegesis* that Calli-

---

[76] "The cutting edge of Callimachus' iambs is not often acknowledged": Clayman (1980) 58, who points to a tradition of presenting Callimachus as "a most mild-mannered iambicist," beginning with F. Jung in 1929 and continuing as recently as Fraser (1972) 733. (In fact, Lafaye [1894] 6 had already spoken of "le délicat, le discret Callimaque.")

[77] Poem 95 on Cinna's *Zmyrna* and Volusius' *Annales*, perhaps inspired in part by this Callimachean passage, highlights Catullus' difference in this regard: Catullus, like Pope in the *Dunciad*, does not hesitate to name other poets by name and to heap the mud of shame on their heads.

[78] See 169–71 above.

[79] *Dieg.* 6.4–6: ἤκουσι δ' αὐτοῖς κατ' εἴλας ἀπαγορεύει φθονεῖν ἀλλήλοις. Clayman (1980) 14 finds in this "a most ironic spectacle." Kerkhecker (1999) 22 acknowledges that "the tone of Hipponax' address is less than flattering," but finds ultimately that Hipponax's "iambic criticism has turned conciliatory" (34).

machus' iambics included blunt and even indecent expression, but
there is no evidence that the diction was at any point other than
intricately learned, or that any living individual was subjected to
verbal abuse by name or under a recognizable pseudonym.[80]

The same can be said, and with even stronger conviction, of the
Ibis, though we possess not a single fragment of that poem. The
Ibis almost certainly contained elaborate and even dire curses, but
"curse poems" (ἀραί) seem to have been at the time a recognized
vehicle for performances of erudite wit.[81] That the poem's internal
addressee was either anonymous or nonexistent is strongly indicated by the oddly roundabout language in which the the text of
the Florentine scholia identifies Ἴβις as Apollonius of Rhodes.[82]
Still more persuasive on this point is Ovid's exilic poem of the
same name, in a passage echoing Poem 116 and making explicit
what Ovid read there, namely a positing of "being Archilochus"
and "being Callimachus" as polar opposite modes of male social
and poetic interaction:

> pax erit haec nobis, donec mihi uita manebit,
>   cum pecore infirmo quae solet esse lupis.
> prima quidem coepto committam proelia uersu,
>   non soleant quamuis hoc pede bella geri,
> utque petit primo plenum flauentis harenae
>   nondum calfacti militis hasta solum,
> sic ego te ferro nondum iaculabor acuto,
>   protinus inuisum nec petet hasta caput,
> et neque nomen in hoc nec dicam facta libello
>   teque breui qui sis dissimulare sinam.
> postmodo, si perges, in te mihi liber iambus
>   tincta Lycambeo sanguine tela dabit.
> nunc quo Battiades inimicum deuouet Ibin,
>   hoc ego deuoueo teque tuosque modo,
> utque ille historiis inuoluam carmina caecis,
>   non soleam quamuis hoc genus ipse sequi.
> illius ambages imitatus in Ibide dicar
>   oblitus moris iudiciique mei,

[80] Clayman (1980) 58: "Callimachus' *Iambi* are full of personal abuse directed at named *or more probably pseudonamed* individuals" (italics mine). Kerkhecker (1999) 59–60 compares Archilochus' "self-assertion against overwhelming odds" with Callimachus' "modest morality of social graces."

[81] On Hellenistic ἀραί, Watson (1991) 131–3. See also Williams (1996) 10–12 who, while conceding that even an erudite and witty curse can take delight in wounding gravely, finds it "hard to believe that Callimachus shared this sadistic relish."

[82] Cameron (1995) 225–6 and references there.

> et, quoniam qui sis nondum quaerentibus edo,
>   Ibidis interea tu quoque nomen habe,
> utque mei uersus aliquantum noctis habebunt,
>   sic uitae series tota sit atra tuae.   (Ovid, *Ibis* 41–64)

As long as I live, we'll have the kind of peace
that obtains between wolves and helpless sheep.
Still, I'll enter the fray in the verse form I've adopted,
though it's an unaccustomed rhythm for waging war.
And, just as a soldier's spear, before he's hot,
is pointed at the ground covered in yellow sand,
so I won't yet hurl at you with an iron point,
and a spear won't head straight for the head I hate.
Your name and your deeds will go unsaid in the present
book. I'll conceal your identity for now.
Later, if you keep it up, free-wheeling *iambus* will give me
shafts against you stained with the blood of Lycambes.
For now, I'll curse you and yours in the mode
the son of Battus used to curse Ibis, his enemy.
I'll wrap my poetry up, like him, in obscure
tales, though I'm unaccustomed to following this genre.
For having imitated his riddles in his *Ibis*
I'll be said to have forgotten my own character and
    judgment.
And since I don't yet give your name when people ask,
meantime take the name of Ibis yourself.
And just as my lines will have some darkness in them,
so may the whole course of your life be blackened over!

Ovid's characterization of *iambus* as "giving shafts soaked in blood" (*tincta … sanguine tela dabit*) openly alludes both to Poem 116 and also, by "window reference," to Catullus' own allusion there to the words spoken by fratricidal Romulus to his brother in Ennius (an anti-neoteric allusion to match the anti-neoteric prosody of the Catullan verse):[83]

> contra nos tela ista tua euitabimus acta
>   at fixus nostris tu dabis supplicium.   (116.7–8)

Every shaft you aim at me, I'll dodge.
But mine will hit. You'll give me satisfaction.

---

[83] On Catullus and Ennius, Zetzel (1983).

nec pol homo quisquam faciet impune animatus
hoc nec tu: nam mi calido dabis sanguine poenas
(Ennius, *Ann.* 94–5 Skutsch)[84]

No man, I swear, will dare this and his daring
go unpunished. Not even you: you'll give me payment
in warm blood.

Ovid seems clear on the point that Callimachus' Ibis remained unidentified and unidentifiable in that poem. He shows as well that a Roman poet could mention Archilochus' deadly iambs in the same breath as Callimachus without feeling impelled to concede that Callimachus too had composed iambs. As a self-proclaimed non-invective poet, Ovid claims that taking even the small first step of following Callimachus' non-defamatory *Ibis* represents a guilty departure from his own good-natured character. For Catullus, conversely, author of the fiercest invective extant in his language, Callimachean "invective" may have seemed to be no invective at all: there is arguably no *convicium* or even *maledictio* where no one is *maledictus*, no aggression where no addressee is exposed to the harm of public shame.

Poem 116's Catullus, then, as Ovid read him, placed Callimachus and Archilochus at opposite ends of a spectrum of manly performance, and what we know or can deduce about Callimachus' poetics of manhood at its most aggressive does not compel us to qualify the justice of that placement. At his most incomparably delicate, as in the following epigram, Callimachus comes very close to a self-allusive unwriting of Archilochus' personated *ethos*, a speaking stance always hubristic in aggressive public shaming and hubristic even in love itself:

Εἰ μὲν ἑκών, Ἀρχῖν', ἐπεκώμασα, μυρία μέμφου,
εἰ δ' ἄκων ἥκω, τὴν προπέτειαν ἔα.
Ἄκρητος καὶ Ἔρως μ' ἠνάγκασαν, ὧν ὁ μὲν αὐτῶν
εἷλκεν, ὁ δ' οὐκ εἴα τὴν προτέτειαν ἐᾶν.
ἐλθὼν δ' οὐκ ἐβόησα, τίς ἢ τίνος, ἀλλ' ἐφίλησα
τὴν φλιήν· εἰ τοῦτ' ἔστ' ἀδίκημ', ἀδικέω.
(Call., *Epigr.* 42 Pfeiffer = *AP* 12.118)

---

[84] First noted by La Penna (1956); see discussion at Newman (1990) 45–6.

> If I came of my will to your house in my cups, Archinus,
> blame me ten thousand blames. If against my will,
> let my rashness be.
> Unmingled wine and Desire compelled me. The one
> drew me on, the other would not let me
> let my rashness be.
> I came. But I never shouted your name, or your father's.
> All I did was post a kiss on your doorpost. If that
> is a crime, I am a criminal.

Eros and waterless wine have here combined forces to drive the Callimachean speaker to a gesture he calls "rash." By so calling it he only throws into sharper relief the restraint, the discretion, the "water-drinking" delicacy of this poetic performance of "mild frenzy."[85] The three extant Augustan elegists would attempt this provocatively delicate mode, with Tibullus perhaps the most successful personator of a "Callimachean" manhood, since he portrays himself as the least successful in love.[86] But Catullus had already shown his mastery of the manhood of delicacy in love, in several of the most exquisite poems of the corpus: the poem of the single kiss, for example, whose speaker describes himself spending over an hour "hanging on the cross" (99.4), begging forgiveness while Juventius purged his lips with water.[87] The poems of the many kisses (Poems 5 and 7 to Lesbia, and Poem 48 to Juventius), and the sparrow poems as well (Poems 2 and 3) can easily be read as partaking of the same mode. Under stress or threat, however, the Catullan persona does not defend himself with quiet Callimachean dignity, but instead snaps like a whip from one end of his spectrum of manly performance to the other, acting out Poem 116's Archilochian threat by hurling iambic shafts of aggression at rivals and enemies.

We might have expected a Callimachean manhood of delicacy to be somewhat differently gendered in the cultural context of Catullus' Rome than at Callimachus' Alexandria, and Catullus' text seems to reflect this. The other reference to "songs of Battus'

[85] Garrison (1978). προπέτεια ("rashness") is a technical term in Stoic moral philosophy (Diogenes Laertius 7.46).

[86] Tibullus, unlike Propertius and Ovid, never enjoys the embrace or even the conversation of either of his *puellae*.

[87] Ross (1969) 24 noted the "tone of delicacy" that distinguishes this most remarkable of the Juventius poems from the other epigrams. Many critics (e.g. Arkins [1982] 114–16) have focused on the poem's literary qualities as a way of "heterosexualizing" Catullus.

son" in the corpus depicts its speaker's farthest "retreat from the male" into a delicious, but also dangerously vulnerable, femininity. In "being Callimachus," Catullus "becomes a woman" more explicitly and insistently here than anywhere else in the corpus:[88]

> numquam ego te, uita frater amabilior,
> aspiciam posthac? at certe semper amabo,
>   semper maesta tua carmina morte canam,
> qualia sub densis ramorum concinit umbris
>   Daulias, absumpti fata gemens Ityli. –
> sed tamen in tantis maeroribus, Ortale, mitto
>   haec expressa tibi carmina Battiadae,
> ne tua dicta uagis nequiquam credita uentis
>   effluxisse meo forte putes animo,
> ut missum sponsi furtiuo munere malum
>   procurrit casto uirginis e gremio,
> quod miserae oblitae molli sub ueste locatum,
>   dum aduentu matris prosilit, excutitur,
> atque illud prono praeceps agitur decursu,
>   huic manat tristi conscius ore rubor.   (65.10–24)

Brother I loved better than life, will I never
see you again? Yet I'll love you forever still,
forever I'll sing my song to mourn your death,
a song like the Daulian bird's, under thick shade of branches,
lamenting the fate of her Itylus, taken away.
Even so, Ortalus, even in sorrow like this,
I send you this rendered song of Battus' son,
for fear you might think your words all vain,
entrusted to sweeping winds, drained from my heart
like the apple her suitor sent, a secret token,
that tumbles from the young girl's virgin lap
(poor thing forgot she hid it beneath the softness
of her cloak). Her mother arrives, she jumps, it's shaken
out, and as its floodtide rushes down,
red shame comes trickling up her saddened cheeks.

In this prologue to an episode translated from Callimachus' *Aetia* and spoken in the voice of a lock of hair cut from a queen's head, the Catullan speaker externalizes his two ruling and conflicting affective states in a pair of extended similes, both in the vehicle of

---

[88] "Retreat from the male": Stehle Stigers (1977). The "feminine" has of course been a central Catullan critical term since Havelock (1939).

a feminine persona and both evoking specifically Callimachean images. First, grief at his brother's death makes Catullus into the "Daulian bird," a woman metamorphosed into the nightingale, her cry an eternal lament for a murdered boy.[89] The tenderest expression of grief in Callimachus' poetry (as we possess it) ruminates, like Poem 65, on a life cut short, on a bereaved poet's lifelong memory, and on poetic remembrance as the only thing to escape death's oblivion:[90]

Εἶπέ τις, Ἡράκλειτε, τεὸν μόρον, ἐς δέ με δάκρυ
ἤγαγεν, ἐμνήσθην δ' ὁσσάκις ἀμφότεροι
ἥλιον ἐν λέσχῃ κατεδύσαμεν· ἀλλὰ σὺ μέν που,
ξεῖν' Ἁλικαρνησεῦ, τετράπαλαι σποδιή·
αἱ δὲ τεαὶ ζώουσιν ἀηδόνες, ἧσιν ὁ πάντων
ἁρπακτὴς Ἀίδης οὐκ ἐπὶ χεῖρα βαλεῖ.
          (Call. *Epigr.* 2[= *AP* 7.80].5–6)

Heraclitus, someone mentioned your death to me.
It brought back a tear and a memory: you and I
together, talking, putting the sun to bed, how many times.
You're ashes now, my friend from Halicarnassus,
ashes long since, and long since four times over.
But your nightingales live on. Hades shall not lay
on them his hand that grasps at everything.

Heraclitus' deathless "nightingales" (ἀηδόνες) are his poems, so called by Callimachus because poets, too, "sing" (ἀείδουσι).[91] Catullus, rather than naming the nightingale outright, hints at it (and at Callimachus as well, I think), spotlighting his own knowledge of the Greek word's etymology by a threefold etymological figure on the Latin equivalent (*carmina, canam, concinit*: 65.12–13),

---

[89] There were at least two ancient versions of the myth (see Zacharia [forthcoming]), and Catullus shows his knowledge of both of them. Interestingly, Parthenius (whom we are sometimes invited to imagine at Catullus' side helping him to construe his Callimachus) makes mention of the similar story of Harpalyce, at *Erotika Pathemata* 13. Parthenius lists Euphorion among the poetic sources of his tale. On Catullus, Callimachus and Parthenius, see Clausen (1964). On nightingales as symbols of maternal grief, Loraux (1990).

[90] Walsh (1990) finds a new kind of relation to the self expressed in this and similar Hellenistic poems.

[91] The etymology is probably correct (Chantraine s. v. ἀηδών). See Santini (1994) on the nightingale-poet speaker of Poem 65 (though without mention of the etymological figure).

and by specific reference to the moment in Homer, on the same mythological exemplum, where the etymology is made explicit:[92]

ὡς δ' ὅτε Πανδαρέου κούρη, χλωρηὶς ἀηδών,
καλὸν ἀείδησιν ἔαρος νέον ἱσταμένοιο
δενδρέων ἐν πετάλοισι καθεζομένη πυκινοῖσιν,
[*sub densis ramorum concinit umbris*, 65.13]
ἥ τε θαμὰ τρωπῶσα χέει πολυηχέα φωνήν,
παῖδ' ὀλοφυρομένη, Ἴτυλον φίλον   (*Od.* 19.518–22)

... as when Pandareus' daughter, the greenwood <u>nightingale</u>,
<u>sings</u> her beautiful song made new with the spring
and, sitting in the trees' thick foliage,
[Catullus: "she sings under thick shade of branches"]
warbling she pours out the rich tones of her voice,
dirging her <u>Itylus</u>, her dear dead son ...

In the second simile (65.15–24), the Catullan speaker's feminization is thrown into still sharper relief. Ortalus had asked Catullus to "bring forth sweet fruits of the Muses" (*dulcis Musarum expromere fetus*, 65.3) – perhaps a hinted suggestion of poetic composition as pregnancy – and Catullus had claimed not to be able to do justice to that request (the claim is itself a performance that does it honor), pleading his mind's "fluctuation" (65.4) in grief at the river of death whose waters have moistened his brother's pallid foot (65.5–6). At the poem's end the images of flowing and exuding are redoubled: Catullus sends "pressed out" or "forced out" (*expressa*, 65.16, a word regularly used of translating) songs of Battus' son to Ortalus lest Ortalus think his own "words" (*dicta*, 65.17) have "flowed out" (*effluxisse*, 65.18) of Catullus' mind.[93] Ortalus' *dicta*, as suggested earlier, probably had taken the form of a poetic epistle, an agonistic performance of the excellence of erudite delicacy, challenging and compelling its recipient to a response in kind. If so, then Ortalus' request is a material artifact – a tablet, or perhaps a

---

[92] The nightingale's common Latin name, *luscinus*, seems to have been excluded from the language's highest dictional registers. We have it attested once in Augustan literature, in Horace's *Satires* (2.3.245). Virgil, in a simile recalling both Homer and Catullus, calls the nightingale *philomela* (*G.* 4.511). Edwards (1994) 822–3 finds in the Virgilian passage a specifically Callimachean "impotence of song."

[93] On poetic composition as pregnancy and "forced out" songs of Battus, Fitzgerald (1995) 189–96.

bookroll like Phaedrus' speech of Lysias in the Platonic dialogue – and the reader is at liberty to imagine it nestled pleasurably in the speaker's lap. Poem 65's Catullus must not let the apple drop, by neglecting to bring forth poetry's fruits. Just as he warns his friends elsewhere, one traitorous lapse and the game is up, everything is known, and delicacy gives way to shame (and thence, in the logic of Catullan friendship, to aggressive shaming). The red moisture that irrigates the virgin's face, with its faint suggestion of a pubescence both psychological and physiological, very likely reflects a moment in the episode of Acontius and Cydippe from Callimachus' *Aetia*, though we are missing the part of the tale where the chaste Cydippe picks up the apple thrown by Acontius and naïvely reads aloud its inscribed oath, counted as binding, to wed Acontius.[94]

In Poem 65, then, two poetic emblems preside over Catullus' Callimachean feminization: a bird connected with death and grief and symbolizing poetry itself, and a deflowering apple both "thrown" and "sent" as love-gift (or love-charm) and epistle (*missum ... malum*, 65.19, opening the simile, has both meanings: the same pun on which Poem 116 turns).[95] It is difficult to attribute to chance the fact that our corpus opens (after the dedication) on a pair of poems formed around that same pair of images, and on a Catullan speaker similarly feminized, or perhaps better to say, similarly occupying the threshold between manhood and womanhood. The pair formed by Poems 2 and 3 begins and ends by apostrophizing Lesbia's pet sparrow.[96] Poem 2's first word seems to have given an ancient Catullan poetry book its name; Catullus' *passer* ("sparrow") is to that extent his poetry. Poem 2's speaker expresses the wish to play with the sparrow just as the girl does;

---

[94] Callimachus has already described Cydippe as "resembling the dawn" (*Aet.* 3. fr. 67.15 Pfeiffer). The *Diegesis* (7.1) assures us that Callimachus recounted the part of the tale where Cydippe reads the apple. Aristaenet. 1.10 ends his encapsulated version with Cydippe throwing down the apple "ashamed." And Ovid's letter from Acontius to Cydippe begins with Acontius remembering how, at the moment of reading his previous missive, Cydippe's "noble cheeks blushed in Diana's temple" (*Ep.* 20.5–6). The most likely source for the Ovidian Acontius's intertextual "memory" is this episode in the *Aetia*. See Johnston (1983) 389 n. 3 for references.

[95] Poem 95 suggests that Catullus' relations with Hortensius, the recipient of Poem 65 and the following *carmina Battiadae*, were not untroubled, though Poem 95's apparent negative judgment on Hortensius' poetry is very far in tone from the aggressive abuse of the poems against Gellius.

[96] The sparrow is Aphrodite's bird, prominently featured in Sappho (fr. 1.10 Lobel Page) drawing the goddess's chariot.

Poem 3 mourns the sparrow, now dead, in language that seems to recall Callimachus' epigram on Heraclitus:[97]

> at uobis male sit, malae tenebrae
> Orci, quae omnia bella deuoratis   (3.13–14)

> Curses on you, wicked darkness
> of Orcus: you devour everything beautiful.

Three verses at the end of the received text of Poem 2 are separated from it in our scholarly editions. Whether Poem 2b stands alone, is a fragment, or (as many distinguished critics have believed) completes Poem 2 as it stands without a lacuna or emendation, it is in any case a placement of the speaking subject in a feminine role nearly as striking as the one that ends Poem 65.[98] An apple once again effects simultaneously a virgin's passage to sexual awakening and the Catullan speaker's passage to the position of an unnamed virgin girl whose identity is left to the reader's learning:

> tam gratum est mihi quam ferunt puellae
> <u>pernici</u> aureolum fuisse malum,
> quod zonam soluit diu ligatam.   Poem 2b

> It gives me joy like the joy they say an apple
> made of gold once gave a <u>fast-running</u> girl:
> it undid her belt, tied tight too long.

The name of Atalanta, like Cydippe a virgin devoted to Artemis, appears once in our extant corpus of Callimachus, in the hymn to that goddess:

> ἤνησας δ' ἔτι πάγχυ <u>ποδορρώρην</u> Ἀταλάντην
> Call. H. 3.215

> ... and you [Artemis] wholeheartedly commended the <u>swift-footed</u> Atalanta

---

[97] The themes are however too commonplace for a direct Callimachean allusion to be posited with certainty. See Hezel (1932) 2–9 and Syndikus (1984) ad loc. on the Hellenistic traditions behind these poems.

[98] Notably Ellis (1876) ad loc., Lieberg (1962) 99–110 and Fitzgerald (1995) 42–4. On the other side are most Catullan editors, including most recently Thomson (1997), who is certain that Poem 2b cannot be part of Poem 2.

ποδορρώρην ("swift-footed"): the Callimachean epithet is exquisitely mellifluous diction, and recondite enough to require a scholiast's gloss. Catullus, in making a synonymous epithet (*pernici*, 2b.2) stand in the name's stead, may possibly have had Callimachus in mind.[99] If so, the antonomasia is erudite indeed, and its learning anything but sterile: where Callimachus had depicted Atalanta eternally frozen in the virgin goddess' entourage, Catullus shows her (and himself) at the precise moment of passage from Diana's sphere into Venus'; his Atalanta is called "fast-running" only when love has caught up with her and stayed her feet.

Poem 65, then, shares with the pair formed by Poems 2 and 3 a group of extraordinary images. Both feature small birds as poetic emblems connected with passage from life to death, and from death to (poetic) immortality.[100] Both feature apples as erotic emblems not only symbolizing but effecting passage from maidenhood to sexual awakening, and from the masculine to the feminine. Both poetic productions, finally, are self-allusive performances of their speaker's own *uenustas*, and both are placed under the special tutelage of Venus: Poem 3 begins on an address to Venus and the Loves, and to those among mortals possessing enough *uenustas* to savor its charm (3.1–2); Poem 65 prefaces a poem narrating a miracle wrought by Venus Zephyritis in answer to a new bride's sacrifice of a lock of hair, and laid (like Poem 65's apple) in a "chaste lap," the goddess's this time (66.56). The connection between a sky goddess and precisely this nexus of images and ideas – apples, small birds, sexual passage and gender liminality – was widespread throughout the Mediterranean, and far more ancient than Greco-Roman culture.[101] Catullus surely had access to that nexus of images, and to the goddess they accompany, by avenues other

---

[99] Though it seems plausible, direct Callimachean reference is once again impossible to establish. Before Callimachus, Hesiod (fr. 76.18–23 Merkelbach-West) had already recounted the episode, with "swift-footed" (ποδώκης) Atalanta forfeiting the race by stopping to pick up the third apple thrown by Hippomenes. Hezel's (1932) 3–4 discussion of Poem 2b adduces, instead of Callimachus or Hesiod, Meleager's epigram (*AP* 7.207) spoken in the persona of a rabbit.

[100] In Poem 65 the poetic immortality is made explicit (*semper maesta tua carmina morte canam*, 65.12). In Poems 2 and 3 less so, but if we take the arrangement of the first three poems to be Catullus' (and the reception evidence makes at least that much hard to deny), then the sparrow poems follow immediately upon a dedication whose speaker has prayed for the immortalization of his *Passer* ("Sparrow").

[101] Friedrich (1978).

than literary ones.[102] Still, I think it would have been as impossible
for ancient readers of Catullus as it is for us to think of those
images together in a poetic context without thinking of Sappho.
We have just enough of Sappho to sense her presence in these
poems (ancient readers of Catullus probably saw more) and
through that presence these poems are in turn linked for a reader
of the collection to the kiss poems to Lesbia and the Sappho
translation to Lesbia (and Calvus), all of them redolent with the
same delicacy that, as readers have long seen, blurs the gender of
their speaking subject.[103] But Catullus, remarkably, never refers to
Sappho directly by name in these poems. When he gives a name to
the code model personated in these and similar poems, agonistic
for all its delicacy and homosocial for all its "femininity," the
name he inscribes in his verses is that of the son of Battus.

CONCLUSION: CATULLAN SELF-PERFORMANCE AND
THE DOUBLE BIND OF ROMAN MANHOOD

The chance discovery celebrated in Benvenuto Campesani's epigram gave to modernity a book of poems whose reception history
presents an extraordinary case in more respects than one. The
poetry itself is of course something extraordinary, and the story of
Catullus' afterlife in the imaginations of great readers, and great
poets, does not appear to be speeding toward narrative closure.[104]
It is a story that can be told, if we choose, as sentimentally as the
warmest "romantic" version of the Lesbia novel. Whether we celebrate his "lyric genius" or resist it by bringing to light the lyric's
"unconscious" (and both those readings have taught us something
new about "our Catullus" and made him into something new), it
remains that the Catullan text, the fabric of poems and reception
woven together, continues widely to elicit (or compel) reader
responses of a very particular and passionate kind.

Certainly Catullus the "lyric darling" has no rivals among

---

[102] On erotic magic in the form of prayers to Aphrodite involving "apples" (fruits of other
kinds as well) thrown and birds crucified on the *iunx*, Faraone (1999) 64–80.
[103] On Sappho's presence in Poem 65 alongside that of Callimachus, Johnston (1983),
Edwards (1994).
[104] Among the great poets whose work has added lustre to Catullus' reception history I cite
the recent versions of Carson (2000).

Roman poets for the affections of lovers of (lyric) poetry outside classical scholarship. For much of the twentieth century, the old lyric voice, with its high decorum and rhetorical urgency, was largely a missing dictional register in Anglophone poetry, being replaced for the most part by "poetry of talk." And Catullus, so strangely and unthinkably, and in a way so unlike (for example) the Augustan poets, often seems to be giving us just that, to be talking to his reader, to *us*.[105] How much of this effect is individually, originally Catullus', and how much of it has to do with his moment in literary history and the conventions of the genres in which he wrote, is impossible to say. Calvus and the other "neoterics" are lost to us; Lucretius, whom Catullus probably knew, is a "contemporary poet" by the calendar alone. (And I suppose few will put forward Cicero's poetry for comparison.) Accident of history though it is, the empty sky into which he seems to rise has undoubtedly given special luster to Catullus' reputation among readers who take it that "originality" is central to the greatness of a great poet. Conversely, if we know very little about what Catullus' fellow poets were writing, his poetic production happens to coincide with one of the moments of antiquity about which we have the richest body of historical evidence. Late republican prosopography and the lure of the "conspicuous source" have clearly gone a long way toward "resurrecting" Catullus, injecting his *corpus* with a life partly his own and partly borrowed, to satisfy the curiosity that every reader (stern warnings against the "biographical fallacy" notwithstanding) feels toward a poet whose work has given genuine poetic pleasure.

If we extend the field to include Greek poets, we have to admit that Sappho's name far outshines that of her Latin translator, but it is precisely around her *name* that Sappho's modern reception history has gathered its sparkling brilliance. Paul Allen Miller is surely right that Catullus is "lyric" – a "consciousness" that we create and interact with through the act of reading – in a way that Sappho cannot be, for us. It may be true, and probably is true, that issues of oral performance and written collection situate Sappho's poetry on the other side of a clear divide from Catullus' in this regard. Still, a single complete poem and a series of (stunning)

---

[105] Horace, of course, gives us "poetry of talk" in the *Satires* and *Epistles*, but without the intensity and urgency of the "lyric."

fragments make too little Sappho to judge what effect a reading of
the Alexandrian edition in nine books (arranged editorially by
metre) might have operated on Catullus' own consciousness, and
whether we might be able to discern a "Sapphic consciousness"
present in her work, and reflected in the Catullan collection, if
only we possessed Catullus' Sappho.[106] Sappho and Catullus both
have labored all (long) modernity long under the weight of critics'
adulation. Romanticism made both poets original "geniuses."
Modernism made them both intensely "personal poets." Both lives
have been novelized, but in Sappho's case the distinction between
fictional novel and literary biography is simply harder to blur,
precisely because of our far greater ignorance of Sappho's poetry,
life, and historical and social context.[107]

While Havelock, writing between the world wars, was still romantic in many aspects of his sensibility, he had already satirized
the romantic version of the Catullus novel roundly enough to pre-
vent serious scholars from continuing that nineteenth-century tradition. If the romantic narrative novel had been put to flight from
Catullan scholarship, there was however still room for a novel of a
newer kind, a modernist psychological novel whose burden was
not the story of the life but rather the analysis of the self, of the
personality behind Catullus' "poetry of personality," as Quinn
called it. A modernist self, as unitary and eternally identical to
itself as the God of the schoolmen, was made to stand, transcendent, behind every poem as its unique *sujet d'énonciation* or "speaking subject" (those terms are of course anachronistic: at the time
one said simply Catullus, as opposed to "Catullus," or else "the
poet," as opposed to the "persona"). This self, though unchanging
in itself (even as it passed through the different phases of the Lesbia story), "revealed" itself, as transcendent things will, to greater
or lesser degree from one poem to the next. The result was a hierarchical signifying relation among the poems, and between the
poet's self and his poetic self-revelation. Criticism, while ostensibly explicating it, had in fact authored this relation. Inevitably
that critical explication took the line that allowed us (literary
Catullans) to continue celebrating our Catullus as a secret double

---

[106] On the "double consciousness" that emerges from our reading of Sappho, see the suggestive remarks of Winkler (1990) 162–87.
[107] On Sappho's social context, see Hallett (1979).

agent, our man in Rome: Catullus, long before us, had seen with our eyes and critiqued with our conscience everything that was ethically indigestible in the Roman society whose artifacts we had learned not to take as normative, but still consumed with appetite and love.

The project of questioning modernism's "sweet fiction" of a unitary self began earlier in the twentieth century than is sometimes imagined, and it has taken more forms than those of deconstructionism and the rest of the Anglophone reception of continental poststructuralist thought. Sociology and comparative anthropology offer a language for describing a self that is performed rather than revealed, and I have invoked Herzfeld's model of a "rhetoric of the self" as one way of demodernizing ancient Catullus. And well before postmodern theorists were proclaiming the dispersal into fragments of the modernist speaking subject, postmodern poets were performing that dispersal. I have pointed to some of their work here as offering alternatives to modernist ways of reading Catullus and of thinking and speaking about his poetry, ways based on assumptions that remain unquestioned and even invisible so long as "romantic" is the name given to every mode of reading that has fallen out of critical favor. Modernist constructions of Catullus have given us, I think, the richest critical insights into his poetry to date. Surely the best way to honor those insights is to critique them in turn, and to locate them in their own cultural and historical context.

Catullus, in the reading I have offered, is the name of a performed self, or rather, the name of a performance of multiple selves. The central issue at stake in male self-performance in Catullus' Rome seems by all accounts to have been that of masculinity itself, construed and established through a discourse that I have chosen here to describe in terms of Herzfeld's "poetics of manhood." Every period of Greco-Roman antiquity was in fact characterized, so far as we can tell, by competitive public performance of manhood among adult elite males (probably among non-elite males as well, but we possess few records of their interaction).[108] At Rome, however, and perhaps especially at the end of

---

[108] Performance of manhood in the ancient (Greek-speaking) Mediterranean has been the object of a number of recent studies. See esp. Gleason (1995), Stehle (1997) and Bassi (1998).

the republic, this competition appears to have been rendered problematic and even paradoxical by the coexistence of two divergent models of masculine behavior: one connected ideologically with Roman *mos maiorum* and that can be roughly characterized as archaic and "traditional," the other connected with the prestige of Hellenistic culture and more or less "cosmopolitan."[109] It is tempting, from the present vantage point, to read this coexistence as a dichotomy between public (society) and private (individual), and that is so for at least three reasons: (1) partly because our sources often seem to invite us to read it that way (think of Cicero's characterizations of the "private lives" of Catiline, Piso and Marc Antony); (2) partly owing to recent and ongoing debates concerning the referents of the terms "sex," "gender" and "sexuality"; (3) and partly, I think, because of the recent history of our own cultural reception of classical antiquity. We are still very close in time to a historical moment in which writers and educators could put forward Roman *prisca uirtus* ("old time manliness"), even in its most rebarbative aspects, as normative or at least admirable. The other "style of manhood" (the one attached to the name of Callimachus in the last chapter, with its positive valuation of delicacy and refinement) is conversely one that most contemporary readers of ancient poetry can be counted on to find sympathetic, or at least more sympathetic than the first. (Eventually the poetics of that manhood must come under ethical question too, as Fitzgerald has shown, for its exclusionary elitism – not that we could have expected to find an ancient egalitarianism in Catullus.)[110]

It is appealing, in consequence, to imagine that Roman orators and politicians felt subjectively oppressed and straitjacketed by the cultural obligation to personate constantly a manhood of iron under the public scrutiny of myriad eyes searching out every chink in the armor, and it is appealing to imagine that leisure time pursuit of Hellenistic high culture afforded the Roman elite man not only what Cicero calls *relaxatio mentis* ("mental relaxation"), but also the opportunity to give way privately to a softness that the public gaze disallowed as unseemly. What makes this picture difficult to

---

[109] A synchronic dichotomy. As Feeney (1998) 50–2 points out, Rome is "never pre-Greek": the Rome that negotiates its difference from and likeness to Greek culture *is* the "authentic Rome."

[110] Fitzgerald (1995) 87–113

sustain, I think, is chiefly the fact that the marks of "effeminacy" for which our sources show Roman nobles upbraided are in every case marks that have been discerned in the course of public self-presentation and public performance, often performance of the most deliberate and orchestrated sort.[111] Of course it will some-times have been a slip in word or gesture that provoked the charge of effeminacy, but I seriously doubt, for example, that the young Julius Caesar wore his belt loose in public or scratched his head with one finger through absentmindedness, or for any other reason than that of drawing attention to himself and the exquisite excel-lence of his *cultus* ("grooming"): an instance of what Herzfeld calls the self-allusive "stylistic transformation" of an ordinary act. In Caesar's case (and his is the most conspicuous case), we possess anecdotes in which the pursuit of high culture and all the things that, in Caesar's own words, "effeminize the manly spirits" is made to function simultaneously as a mark of both kinds of excel-lence.[112] By writing his grammatical treatise on analogy with Gal-lic missiles whizzing past his head, or again, by calmly composing poetry when captive on a pirate ship speeding toward Bithynia (or rather, by claiming to have done these things), Caesar personates, in a single gesture, both Hellenistic high cultural excellence and "Roman" heroic fearlessness in the face of death.[113]

To the extent that possession of Hellenistic high culture was part of the symbolic capital for which Roman elite men competed, the performance of that excellence was subject at every point to the compulsion of competitive challenge. It was no less subject at every point to negative valuation and aggressive mockery as a de-fection from proper Roman manly behavior. For the man who played at this level, in an agonistic interaction where judges were also fellow competitors, there was no comfort zone at the center in which he could be certain of being sufficiently cultivated without exposing himself to accusations of effeminacy, or of being suffi-ciently rough-hewn without incurring the charge of rusticity.[114]

---

[111] All our sources, of course, including Cicero's letters, are public rather than private records. It can be argued that there is in fact no "private life," as moderns understand the term, in premodern societies. See, e.g., Ariès (1962).

[112] *BG* 1.1.

[113] Fronto 221N; Plut. *Caes.* 2.5.

[114] Edwards (1993) 96 on the "delicate balance" between rusticity and effeminacy in Roman elite performance of manhood.

Many Roman elites may have nonetheless tried to occupy that center. Perhaps Cicero did, but even Cicero's manhood came under critique.[115] Catullus' response to this double bind, however, the response he performs in his poems, was resolutely centrifugal and (to borrow a term from postmodern psychology) "multiphrenic": the speaking subjects of his poems occupy, from moment to moment, stances of hypermasculine aggression, of provocatively effeminate delicacy, and stances at points in between or located on other axes. The real Catullus, the Catullan self, is not to be found outside the poems, or behind them like a masked actor, or above them like a puppeteer. He is all of the speaking subjects of all the poems, and none of them. Catullus' honor, his manhood (and its poetics), can be said to rest upon that proposition. To gainsay it, to grasp at the Catullus who says "I" and try to halt his oscillation, is to step into the subject position of the addressees of Poem 16.

I close on a pair of anecdotal performances of Roman manhood, both preserved in Aulus Gellius, that seem to me paradigmatic. The first story, one that Catullus' older contemporaries could have witnessed, strikes me as instructively different from anything in his poems, while the second, set two centuries after his death, seems remarkably, illustratively Catullan. These vignettes illustrate, respectively, a charge of effeminacy and a charge of rusticity, the dangers at the two opposite ends of elite Roman manhood's double bind. Each shows a Roman man under stress of what Latin calls *lacessatio* or *compellatio*: an aggressive challenge whose addressee is thereby compelled to a performance of wit on his feet and on the defensive. The protagonist of the first anecdote is Cicero's oratorical rival Hortensius, almost certainly Catullus' sometime friend, the recipient of the Callimachean translation with its exquisitely delicate covering letter (Poems 65 and 66), and the recipient as well of Catullus' literary criticism, in the form of a highly unfavorable comparison of Hortensius' prolific verse production to Cinna's newly published masterpiece, the slender and exquisite culling of nine harvests (Poem 95).[116] Hortensius' antagonist, named Torquatus, is presumably an elder kinsman of the

---

[115] Brutus in Tacitus, *Dial.* 18.5.
[116] We are missing the single verse that would show precisely how aggressive a sting Hortensius received at Catullus' hands.

bridegroom whose wedding Catullus was to celebrate in Poem 61. Torquatus' aggression takes the form of an *interpellatio* ("interruption"), a speech genre of which Catullus gives us an example directed anonymously at Calvus and poetically memorialized in Poem 53.[117] The insult hurled at Hortensius, however, cuts far deeper, into the marrow of his manhood, and the narrator, unlike Catullus in Poem 53, gives us the injured party's riposte. It is a surprising one:

... Q. Hortensius omnibus ferme oratoribus aetatis suae, nisi M. Tullio, clarior, quod multa munditia et circumspecte compositeque indutus et amictus esset manusque eius inter agendum forent argutae admodum et gestuosae, maledictis compellationibusque probris iactatus est multaque in eum, quasi in histrionem, in ipsis causis atque iudiciis dicta sunt. sed cum L. Torquatus, subagresti homo ingenio et infestiuo, grauius acerbiusque apud consilium iudicum, cum de causa Sullae quaereretur, non iam histrionem eum esse diceret sed gesticularium Dionysiamque eum notissimae saltatriculae nomine appellaret, tum uoce molli atque demissa Hortensius, 'Dionysia,' inquit, 'Dionysia malo equidem esse quam quod tu, Torquate, ἄμουσος ἀναφρόδιτος ἀπροσδιόνυσος.' (Gell. 1.5.2–3)

Quintus Hortensius was more celebrated than nearly all the orators of his generation, Cicero excepted. He dressed with great elegance, arranging his toga with precise care, and his hands were given to flashy, broad gestures when he delivered a speech. Because of this he was the butt of verbal abuse, challenging insults and humiliating remarks. Even during court proceedings, people often shouted out at him as though he were a stage actor. Once, however, during the trial of Sulla, Lucius Torquatus (a person of rather uncouth and inelegant manners) began, during the jurors' deliberation, to insult Hortensius in more serious and bitter terms, saying that he was not just a stage actor but a mime actor, and calling him "Dionysia" (the name of a dancing girl). At this, Hortensius answered in a soft, meek voice: "Dionysia indeed. Torquatus, I would rather be Dionysia than be what you are [and here Hortensius breaks into Greek]: no friend of the Muses, of Aphrodite, of Dionysus."

Of this "soft voice, a rare one, that spoke for sophistication, philhellenism and even the feminine," Catharine Edwards has suggested that "this may be as close as a Roman text ever comes to suggesting virility need not be the ultimate virtue."[118] Indeed, Hortensius' words are very far from what we might have expected. Very far too, I think, from anything in Catullus. Catullus goes

---

[117] *di magni salaputium disertum* (53.5) See Thomson (1997) ad loc. and references there.
[118] Edwards (1993) 97.

considerably deeper than Hortensius into a performance of "the feminine," certainly, but never under stress: when challenged, he never fails to show his colors, to give an opponent the lie Priapic. Edwards' sympathetic reading is not only understandable, it is difficult not to share. At the same time, I do not think that Hortensius is calling off the Roman manhood game, or even refusing to play it, but merely defending himself with the only arrow in his quiver.[119] We know far less about Hortensius than did Gellius and his second-century readers, but we do know that he was the descendant of an old (plebeian) Roman family, that he was a friend of Lucullus and shared Lucullus' reputation for gourmandise, and that, although a chief proponent of the florid "Asiatic" style in oratory, he had never studied in the east.[120] If Gellius' anecdote is authentic, it gives the sense of Hortensius' self-performance as being far more of a piece, far less volatile and multiphrenic – far more "modernist," if you will – than that of Catullus, whose friendship he seems not to have kept. In that sense, Hortensius' response seems remarkable precisely for its refusal to *play* with Torquatus, and with his audience, by raising a laugh at Torquatus' expense: it is hard to imagine Cicero's Caesar Strabo holding up Hortensius' mild wordplay on Dionysia/Dionysus as an example of the clever riposte. Hortensius' (and the narrator's) point about Torquatus' boorishness stands, but Hortensius' response surprises precisely by its lack of *uenustas* in the sense of verbal wit.[121] One could even speculate that Hortensius' choice of a soft and meek voice under stress was one more of strategy than of "personality": if his formation in the Greek language and its culture was somewhat second-hand and so subject to the accusation of pose, then leaving himself open to the charge of effeminacy may have been a wiser course than answering an insult "like a man," momentarily personating the home-grown ethos of his hirsute ancestors, and so running the risk of cutting the figure of a bumpkin in expensive clothes who likes to pretend that his Greek is better than his Latin, but whose true character is brought instantly to the surface by a prick to the skin: material for a particularly

---

[119] For another instance of a charge of effeminacy answered by impersonating the feminine, see the anecdote on Egilius' *bellus* riposte at Cic. *de Orat.* 2.277.

[120] *OCD* s.v. Hortensius.

[121] In the anecdote to follow, Hortensius' poetry is criticized by learned Greek readers on precisely this count.

delightful (to an audience) and memorable form of the charge of rusticity, and one that might have been harder to shrug off than Torquatus' name calling.

A charge of rusticity deftly deflected provides the action of the second anecdote. Its protagonist is Antonius Julianus, a professor of rhetoric and a friend and teacher of Gellius (who tells us he was present as well). Earlier books of the *Attic Nights* have given their reader proofs of Julianus' affability and discretion, his wide learning, and his ready wit. The setting is a young equestrian's birthday party at his villa outside Rome, where a chorus of boys and girls has just given an exquisite performance of some Anacreontic poems. The Greeks among the symposiasts take the opportunity to make trial of Julianus' *uenustas* by subjecting it to the aggressive sting of Greek sympotic raillery, calling him nothing more or less than a barbarian. By the end of the vignette, interestingly, Julianus' voice will have become as gentle as that of Hortensius, and almost certainly more pleasing to the ear, since by now he is no longer on the defensive but is instead delighting and instructing his audience with poetic recitation, having sent the charge of rusticity to rout through a fiercely erudite, allusive and self-allusive, outrageously kaleidoscopic performance of aggression and delicacy:

... Graeci plusculi, qui in eo conuiuio erant, homines amoeni et nostras quoque litteras haut incuriose docti, Iulianum rhetorem lacessere insectarique adorti sunt tamquam prorsus barbarum et agrestem, qui ortus terra Hispania foret clamatorque tantum et facundia rabida iurgiosaque esset eiusque linguae exercitationes doceret, quae nullas uoluptates, nullamque mulcedinem Veneris atque Musae haberet; saepeque eum percontabantur, quid de Anacreonte ceterisque id genus poetis sentiret et ecquis nostrorum poetarum tam fluentes carminum delicias fecisset, 'nisi Catullus' inquiunt, 'forte pauca et Caluus itidem pauca. nam Laeuius implicata et Hortensius inuenusta et Cinna illepida et Memmius dura ac deinceps omnes rudia fecerunt atque absona.'

Tum ille pro lingua patria tamquam pro aris et focis animo irritato indignabundus 'cedere equidem' inquit 'uobis debui, ut in tali asotia atque nequitia Alcinoum uinceretis et sicut in uoluptatibus cultus atque uictus, ita in cantilenarum quoque mollitiis anteiretis. sed ne nos, id est nomen Latinum, tamque profecto uastos quosdam et insubidos ἀνα-φροδισίας condemnetis, permittite mihi, quaeso, operire pallio caput, quod in quadam parum pudica oratione Socraten fecisse aiunt, et audite ac discite nostros quoque antiquiores ante eos, quos nominastis, poetas amasios ac uenerios fuisse.'

Tum resupinus capite conuelato uoce admodum quam suaui uersus cecinit Valerii Aeditui, ueteris poetae, item Porcii Licini et Q. Catuli, quibus mundius, uenustius, limatius, tersius Graecum Latinumue nihil quicquam reperiri puto. (Gell. 19.9.7–10)

A fair number of Greeks were present at this symposium, persons of affable elegance and no small learning in our own literature. They began to challenge and taunt Julianus the rhetor, calling him a barbarian outright, a hayseed out of Spain, [no declaimer (*declamator*) but] merely a shouter (*clamator*) whose "eloquence" was rabid and vicious, and pointing out that he taught oratorical proficiency in a language possessing no pleasures, no sweet blandishment of Venus and the Muse. And they asked him, again and again, for his critical opinion on Anacreon and other poets of that sort, and whether any of our own poets at all had composed such mellifluous delicacies in verse, "except," they added, "for Catullus, but only a few of his pieces, and Calvus, but likewise only a few. For Laevius' compositions are tortured, Hortensius' charmless, Cinna's unpolished, Memmius' harsh and, in a word, all of them are primitive and discordant."

Then Julianus, indignant, his animus piqued in defense of his native tongue, as though it were his altars and hearths under attack, said: "Yes, I suppose I would have to concede to you that in point of *asotia* (profligacy) and depravity you would surpass Alcinous, and that you would excel at the effeminate softness of your little songs just as much as in your "pleasures" of grooming, diet and mode of living. Even so, to keep you from condemning us – the Latin name, I mean – on the charge of *anaphrodisia* (insensitivity to Aphrodite), as an uncivilized lot of dolts, pray allow me to cover my head with my cloak, as they say Socrates did in making a certain improper speech, and then listen, and learn that there have been poets among us, older than the ones you named, who were friends of Love and of Venus."

Then, reclining back, his head veiled, in the sweetest voice imaginable he sang verses of the old poet Valerius Aedituus, and verses of Porcius Licinius and Quintus Catulus. And I think that nothing can be found, in Greek or in Latin, to surpass them in refinement, charm, polish and concision.

I can point to no moment of self-performance more Catullan than this in Latin literature after Catullus. Catullus is of course among the poets whose "honor" Julianus is defending, though the Greek antagonists, themselves knowledgeable readers of Latin poetry, have set Catullus aside as a special case (already), along with his friend Calvus. When Julianus first begins to speak, it seems that he has already lost the encounter – as in the African-American "Dozens" – by being the first to give in to rage and lose his cool (the narrator conspires with his character against us to create this impression, allowing us to share the internal audience's surprise when it is proved false).[122] His first Hellenizing reference, the word *asotia* (immediately glossed by the Latin *nequitia*, "depravity") is construable as typically Roman moralizing bluster, the old line about decadence being a Greek invention and import. The reference to the Homeric Alcinous is slyer and subtler – picking up on his Greek interlocutors' use of the Epicureanism's central term (*uoluptas*, "pleasure"), Julianus invokes the commonplace of Alcinous, and the golden verses on the pleasures of the table spoken at his palace by the "gluttonous" Odysseus, as forerunners of that philosophy – but its content is still ultimately not out of keeping with a Roman orator at his most forensically moralizing.

With the dramatic business of the pallium comes the flash, the stylistic transformation and stroke of (lyric) genius. The triclinium has fallen silent, with every eye fixed on the speaker whose face, whose persona, is about to be eclipsed. By recalling Socrates in the *Phaedrus*, Julianus has both invoked the most delicate (and culturally prestigious) of erotic contexts and simultaneously preempted every observation about his veiled head that wit might have devised (concerning, say, Roman augurs or virgin brides). He has also put himself, allusively and self-allusively, in the position of Poem 16's speaker, since he too will give voice to "impure speech" (*parum pudica oratione*) spoken with no loss or taint to his own impenetrable *pudicitia*.[123] Julianus is about to rise, or rather recline, to the defense of himself and the entire *nomen Latinum* (Catullus and Calvus partially exempted) on the charge of *anaphrodisia*: a boorish insensitivity to every delicate charm and choice delight of the honey-sweet gifts shared by the goddess and her son with those who can savor their taste. Hortensius had defended himself by turning the same charge, in the same terms, upon Torquatus. Catullus, of course, proclaims and performs his indemnity to the charge of *anaphrodisia* in some of the best known of his poems, and as the last chapter argued, several of those poetic performances of Hellenistic delicacy directly or indirectly invoke Callimachus as

---

[122] On the game of verbal abuse known as the "Dozens," see Levine (1977) 344–58.

[123] 16.7–8: *qui tum denique habent salem ac leporem, | si sunt molliculi ac parum pudici* ("[light verses] have salt and charm only when they are a bit soft (effeminate) and none too modest"). See discussion at Selden (1992) 484–5.

their code model. What Julianus proceeds to sing, in a "voice amazingly (how) sweet" (Gellius' grammar here calques on a Greek construction favored by Plato) is a series of Latin poems that gives us all but one of our entire extant corpus of erotic epigram before Catullus.[124] Julianus' performance, one that began with his *animus* (so it seemed, and indeed perhaps it was) irritated to hypermasculine aggression in the old Roman moralizing satiric vein, ends on a poem whose speaker laments an exquisitely helpless submission to love: his *animus* has run away like a fugitive slave, finding refuge in a beautiful boy. It is surely no accident that the last shameless words to fly from Julianus' lips behind the veil of shame perform their speaker's own delicate *uenustas* by personating a hapless lover's prayer to Venus: "What shall I do? Grant me, Venus, your counsel."[125] And I think it no accident that this last poem, Julianus' parting shot, is a Latin adaptation of an epigram by Callimachus.[126]

Julianus, like Catullus, could claim membership in three distinct and overlapping discursive communities: *nomen Latinum*, Hellenistic culture, and provincial origin (a province long and nobly romanized, it is true, but his Greek interlocutors found it good enough for throwing in Julianus' face). Cosmopolitan complexity of affiliation and identity, the rule rather than the exception for "Roman" poets, of course explains nothing of itself (and the search for the poet's psychogenesis, happily, has long since been called off). Still, Julianus' relation to his complex identity resonates interestingly with Catullus'. The standard anxieties and defensive aggressions of Roman manhood are palpably expressed by both speakers, but the fact of having (at least) "three brains," like Ennius, and liking it, seems have served both Julianus and Catullus well in poetic performance of manly excellence, an excellence, that is, that we are invited to view and applaud as an attribute not so much of the "man" as of the "maelstrom" of the poetic performance, the "acting out" of the "insane self."[127]

Kenneth Koch, a similarly three-souled postmodern American poet, gives such a performance:

---

[124] The other is preserved by Cicero at *N.D.* 1.79 (= Catulus 2 Courtney).
[125] *quid ago? da, Venus, consilium.* Gell.19.9.14.6 (= Catulus 1.6 Courtney).
[126] Call. *Epigr.* 41 Pfeiffer.
[127] On Ennius' *tria corda*: Gell. 17.17.

I have a bird in my head and a pig in my stomach
And a flower in my genitals and a tiger in my genitals
And a lion in my genitals and I am after you but I have a
    song in my heart
And my song is a dove
I have a man in my hands I have a woman in my shoes
I have a landmark decision in my reason
I have a death rattle in my nose I have summer in my brain
    water
I have dreams in my toes
This is the matter with me and the hammer of my mother
    and father
Who created me with everything
But I lack calm I lack rose
Though I do not lack extreme delicacy of rose petal
Who is it that I wish to astonish?
. . .
I have a knocking woodpecker in my heart and I think I have
    three souls
One for love one for poetry and one for acting out my insane
    self
Not insane but boring but perpendicular but untrue but true
The three rarely sing together take my hand it's active
The active ingredient is a touch
I am Lord Byron I am Percy Shelley I am Ariosto
I eat the bacon I went down the slide I have a thunderstorm
    in my inside I will never hate you
But how can this maelstrom be appealing? do you like
    menageries? my god
Most people want a man! So here I am

These verses, monstrously ithyphallic and just as monstrously tender, spell out a love poem, of course, and it is a love poem as outrageous as anything in our Catullus. The last two verses I cited are in their way the most outrageous of all. Certainly their estimation of what "most people want" is the least credible of the poem's assertions. The maelstrom, the menagerie, is in fact considerably more appealing than the man, whoever he may be, and every verse of the poem tells us that fact, performs it. The same, I think, could be said of the man from Verona. But then, a reader of Catullus needs no warning against the indirections of lovers, or of poets.

Works cited

Adams, James Eli (1995) *Dandies and Desert Saints: Styles of Victorian Masculinity*. Ithaca

Adams, J. N. (1982) *The Latin Sexual Vocabulary*. Baltimore

Adler, Eve (1981) *Catullan Self-Revelation*. New York

Ahearn, Barry (1983) *Zukofsky's "A": An Introduction*. Berkeley

Allen, Archibald (1984) "Catullus' Little White Dove [29.8]," *Maia* 36:243–5

Anderson, W. S. (1964) *Anger in Juvenal and Seneca*. Berkeley

André, J.-M. (1966) *L'otium dans la vie morale et intellectuelle romaine, des origines à l'époque républicaine*. Paris

Andrews, Bruce and Charles Bernstein, eds. (1984) *The L=A=N=G=U=A=G=E Book*. Carbondale, Ill.

Antin, David (1972) "Modernism and Postmodernism: Approaching the Present in American Poetry," *boundary 2: A Journal of Postmodern Literature* 1:98–9, 109–12

Arditi, Jorge (1998) *A Genealogy of Manners: Transformations of Social Relations in France and England from the Fourteenth to the Eighteenth Century*. Chicago

Ariès, Philippe (1962) *Centuries of Childhood: A Social History of Family Life*. New York

Arkins, Brian (1982) *Sexuality in Catullus*. Hildesheim

Austin, J. L. (1962) *How To Do Things With Words*. Cambridge, Mass.

Austin, R. G. (1960) *M. Tulli Ciceronis Pro M. Caelio Oratio* (3rd edn). Oxford

(1968) "Ille ego qui quondam," *CQ* 18:107–15

Badian, Ernst (1977) "Mamurra's Fourth Fortune," *CP* 72:320–2

Bahti, Timothy (1996) *Ends of the Lyric: Direction and Consequence in Western Poetry*. Baltimore

Bakhtin, Mikhail (1981) *The Dialogic Imagination: Four Essays*. Austin

(1984) *Rabelais and His World*. Bloomington

(1986) "The Problem of Speech Genres," in *Speech Genres and Other Late Essays*. Austin. 60–102

Barchiesi, Alessandro (1984) *La traccia del modello: Effetti omerici nella narrazione virgiliana*. Pisa

Bardon, Henri (1943) *L'art de la composition chez Catulle*. Paris
Barthes, Roland (1970) *S/Z*. Paris (= [1974] *S/Z*. New York)
  (1973) *Le plaisir du texte*. Paris (= [1976] *The Pleasure of the Text*. London)
  (1977) *Roland Barthes* (trans. R. Howard). New York
Barton, Carlin A. (1993) *The Sorrows of the Ancient Romans: The Gladiator and the Monster*. Princeton
Bartsch, Shadi (1994) *Actors in the Audience: Theatricality and Doublespeak from Nero to Hadrian*. Cambridge, Mass.
Bassi, Karen (1998) *Acting Like Men: Gender, Drama, and Nostalgia in Ancient Greece*. Ann Arbor
Batstone, William (1993) "Logic, Rhetoric and Poesis," *Helios* 20:143–71
Bayet, Jean (1956) "Catulle, la Grèce et Rome," in *L'Influence grècque sur la poésie latine de Catulle à Ovide (Hardt Entretiens 2)*. Berne. 3–55
Beck, Jan-Wilhelm (1996) *"Lesbia" und "Juventius": Zwei libelli im Corpus Catullianum*. Göttingen
Belsey, Catherine (1980) *Critical Practice*. London
Benjamin, Walter (1974) "Über einige Motive bei Baudelaire," in R. Tiedemann and H. Schweppenhäuser (eds.), *Gesammelte Schriften*, vol. 1.2. Frankfurt. 605–53
Bidart, Frank (1997) *Desire*. New York
Bing, Peter (1988) *The Well-Read Muse: Present and Past in Callimachus and the Hellenistic Poets*. Göttingen
Blaiklock, E. M. (1959) *The Romanticism of Catullus*. Auckland
Blodgett, E. D. (1988) "Wiseman's Catullus: The Darkness Beyond the Window," *AC* 57:290–5
Bloom, Harold (1973) *The Anxiety of Influence: A Theory of Poetry*. Oxford
  (1975) *A Map of Misreading*. New York
  (1977) *Wallace Stevens: The Poems of Our Climate*. Ithaca
Booth, Joan (1993) *Latin Love Elegy: A Companion to Translations of Guy Lee with Introduction and Commentary*. Bristol
  (1997) "All in the Mind: Sickness in Catullus 76," in S. Braund and C. Gill (eds.), *The Passions in Roman Thought and Literature*. Cambridge. 150–68
Booth, Wayne (1974) *The Rhetoric of Fiction* (2nd edn). Chicago
Bossi, Francesco (1990) *Studi su Archiloco*. Bari
Bourdieu, Pierre (1972) *Esquisse d'une théorie de la pratique*. Geneva
  (1979) *La distinction: critique sociale du jugement*. Paris
  (1998) *La domination masculine*. Paris
  (1999) "The New Global Vulgate," *The Baffler* 12:69–78
Bradley, Keith (1994) *Slavery and Society at Rome*. Cambridge
Brooks, Peter (1984) *Reading for the Plot: Design and Intention in Narrative*. New York
Bruns, Gerald (1999) *Tragic Thoughts at the End of Philosophy: Language, Literature and Ethical Theory*. Evanston
Bryson, Norman (1990) *Looking at the overlooked: Four Essays in Still Life Painting*. London

Buchheit, Vinzenz (1959) "Catulls Dichterkritik in c. 36," *Hermes* 87:309–27 (= R. Heine [ed.], *Catull, Wege der Forschung* 308. Darmstadt [1975] 36–61)

(1976) "Catulls c. 50 als Programm und Bekenntnis," *RhM* 119:162–80

Burgess, Dana L. (1986) "Catullus c. 50: The Exchange of Poetry," *AJP* 107:576–86

Burnett, Anne Pippin (1983) *Three Archaic Poets: Archilochus, Alcaeus, Sappho.* Cambridge, Mass.

Burzachechi, M. (1962) "Oggetti parlanti nelle epigrafi greche," *Epigraphica* 24:3–54

Buss, Arnold H. (1961) *The Psychology of Aggression.* New York

Butler, Judith (1993) *Bodies That Matter: On the Discursive Limits of "Sex."* New York

Cage, John (1967) *A Year from Monday: New Lectures and Writings.* Middleton

Cairns, Francis (1972) *Generic Composition in Greek and Roman Poetry.* Edinburgh

(1973) "Catullus' *Basia* Poems (5, 7, 48)," *Mnemosyne* 26:15–22

Calinescu, Matei (1987) *Five Faces of Modernity.* Durham, N.C.

Calvino, Italo (1973) *Il Castello dei destini incrociati.* Torino (= [1977] *The Castle of Crossed Destinies.* New York)

Cameron, Alan (1976) "Catullus 29," *Hermes* 104:155–63

(1995) *Callimachus and His Critics.* Princeton

Campbell, P. Michael (1997) "The Comedian as the Letter Z: Reading Zukofsky Reading Stevens Reading Zukofsky," in M. Scroggins (ed.), *Upper Limit Music: The Writing of Louis Zukofsky.* Tuscaloosa. 175–91

Cantarella, Eva (1992) *Bisexuality in the Ancient World* (trans. C. Cuilleanáin). New Haven

Carson, Anne (1999) *Economy of the Unlost: Reading Simonides of Keos with Paul Celan.* Princeton

(2000) *Men in the Off Hours.* New York

Castronovo, David (1987) *The English Gentleman: Images and Ideals in Literature and Society.* New York

(1991) *The American Gentleman: Social Prestige and the Modern Literary Mind.* New York

Cenerini, Francesca (1989) *"O colonia quae cupis ponte ludere longo* (Catullus 17): Cultura e politica," *Athenaeum* 67:41–55

Chantraine, Pierre (1984–1990) *Dictionnaire étymologique de la langue grecque: histoire des mots* (4 vols.). Paris

Cheah, Pheng and Elizabeth Grosz (1998) "The Future of Sexual Difference: An Interview with Judith Butler and Drucilla Cornell," *Diacritics* 28:19–42

Cherniss, H. W. (1962) *"Me ex versiculis parum pudicum,"* in J. P. Sullivan (ed.), *Critical Essays on Roman Literature.* London. 15–30

Clack, J. (1976) *"Otium tibi molestum est* – Catullus 50 and 51," *CB* 52:50–53

Clare, R. J. (1996) "Catullus 64 and the *Argonautica* of Apollonius Rhodius: Allusion and Exemplarity," *PCPS* 42:60–88

Clausen, Wendell (1964) "Callimachus and Latin Poetry," *GRBS* 5:181–96

(1987) *Virgil's* Aeneid *and the Traditions of Hellenistic Poetry.* Berkeley

Clayman, Dee L. (1980) *Callimachus' Iambi* (Mnemosyne Suppl. 59) Leiden

Coarelli, F. (1983). "I santuari del Lazio e della Campania tra i Gracchi e le guerre civili," in *Les "bourgeoisies" municipales italiennes aux IIe et Ier siècles av. J.-C.* (Paris and Naples) 217–40

(1985) "Architettura e arti figurative in Roma: 150–50 a.C.," in P. Zanker (ed.), *Hellenismus in Mittelitalien (Abhandlungen der Akademie der Wissenschaften in Göttingen*, ser. 3 v. 97) 21–51

Connelly, Jill L. (2000) "Renegotiating Ovid's *Heroides.*" Diss., University of Chicago

Conte, Gian Biagio (1986) *The Rhetoric of Imitation: Genre and Poetic Memory in Virgil and Other Latin Poets.* Ithaca

(1994) *Genres and Readers: Lucretius, Love Elegy, Pliny's Encyclopedia.* Baltimore

Conte, Joseph M. (1991) *Unending Design: The Forms of Postmodern Poetry.* Ithaca

Copley, F. O. (1949) "Emotional Conflict and its Significance in the Lesbia-Poems of Catullus," *AJP* 70:22–40 (=K. Quinn [ed.], *Approaches to Catullus.* Cambridge [1972] 78–96)

Corbeill, Anthony (1996) *Controlling Laughter: Political Humor in the Late Roman Republic.* Princeton

Courtney, Edward (1993) *The Fragmentary Latin Poets.* Oxford

Crawford, J. (1994) *M. Tullius Cicero, the fragmentary speeches: an edition with commentary.* Atlanta

Creeley, Robert (1989) *Collected Essays.* Berkeley

Crook, J. A. (1967) "A Study in Decoction," *Latomus* 26:363–376

Crowther, N. B. (1979) "Water and Wine as Symbols of Inspiration," *Mnemosyne* 23:1–11

Culler, Jonathan (1981) *The Pursuit of Signs: Semiotics, Literature, Deconstruction.* Ithaca

Daniels [Kuntz], Marion L. (1967) "Personal Revelation in *Carmen* 64 of Catullus," *CJ* 62:351–6

Daube, D. (1948) "*Ne quid infamandi causa fiat*: The Roman Law of Defamation," *Atti del congresso internazionale di diritto romano e di storia del diritto* vol. III (Milan) 413–50

Davenport, Guy (1981) "Zukofsky," in *The Geography of the Imagination.* New York. 100–13

Degani, Enzo (1977) *Poeti greci giambici ed elegiaci: letture critiche.* Milan

de Jong, Irene J. F. (1987) *Narrators and Focalizers: The Presentation of the Story in the "Iliad."* Amsterdam

de Lauretis, Teresa (1998) "The Stubborn Drive," *Critical Inquiry* 24:851–77

de Man, Paul (1979) *Allegories of Reading.* New Haven
  (1984) *The Rhetoric of Romanticism.* New York
  (1986) *The Resistance to Theory.* Minneapolis
Dettmer, Helena (1997) *Love by the Numbers: Form and Meaning in the Poetry of Catullus.* New York
Devereux, G. (1970) "The Nature of Sappho's Seizure in Fr. 31 LP as Evidence of her Inversion," *CP* 20:17–31
Diehl, Ernst (1922) *Anthologia Lyrica Graeca.* Leipzig
Diels, Hermann and Walther Kranz, eds. (1937) *Die Fragmente der Vorsokratiker.* Berlin
Di Stasi, Lawrence (1981) *Mal Occhio: The Underside of Vision.* New Haven
Dover, Kenneth J. (1964) "The Poetry of Archilochus," in *Archiloque (Entretiens de la Fondation Hardt 10).* Vandœuvres-Geneva. 181–212
duBois, Page (1995) *Sappho Is Burning.* Chicago
Dubuisson, M. (1981) "Problèmes du bilinguisme romain," *Les Etudes Classiques* 49:27–45
Dumézil, Georges (1943) *Servius et la fortune: essai sur la fonction sociale de louange et de blâme et sur les éléments indo-européens du cens romain.* Paris
  (1969) *Idées romaines.* Paris
Dundes, Alan (1992) *Interpreting Folklore.* Bloomington
Dundes, Alan, et al. (1970) "The Strategy of Turkish Boys' Dueling Rhymes," *Journal of American Folklore* 83 (1970) 325–49
Dupont, Florence (1994) *L'invention de la littérature: de l'ivresse grecque au livre latin.* Paris
Edmunds, Lowell (1982) "The Latin Invitation Poem: What Is It? Where Did It Come From?" *AJP* 103:184–8
Edwards, Catharine (1993) *The Politics of Immorality in Ancient Rome.* Cambridge
Edwards, M. J. (1994) "Callimachus, Roman Poetry and the Impotence of Song," *Latomus* 53:806–23
Elias, Norbert (1994) *The Civilizing Process.* Oxford (= *Über den Prozess der Zivilisation* [1939] Basel. 2 vols.)
Eliot, T. S. (1950) *Collected Essays.* New York
  (1961) "The Three Voices of Poetry," in *On Poetry and Poets.* New York. 96–112
  (1975) "Hamlet," in F. Kermode (ed.), *Selected Prose of T. S. Eliot.* London. 45–9
Elliott, Robert C. (1982) *The Literary Persona.* Chicago
Ellis, Robinson (1876) *A Commentary on Catullus.* Oxford
Fantham, Elaine (1989) "Mime: The Missing Link in Roman Literary History," *CW* 82:153–63
  (1996) *Roman Literary Culture: From Cicero to Apuleius.* Baltimore
Faraone, Christopher A. (1999) *Ancient Greek Love Magic.* Cambridge, Mass.
Farrell, Joseph (1991) *Vergil's* Georgics *and the Traditions of Ancient Epic.* Oxford

Fedeli, Paolo (1972) *Il carme 61 di Catullo*. Freiburg

    (1991) "Il carme 17 di Catullo e i sacrifici edilizi," in *Studi di filologia classica in onore di Giusto Monaco*. Palermo. 707–22

Feeney, Denis (1998) *Literature and Religion at Rome: Cultures, Contexts and Beliefs*. Cambridge

Ferguson, John (1985) *Catullus*. Lawrence, Kansas

Ferrari, Walter (1938) "Il carme 51 di Catullo," *Annali della Scuola Normale Superiore di Pisa* 7:59–72 (= "Catulls Carmen 51," in R. Heine [ed.], *Catull, Wege der Forschung* 308. Darmstadt [1975] 241–61)

Fish, Stanley (1980) *Is There a Text in This Class?: The Authority of Interpretive Communities*. Cambridge, Mass.

Fitzgerald, William (1995) *Catullan Provocations: Lyric Poetry and the Drama of Position*. Berkeley

Fordyce, C. J. (1961) *Catullus: A Commentary*. Oxford

Foucault, Michel (1966) *Les mots et les choses: Une archéologie des sciences humaines*. Paris

    (1970) *The Order of Things: An Archaeology of the Human Sciences* (A translation of *Les mots et les choses*). New York

    (1979) "What Is an Author?" in Josue Harari (ed.), *Textual Strategies: Perspectives in Post-Structuralist Criticism*. Ithaca. 141–60

    (1980) *The History of Sexuality. Volume 1: An Introduction*. New York.

Fraenkel, Eduard (1957) *Horace*. Oxford

Fraistat, Neil, ed. (1986) *Poems in Their Place: The Intertextuality and Order of Poetic Collections*. Chapel Hill

Fraser, P. M. (1972) *Ptolemaic Alexandria* (vol. 1). Oxford

Fredricksmeyer, E. A. (1970) "Observations on Catullus 5," *AJP* 91:431–45

    (1993) "Method and Interpretation: Catullus 11," *Helios* 20:89–105

Frevert, Ute (1998) "The Taming of the Noble Ruffian: Male Violence and Dueling in Early Modern and Modern Germany," in P. Spierenburg (ed.), *Men and Violence: Gender, Honor, and Rituals in Modern Europe and America*. Columbus, Ohio. 37–63

Friedl, Ernestine (1961) *Vasilika, A Village in Modern Greece*. New York

Friedrich, Gustav (1908) *Catulli Veronensis Liber*. Leipzig

Friedrich, Paul (1978) *The Meaning of Aphrodite*. Chicago

Fry, Paul H. (1995) *A Defense of Poetry: Reflections of the Occasion of Writing*. Stanford

Frye, Northrop (1957) *Anatomy of Criticism*. Princeton

Fusillo, M. (1985) *Il tempo delle Argonautiche: Un' analisi del racconto in Apollonio Rodio*. Rome.

Gaisser, Julia Haig (1993) *Catullus and his Renaissance Readers*. Oxford

Garrison, Daniel (1978) *Mild Frenzy: A Reading of the Hellenistic Love Epigram* (Hermes Einzelschriften vol. 41) Wiesbaden

Geffcken, Katherine A. (1973) *Comedy in the "Pro Caelio." Mnemosyne*, suppl. 30. Leiden

Genette, Gérard (1980) *Narrative Discourse: An Essay in Method*. Ithaca
(1982) *Palimpsestes: la littérature au second degré*. Paris

Gill, Christopher (1988) "Personhood and Personality: The Four-*Personae* in Cicero, *De Officiis* I," *Oxford Studies in Ancient Philosophy* 6:169–99

Gilmore, David D. (1987) *Aggression and Community: Paradoxes of Andalusian Culture*. New Haven
(1990) *Manhood in the Making: Cultural Concepts of Masculinity*. New Haven

Giuffrida, Pasquale (1948) *L'epicureismo nella letteratura latina nel I secolo a. C* (vol. I): *Lucrezio e Catullo*. Turin

Gleason, Maud W. (1995) *Making Men: Sophists and Self-Presentation in Ancient Rome*. Princeton

Goffman, Erving (1959) *The Presentation of Self in Everyday Life*. Garden City, New York

Gold, Barbara K. (1999) "Which Juvenal? Performing Subjectivity," *APA* conference paper read 30 December. Dallas

Goldhill, Simon (1991) *The Poet's Voice: Essays on Poetics and Greek Literature*. Cambridge

Gowers, Emily (1993) *The Loaded Table: Representations of Food in Roman Literature*. Oxford

Granarolo, Jean (1957) "Catulle, ce vivant," *Annales de l'Académie du Var* 125:153–70
(1967) *L'Oeuvre de Catulle*. Paris

Greeley, Andrew M. (1995) *Religion as Poetry*. New Brunswick

Greenblatt, Stephen (1980) *Renaissance Self-Fashioning: From More to Shakespeare*. Chicago

Greene, Ellen (1998) *The Erotics of Domination*. Baltimore
(1999) "Re-figuring the Feminine Voice: Catullus Translating Sappho," *Arethusa* 32:1–18

Griffin, Jasper (1985) *Latin Poets and Roman Life*. London

Gruen, Erich S. (1990) *Studies in Greek Culture and Roman Policy*. Berkeley
(1992) *Culture and National Identity in Republican Rome*. Ithaca

Gunderson, Erik (1997) "Catullus, Pliny, and Love-Letters," *TAPA* 127:201–31

Gutzwiller, Kathryn (1998) *Poetic Garlands: Hellenistic Epigrams in Context*. Berkeley

Habinek, Thomas N. (1992) "Grecian Wonders and Roman Woe: The Romantic Rejection of Rome and Its Consequences for the Study of Roman Literature," in K. Galinsky (ed.), *The Interpretation of Roman Poetry: Empiricism or Hermeneutics?* Frankfurt. 227–42
(1998) *The Politics of Latin Literature: Writing, Identity, and Empire in Ancient Rome*. Princeton

Hallett, Judith P. (1978) "Divine Unction: Some Further Thoughts on Catullus 13," *Latomus* 37:747–8
(1979) "Sappho and Her Social Context," *Signs* 4:447–64 (= [1996] "Sappho and Her Social Context: Sense and Sensuality," in E.

Greene (ed.), *Reading Sappho: Contemporary Approaches*. Berkeley. 125–42)

(1996) "*Nec castrare velis meos libellos*: Sexual and Poetic Lusus in Catullus, Martial and the Carmina Priapea," in C. Klodt (ed.), *Satura Lanx: Festschrift für Werner A. Krenkel zum 70 Geburtstag*. Zürich. 321–44

Halpern, Daniel (1995) *Who's Writing This?: Notations on the Authorial I with Self-Portraits*. Hopewell, N.J.

Hamburger, Michael (1993) *Das Überleben der Lyrik: Berichte und Zeugnisse*. Munich

Harvey, David (1989) *The Condition of Postmodernity: An Enquiry into the Origins of Cultural Change*. Oxford

Harvey, Elizabeth D. (1996) "Ventriloquizing Sappho, or the Lesbian Muse," in E. Greene (ed.), *Re-reading Sappho: Reception and Transmission*. Berkeley. 79–104

Havelock, Eric A. (1939) *The Lyric Genius of Catullus*. Oxford

Heaney, Seamus (1995) "Extending the Alphabet: On Christopher Marlowe's 'Hero and Leander'," in *The Redress of Poetry*. New York. 17–37

Heath, J. R. (1986) "The Supine Hero in Catullus 32," *CJ* 82:28–36

Hendrickson, G. L. (1925) "Archilochus and Catullus," *CP* 20:155–7

Herescu, N. J. (1959) "Sur le sens 'érotique' de *sedere*," *Glotta* 38:125–34

(1960) "Autour de la Salax Taberna (Catulle, 37)," in *Hommages à Léon Hermann*. Brussels. 431–5

Herzfeld, Michael (1981) "Meaning and Morality: A Semiotic Approach to Evil Eye Accusations in a Greek Village." *American Ethnologist* 8:560–74

(1985) *The Poetics of Manhood: Contest and Identity in a Cretan Mountain Village*. Princeton

Hezel, Oskar (1932) *Catull und das griechische Epigramm*. Stuttgart

Highet, Gilbert (1974) "Masks and Faces in Satire," *Hermes* 102:321–37

Hinds, Stephen (1998) *Allusion and Intertext: Dynamics of Appropriation in Roman Poetry*. Cambridge

Horsfall, Nicholas (1979) "Doctus sermones utriusque linguae?" *Echos du monde classique* 23:79–95

Hubbard, Thomas K. (1983) "The Catullan Libellus," *Philologus* 127:218–37

Hughes, Steven (1998) "Men of Steel: Dueling, Honor, and Politics in Liberal Italy," in P. Spierenburg (ed.), *Men and Violence: Gender, Honor, and Rituals in Modern Europe and America*. Columbus, Ohio. 64–81

Hunter, Richard (1993) *The Argonautica of Apollonius: Literary Studies*. Cambridge

(1996) *Theocritus and the Archaeology of Greek Poetry*. Cambridge

Irwin, Elizabeth (1998) "Biography, Fiction, and the Archilochean Ainos," *JHS* 118:177–83

Iser, W. (1978) *The Act of Reading: A Theory of Aesthetic Response*. Baltimore

Jacoby, Felix (1914) "Drei Gedichte des Properz," *RhM* 69:393–413

Jakobson, Roman (1987) "Linguistics and Poetics," in K. Pomorska and S. Rudy (eds.), *Language in Literature*. Cambridge, Mass. 62–94

Jameson, Fredric (1985) "Baudelaire as Modernist and Postmodernist: The Dissolution of the Referent and the Artificial 'Sublime'," in C. Hosek and P. Parker (eds.), *Lyric Poetry: Beyond New Criticism*. Ithaca. 247–63

(1991) *Postmodernism, or, The Cultural Logic of Late Capitalism*. Durham, N.C.

Janan, Micaela (1994) *"When the lamp is shattered": Desire and Narrative in Catullus*. Carbondale, Ill.

Jauss, Hans Robert (1990) "The theory of reception: a retrospective of its unrecognized prehistory," in Peter Collier and Helga Geyer-Ryan (eds.), *Literary Theory Today*. Cambridge. 53–73

Jeffreys, Mark, ed. (1998) *New Definitions of Lyric: Theory, Technology, and Culture*. New York

Jenkyns, Richard (1982) *Three Classical Poets: Sappho, Catullus and Juvenal*. Cambridge, Mass.

Jenny, Laurent (1976) "La stratégie de la forme," *Poétique* 27:257–81

Jocelyn, H. D. (1980) "On Some Unnecessarily Indecent Interpretations of Catullus 2 and 3," *AJP* 101:421–41

(1999) "The Arrangement and the Language of Catullus' so-called *polymetra* with Special Reference to the Sequence 10–11–12," in J. N. Adams and R. G. Mayer (eds.), *Aspects of the Language of Latin Poetry (Proceedings of the British Academy 93)*. Oxford. 335–75

Johnson, Barbara (1994) *The Wake of Deconstruction*. Oxford

Johnson, Marguerite (1999) "Catullus, c. 37, and the Theme of *Magna Bella*," *Helios* 26:85–96

Johnson, W. R. (1982) *The Idea of Lyric: Lyric Modes in Ancient and Modern Poetry*. Berkeley

Johnston, Patricia A. (1983) "An Echo of Sappho in Catullus 65," *Latomus* 42:388–94

Keil, Heinrich, ed. (1822) *Grammatici Latini* (vol. 1). Leipzig

Kelly, J. M. (1966) *Roman Litigation*. Oxford

(1976) *Studies in the Civil Judicature of the Roman Republic*. Oxford

Kennedy, Duncan F. (1993) *The Arts of Love: Five Studies in the Discourse of Roman Love Elegy*. Cambridge

Kenner, Hugh (1971) *The Pound Era*. Berkeley

Kerkhecker, Arnd (1999) *Callimachus' Book of Iambi*. Oxford

Kermode, Frank (1966) *The Sense of an Ending: Studies in the Theory of Fiction*. Oxford

Kloss, Gerrit (1998) "Catullus Brückengedicht (c. 17)," *Hermes* 126:58–79

Knox, Peter (1984) "Sappho fr. 31 LP and Catullus 51: A Suggestion," *QUCC* 46:97–102

(1985) "Wine, Water and Callimachean Poetics," *HSCP* 89:107–19

Konstan, David (1977) *Catullus' Indictment of Rome*. Amsterdam
Koster, Severin (1980) *Die Invektive in der griechischen und römischen Literatur (Beiträge zur classischen Philologie* 99*)* Meisenheim am Glan
Kroll, Wilhelm (1968) *C. Valerius Catullus*. Stuttgart
Krostenko, Brian (2001) *Cicero, Catullus and the Language of Social Performance*. Chicago
Lacan, Jacques (1986) *Séminaire* VII: *L'éthique de la psychanalyse*. Paris
Lafaye, Georges (1894) *Catulle et ses modèles*. Paris
Laird, Andrew (1997) "Approaching Characterisation in Virgil," in C. Martindale (ed.), *The Cambridge Companion to Virgil*. Cambridge. 282–93
La Penna, Antonio (1956) "Problemi di stile catulliano (con una breve discussione sulla stilistica)," *Maia* 8:141–60
Lateiner, Donald (1977) "Obscenity in Catullus," *Ramus* 6:15–32
Lattimore, Richmond (1944) "Sappho 2 and Catullus 51," *CP* 39:184–7
(1962) *Themes in Greek and Latin Epitaphs*. Urbana
Lavency, Marius (1965) "L'ode à Lesbie et son billet d'envoi (Catulle, L et LI)," *AC* 34:175–82
Lenchantin de Gubernatis, Massimo (1945) *Il libro di Catullo*. Turin
Leo, Friedrich (1912) *Plautinische Forschungen zur Kritik und Geschichte der Komödie*. Berlin
Levine, Lawrence W. (1977) *Black Culture and Black Consciousness: Afro-American Folk Thought from Slavery to Freedom*. Oxford
Levy, H. L. (1941) "Catullus 5, 7–11 and the Abacus," *AJP* 62:222–4
Lieberg, Godo (1962) *Puella Divina: Die Gestalt der Göttlichen Geliebten bei Catull im Zusammenhang der Antiken Dichtung*. Amsterdam
Lintott, A. W. (1968) *Violence in Republican Rome*. Oxford
Littman, R. J. (1977) "The Unguent of Venus: Catullus 13," *Latomus* 36:123–6
Lobel, Edgar and Denys Page, eds. (1955) *Poetarum Lesbiorum fragmenta*. Oxford
Loraux, Nicole (1990) *Les mères en deuil*. Paris
Lyne, R. O. A. M. (1978) "The Neoteric Poets," *CQ* 28:167–87
(1980) *The Latin Love Poets: From Catullus to Horace*. Oxford
Lyotard, Jean-François (1984) *The Postmodern Condition: A Report on Knowledge*. Minneapolis
Macherey, Pierre (1966) *Pour une théorie de la production littéraire*. Paris (= [1978] *A Theory of Literary Production*. London)
Macleod, C. W. (1973) "Catullus 116," *CQ* 23:304–9 (= [1983] *Collected Essays*. Oxford. 181–6)
MacMullen, Ramsay (1991) "Hellenizing the Romans," *Historia* 40:419–38
Mallarmé, Stéphane (1982) "The Book: A Spiritual Instrument," in B. Cook (trans.), *Selected Poetry and Prose*. New York. 80–4
Maloney, Clarence, ed. (1976) *The Evil Eye*. New York

Martin, Charles (1992) *Catullus*. New Haven

Martindale, Charles (1993) *Redeeming the Text: Latin Poetry and the Hermeneutics of Reception*. Cambridge

Marx, Karl (1963) *Early Writings*, ed. T. B. Bottomore. London

Maselli, Giorgio (1994) *Affari di Catullo: Rapporti di proprietà nell'immaginario dei Carmi*. Bari

Mauss, Marcel (1938) "Une catégorie de l'esprit humain: la notion de personne, celle de 'moi'," *Journal of the Royal Anthropological Institute* 68:263–81

McKeown, J. C. (1987) *Ovid, Amores: Text, Prolegomena, and Commentary* (4 vols). Liverpool

McKie, D. S. (1977) *The Manuscripts of Catullus: Recension in a Closed Tradition*. Cambridge

Meltzer, Françoise (1994) *Hot Property: The Stakes and Claims of Literary Originality*. Chicago

Merkelbach, Reinhold and M. L. West (1967) *Fragmenta Hesiodea*. Oxford
    (1974) "Ein Archilochus-Papyrus," *ZPE* 14:97–113

Merrill, E. T. (1983) *Catullus*. Boston

Meschonnic, Henri (1995) *Politique du rhythme: politique du sujet*. Lagrasse
    (1996) "Le sujet comme récitatif ou le continu du langage," in D. Rabaté, J. de Sermet and Y. Vadé (eds.), *Le Sujet lyrique en question*. Bordeaux

Michelini, Ann (1987) *Euripides and the Tragic Tradition*. Madison

Miles, Josephine (1974) *Poetry and Change*. Berkeley

Mill, John Stuart (1976) *Essays on Poetry*. Columbia, S.C.

Miller, James E., Jr. (1977) *T. S. Eliot's Personal Wasteland*. Pa.

Miller, Paul Allen (1993a) "Beauty, Tragedy and the Grotesque: A Dialogical Aesthetics in Three Sonnets by Baudelaire," *French Forum* 18:319–33
    (1993b) "Sappho 31 and Catullus 51: The Dialogism of Lyric," *Arethusa* 26:183–99
    (1994) *Lyric Texts and Lyric Consciousness: The Birth of a Genre from Archaic Greece to Augustan Rome*. London
    (1998) "Catullan Consciousness, the 'Care of the Self,' and the Force of the Negative in History," in P. A. Miller and C. Platter (eds.), *Rethinking Sexuality: Foucault and Classical Antiquity*. Princeton. 171–203

Mintz, Jerome R. (1997) *Carnival Song and Society: Gossip, Sexuality and Creativity in Andalusia*. Oxford

Morgan, M. G. (1977) "*Nescio quid febriculosi scorti*: A Note on Catullus 6," *CQ* 27:338–41

Most, Glenn W. (1998) "With Fearful Steps Pursuing Hopes of High Talk with the Departed Dead," *TAPA* 128:311–24

Mynors, R. A. B., ed. (1958) *Catulli carmina*. Oxford

Nagy, Gregory (1976) "Iambos: Typologies of Invective and Praise," *Arethusa* 9:191–205

(1979) *The Best of the Achaeans: Concepts of the Hero in Archaic Greek Poetry.* Baltimore

(1990) *Pindar's Homer: The Lyric Possession of an Epic Past.* Baltimore

Nappa, Christopher (forthcoming) *The Man and the Mask: Aspects of Catullus' Social Fiction.*

Newman, J. K. (1990) *Roman Catullus and the Modification of the Alexandrian Sensibility.* Hildesheim

Nicolet, Claude (1976) "Le cens sénatorial sous la république et sous Auguste," *JRS* 66:20–38

Nussbaum, Martha C. (1994) *The Therapy of Desire: Theory and Practice in Hellenistic Ethics.* Princeton

Nye, Robert A. (1998) *Masculinity and Male Codes of Honor in Modern France.* Berkeley

(1999) "The End of the Modern French Duel," in P. Spierenburg (ed.), *Men and Violence: Gender, Honor, and Rituals in Modern Europe and America.* Columbus, Ohio. 82–95

Obbink, Dirk, ed. (1995) *Philodemus and Poetry: Poetic Theory and Practice in Lucretius, Philodemus, and Horace.* Oxford

Olson, Charles (1974) *Additional Prose.* Bolinas

(1983) *The Maximus Poems.* Berkeley

Opelt, Ilona (1965) *Die lateinischen Schimpfwörter und verwandte sprachliche Erscheinungen: eine Typologie.* Heidelberg

Page, T. E. (1896) *Horace.* London

Palgrave, Francis Turner (1861) *The Golden Treasury of the Best Songs and Lyric Poems in the English Language.* London

Papanghelis, T. D. (1991) "Catullus and Callimachus on Large Women," *Mnemosyne* 44:372–86

Paratore, Ettore (1950) *Una nuova ricostruzione del "De poetis" di Suetonio.* Bari

Parker, Holt N. (1997) "The Teratogenic Grid," in J. Hallett and M. Skinner (eds.), *Roman Sexualities.* Princeton. 47–65

Passerini, Alfredo (1934) "La τρυφή nella storiografia ellenistica," *SIFC* 11:35–56

Pedrick, Victoria (1993) "The Abusive Address and the Audience in Catullan Poems," *Helios* 20:173–96

Perloff, Marjorie (1985) *The Dance of the Intellect: Studies in the Poetry of the Pound Tradition.* Cambridge

(1999) "Postmodernism/'fin de siècle': Defining 'Difference' in Late Twentieth Century Poetics," in E. Larrissy (ed.), *Romanticism and Postmodernism.* Cambridge. 179–209

Petrini, Mark (1997) *The Child and the Hero: Coming of Age in Catullus and Vergil.* Ann Arbor

Pfeiffer, R. (1955) "The Future of Studies in the Field of Hellenistic Poetry," *JHS* 75:69–73

(1979) *Callimachus.* New York (= [1949] and [1953] Oxford)

Pitt-Rivers, Julian A. (1961) *The People of the Sierra.* Chicago
 (1966) "Honour and Social Status," in J. Peristiany (ed.), *Honour and Shame: The Values of Mediterranean Society.* Chicago
 (1977) *The Fate of Shechem.* Cambridge
Platter, C. (1995) "*Officium* in Catullus and Propertius: A Foucauldian Reading," *CP* 90:211–24
Porter, James (1995) "Content and Form in Philodemus: The History of an Evasion," in D. Obbink, ed., *Philodemus and Poetry: Poetic Theory and Practice in Lucretius, Philodemus and Horace.* Oxford. 97–147
Pound, Ezra (1934) *ABC of Reading* (repr. 1960). New York
Pucci, Pietro (1961) "Il carme 50 di Catullo," *Maia* 13:249–56
Puelma, Mario (1982) "Die *Aitien* des Kallimachos als Vorbild der römischen Amores-Elegie," 39:221–46 (Part 1); 285–304 (Part 2)
Puelma Piwonka, Mario (1949) *Lucilius und Kallimachos: Zur Geschichte einer Gattung der hellenistisch-römischen Poesie.* Frankfurt
Putnam, Michael C. J. (1961) "The Art of Catullus 64," *HSCP* 65:165–205 (= [1972] K. Quinn, ed., *Approaches to Catullus.* Cambridge and New York. 225–65)
Quinn, Kenneth (1959) *The Catullan Revolution.* Melbourne
 (1970) *Catullus: The Poems.* London
 (1972) *Catullus: An Interpretation.* London
Quinney, Laura (1999) *The Poetics of Disappointment: Wordsworth to Ashbery.* Charlottesville
Rabinowitz, Nancy Sorkin (1993) *Anxiety Veiled: Euripides and the Traffic in Women.* Ithaca
Rajan, Tilottama (1985) "Romanticism and the Death of Lyric Consciousness," in C. Hosek and P. Parker (eds.), *Lyric Poetry: Beyond New Criticism.* Ithaca. 194–207
Ramage, E. (1973) *Urbanitas: Ancient Sophistication and Refinement.* Norman, Oklahoma
Randall, J. G. (1979) "Mistresses' Pseudonyms in Latin Elegy," *LCM* 4:27–35
Rankin, H. D. (1972) "The Progress of Pessimism in Catullus, Poems 2–11," *Latomus* 31:744–51
 (1977) *Archilochus of Paros.* Park Ridge, N.J.
Rawson, Elizabeth (1985) *Intellectual Life in the Late Republic.* London
Ribbeck, Otto (1863) *C. Valerius Catullus, eine literar-historische Skizze.* Kiel
Richlin, Amy (1981) "The Meaning of *Irrumare* in Catullus and Martial," *CP* 76:40–46
 (1988) "Systems of Food Imagery in Catullus," *CW* 81:355–63
 (1992) *The Garden of Priapus: Sexuality and Aggression in Roman Humor.* New York
 (1993) "Not Before Homosexuality: The Materiality of the *Cinaedus* and the Roman Law Against Love Between Men," *Journal of the History of Sexuality* 3:523–73

Riffaterre, Michael (1980a) "Syllepsis," *Critical Inquiry* 6:625–38
  (1980b) "La trace de l'intertexte," *La Pensée* 215:4–18
  (1990) "Compulsory reader response: the intertextual drive," in
    Worton and Still (eds.), *Intertextuality: Theories and Practices.* Man-
    chester. 56–78
Ross, David O. (1969) *Style and Tradition in Catullus.* Cambridge, Mass.
Rudd, Niall (1986) *Themes in Roman Satire.* London
Saller, Richard P. (1994) *Patriarchy, Property and Death in the Roman Family.*
  Cambridge
Santini, P. (1994) "Il poeta-usignolo (Catullo 65, 13)," *Prometheus* 20:265–
  8
Sarkissian, John (1983) *Catullus 68: An Interpretation.* Leiden
Schmidt, E. A. (1973) "Catulls Anordnung seiner Gedichte," *Philologus*
  117:215–42
Schwabe, Ludwig (1862) *Quaestiones Catullianae.* Giessen
Scott, W. C. (1971) "Catullus and Caesar (c. 29)," *CP* 66:17–25
Scroggins, Mark, ed. (1997) *Upper Limit Music: The Writing of Louis Zukof-
  sky.* Tuscaloosa
  (1998) *Louis Zukofsky and the Poetry of Knowledge.* Tuscaloosa
Seager, Robin (1974) "*Venustus, lepidus, bellus, salsus*: Notes on the Lan-
  guage of Catullus," *Latomus* 33:891–4
Sedgwick, Eve (1985) *Between Men: English Literature and Male Homosocial
  Desire.* New York
Segal, Charles (1970) "Catullan *Otiosi*: The Lover and the Poet," *G&R*
  17:25–31
Segal, Erich (1968) *Roman Laughter: The Comedy of Plautus.* Cambridge,
  Mass.
Selden, Daniel L. (1992) "*Ceveat lector*: Catullus and the Rhetoric of Per-
  formance," in R. Hexter and D. Selden (eds.), *Innovations of Antiquity.*
  New York. 461–512
Shatzman, Israël (1975) *Senatorial Wealth and Roman Politics.* Collection
  Latomus 142. Brussels
Shipton, K. M. W. (1980) "Catullus 51: Just Another Love Poem?" *LCM*
  5:73–6
Sider, David (1997) *The Epigrams of Philodemos: Introduction, Text and Com-
  mentary.* Oxford
Simpson, David (1995) *The Academic Postmodern and the Rule of Literature: A
  Report on Half-Knowledge.* Chicago
Skinner, Marilyn B. (1971) "Catullus VIII: The Comic Amator as Eiron,"
  CJ 66:298–305
  (1979) "Ameana, Puella Defututa," *CJ* 74:110–14
  (1980) "Parasites and Strange Bedfellows: A Study in Catullus' Politi-
    cal Imagery," *Ramus* 8:137–52
  (1981) *Catullus' Passer: The Arrangement of the Book of Polymetric Poems.*
    New York

(1982) "Pretty Lesbius," *TAPA* 112:197–208

(1983) "Clodia Metelli," *TAPA* 113:273–87

(1988) "Aesthetic Patterning in Catullus: Textual Structures, Systems of Imagery and Book Arrangements: Introduction," *CW* 81:337–40

(1989) "*Ut decuit cinaediorem*: Power, Gender and Urbanity in Catullus 10," *Helios* 16:7–23

(1992) "The Dynamics of Catullan Obscenity: cc. 37, 58 and 11," *Syllecta Classica* 3:1–11

Skutsch, Otto (1970) "The Book under the Bushel," *BICS* 17:148

(1985) *The Annals of Q. Ennius.* Oxford

Sperber, Dan (1975) *Rethinking Symbolism.* Cambridge

Stanley, S. (1994) *Louis Zukofsky and the transformation of a modern American poetics.* Berkeley

Stehle Stigers, Eva (1977) "Retreat from the Male: Catullus 62 and Sappho's Erotic Flowers," *Ramus* 6:83–102

Stehle, Eva (1990) "Sappho's Gaze: Fantasies of a Goddess and Young Man," in D. Konstan and M. Nussbaum (eds.), *Differences* 2.1: *Sexuality in Greek & Roman Society.* 88–125

(1997) *Performance and Gender in Ancient Greece: Nondramatic Poetry in its Setting.* Princeton

Stevens, Wallace (1957) *Opus Posthumous.* New York

Stewart, Frank Henderson (1994) *Honor.* Chicago

Still, Judith and Michael Worton (1990) "Introduction," in Worton and Still (eds.), *Intertextuality: Theories and Practice.* Manchester. 1–45

Stoevesandt, M. (1995) "Catull 64 und die Ilias: Die Peleus-Thetis-Epyllion im Lichte der neuren Homer-Forschung," *WJA* n.s. 20:167–205

Strier, Richard (1995) *Resistant Structures: Particularity, Radicalism, and Renaissance Texts.* Berkeley

Sullivan, J. P. (1964) *Ezra Pound and Sextus Propertius; a study in creative translation.* London

Suolahti, J. (1963) *The Roman Censors: A Study on Social Structure.* Helsinki

Svenbro, Jesper (1993) *Phrasikleia: An Anthropology of Reading in Ancient Greece.* Ithaca

Syme, Ronald (1939) *The Roman Revolution.* Oxford

(1956) "Piso and Veranius in Catullus," *C&M* 17:129–34

Syndikus, Hans Peter (1984) *Catull: Eine Interpretation* (3 vols.). Darmstadt

Taggart, John (1994) *Songs of Degrees: Essays on Contemporary Poetry and Poetics.* Tuscaloosa

Tarditi, Giovanni (1968) *Archilochus.* Rome

Tatum, W. J. (1988) "Catullus' Criticism of Cicero in Poem 49," *TAPA* 118:179–84

(1997) "Friendship, Politics and Literature in Catullus: Poems 1, 65 and 66, 116," *CQ* 47:482–500

Terrell, Carroll F. (1980) *A Companion to* The Cantos *of Ezra Pound.* Berkeley

Thomas, Richard F. (1982) "Catullus and the Polemics of Poetic Reference," *AJP* 103:144–64

(1984) "Menander and Catullus 8," *RhM* 127:308–16

(1986) "Virgil's *Georgics* and the Art of Reference," *HSCP* 90:171–98

(1988) "Turning Back the Clock," *CP* 83:54–69

(1991) "'Death,' Doxography and the 'Termerian Evil'. Philodemus 27 Page = *A.P.* 11.30," *CQ* 41:130–7

(1993) "Sparrows, Hares and Doves: A Catullan Metaphor and its Tradition," *Helios* 20:131–42

(1998) "'Melodious Tears': Sepulchral Epigram and Generic Mobility," in Harder, Regtuit and Wakker (eds.), *Genre in Hellenistic Poetry (Hellenistica Groningana 3)*. 205–23

Thomsen, O. (1992) *Ritual and desire: Catullus 61 and 62 and other ancient documents on wedding and marriage*. Aarhus

Thomson, D. F. S. (1973) "A New Look at the Manuscript Tradition of Catullus," *YCS* 23:113–29

(1978) *Catullus: A Critical Edition*. Chapel Hill

(1997) *Catullus: Edited with a Textual and Interpretive Commentary*. Toronto

Todorov, Tzvetan (1977) "La Crise romantique," in *Théories du symbole*. Paris. 179–260 (= "The Romantic Crisis," in *Theories of the Symbol*. Ithaca. 147–221)

Treggiari, Susan (1991) *Roman Marriage: "Iusti Coniuges" from the Time of Cicero to the Time of Ulpian*. Oxford

(1998) "Home and Forum: Cicero Between 'Public' and 'Private'," *TAPA* 128:1–23

Trendelenburg, Adolf (1910) "A Contribution to the History of the Word Person," *The Monist* 20:336–63

Treu, Max (1959) *Archilochos*. Göttingen

Usener, Hermann (1901) "Italische Volksjustiz," *RhM* 56:1–28

Vandiver, Elizabeth (1990) "Sound Patterns in Catullus 84," *CJ* 85:337–40

(1999) "The Way Their Catullus Walked: Changing Strategies of Translation," *APA* conference paper read 29 December. Dallas

Van Sickle, John (1980) "The Book-Roll and Some Conventions of the Poetic Book," *Arethusa* 13:5–40

Vattimo, Gianni (1985) *La fine della modernità*. Milan

Veyne, Paul (1979) "The Hellenization of Rome and the Question of Acculturations," *Diogenes* 106:1–27

(1988a) *Roman Erotic Elegy: Love, Poetry and the West*. Chicago

(1988b) *Did the Greeks Believe in their Myths? An Essay on the Constitutive Imagination*. Chicago

Vine, Brent (1992) "On the Missing Fourth Stanza of Catullus 51," *HSCP* 94:251–8

von Hallberg, Robert (1978) *Charles Olson: The Scholar's Art*. Cambridge, Mass.

Vretska, K. (1966) "Das Problem der Einheit von Catull c. 68," *WS* 79:313–30

Wallace-Hadrill, Andrew (1994) *Houses and Society in Pompeii and Herculaneum*. Princeton

(1997) "*Mutatio morum*: the idea of a cultural revolution," in T. Habinek and A. Schiesaro (eds.), *The Roman Cultural Revolution*. Cambridge. 3–22

Walsh, George (1990) "Surprised by Self: Audible Thought in Hellenistic Poetry," *CP* 85:1–21

Walters, Jonathan (1997) "Invading the Roman Body: Manliness and Impenetrability in Roman Thought," in M. Skinner and J. Hallett (eds.), *Roman Sexualities*. Princeton. 29–43

Ward, Donald (1973) "On the Poets and Poetry of the Indo-Europeans," *Journal of Indo-European Studies* 1:127–44

Watkins, Calvert (1990) "What is Philology?" in J. Ziolkowski (ed.), *On Philology*. University Park, Pa. (= [1990] *Comparative Literature Studies* 27). 21–5

Watson, L. C. (1991) *Arae: The Curse Poetry of Antiquity*. Leeds

West, M. L. (1974) *Studies in Greek Elegy and Iambus*. Berlin

(1989) ed., *Iambi et elegi Graeci ante Alexandrum cantati*, vol. 1. Oxford

Westphal, Rudolf (1867) *Catulls Gedichte in ihrem geschichtlichen Zusammenhange*. Breslau

Wheeler, Arthur L. (1934) *Catullus and the Traditions of Ancient Poetry*. Berkeley

White, Peter (1993) *Promised Verse: Poets in the Society of Augustan Rome*. Cambridge, Mass.

Wiener, Martin J. (1998) "The Victorian Criminalization of Men," in P. Spierenburg (ed.), *Men and Violence: Gender, Honor, and Rituals in Modern Europe and America*. Columbus, Ohio. 197–212

Wilamowitz-Moellendorff, Ulrich von (1913) *Sappho und Simonides*. Berlin

Williams, Craig A. (1999) *Roman Homosexuality: Ideologies of Masculinity in Classical Antiquity*. Oxford

Williams, Gareth D. (1996) *The Curse of Exile: A Study of Ovid's* Ibis (Cambridge Philological Society Suppl. 19). Cambridge

Williams, Gordon (1968) *Tradition and Originality in Roman Poetry*. Oxford

(1980) *Figures of Thought in Roman Poetry*. New Haven

Williams, Mark (1988) "Catullus 50 and the Language of Friendship," *Latomus* 47:69–73

Williams, William Carlos (1992) *Paterson*. New York

Wimmel, Walter (1960) *Kallimachos in Rom* (Hermes Einzelschriften 16). Wiesbaden

Winkler, John J. (1985) *Auctor & Actor: A Narratological Reading of Apuleius' Golden Ass*. Berkeley

(1990) *The Constraints of Desire*. New York

Wiseman, T. P. (1969) *Catullan Questions*. Leicester

(1974) *Cinna the Poet and Other Roman Essays*. Leicester
(1979) *Clio's Cosmetics: Three Studies in Greco-Roman Literature*. Leicester
(1985) *Catullus and His World: A Reappraisal*. Cambridge
(1987) *Roman Studies: Literary and Historical*. Liverpool
Witke, Charles (1980) "Catullus 13: A Reexamination," *CP* 75:325–31
Wray, David (forthcoming) "Apollonius' Masterplot: Narrative Strategy in *Argonautica* 1," in M. A. Harder et al. (eds.), *Apollonius Rhodius: Hellenistica Groningana* 4. Groningen
Wyke, Maria (1987) "Written Woman: Propertius' *Scripta Puella*," *JRS* 77:47–61
Young [Forsyth] P. R. (1969) "Catullus 29," *CJ* 64:327–8
Zacharia, Katerina (forthcoming) "'The rock of the nightingale': Kinship Diplomacy and Sophocles' *Tereus*"
Zanker, P. (1983) "Zur Bildnisrepräsentation führender Männer in Mittelitalischen und Campanischen Städten zur Zeit der Späten Republik und der Julisch-Claudischen Kaiser," in *Les "bourgeoisies" municipales italiennes aux IIe et Ier siècles av. J.-C.* (Paris and Naples) 251–66
Zetzel, J. E. G. (1983) "Catullus, Ennius and the Poetics of Allusion," *ICS* 8:251–66
Zizek, Slavoj (1989) *The Sublime Object of Ideology*. London
(1991) *For They Know Not What They Do: Enjoyment as a Political Factor*. London
(1994) *The Metastases of Enjoyment: Six Essays on Woman and Causality*. London
Zukofsky, Celia and Louis Zukofsky (1969) *Catullus (Gai Valeri Catulli Veronensis Liber) translated by Celia and Louis Zukofsky*. London
Zukofsky, Louis (1993) *"A"*. Baltimore

Passages discussed

General index

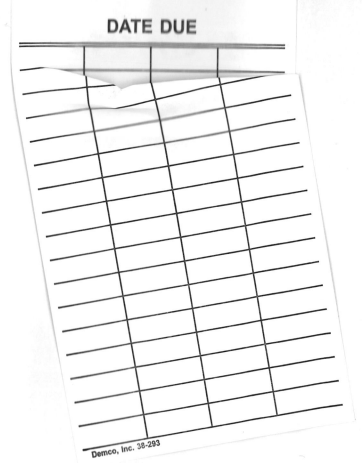

DATE DUE